THE

THEOLOGY

OF THE

NEW TESTAMENT.

A Handbook for Bible Students.

BY THE REV. J. J. VAN OOSTERZEE, D.D.,
Professor of Theology in the University of Utrecht.

TRANSLATED FROM THE DUTCH, BY
MAURICE J. EVANS, B.A.,
Translator of Dr. Hoffmann's "Prophecies of Our Lord and His Apostles."

WIPF & STOCK · Eugene, Oregon

Wipf and Stock Publishers
199 W 8th Ave, Suite 3
Eugene, OR 97401

The Theology of the New Testament
A Handbook for Bible Students
By Van Oosterzee, J. J. and Evans, Maurice J.
Softcover ISBN-13: 978-1-7252-9984-9
Hardcover ISBN-13: 978-1-7252-9986-3
eBook ISBN-13: 978-1-7252-9985-6
Publication date 2/4/2021
Previously published by Dodd, Mead, & Company, 1871

This edition is a scanned facsimile of
the original edition published in 1871.

Original language edition,
De Theologie des Nieuwen Verbonds,
published by Kemink en Zoon, 1869

INTRODUCTORY NOTE
TO THE
AMERICAN EDITION.

The author of this volume is very generally regarded as the ablest living Dutch divine of the evangelical school. He is already well known in this country by his contributions to Lange's Commentary, viz: on Luke, the Pastoral Epistles, Philemon, and James. These expositions are among the very best in this comprehensive Bible Work, edited by Dr. Schaff. A small treatise of his, *History or Romance*, in reply to Renan, has been published by the American Tract Society. Besides these works, Dr. Van Oosterzee has also written a *Life of Jesus*, 3 vols., 2d ed., 1863–1865; a *Christology; or, Manual for Christians*, 3 vols., 1855–1861, and several other essays and articles, and he has vigorously defended the Christian faith against the assaults of rationalism. He is at present engaged upon a manual of *Dogmatics*, a translation of which is already announced in England, and which will be, in some sort, a continuation of the present volume.

Dr. Van Oosterzee was born at Rotterdam, Holland, in 1817; studied at the University of Utrecht; was pastor of one of the chief churches in Rotterdam for eighteen years; and, since 1862, he has been a Professor of Theology in the University of Utrecht. He is no less distinguished in the pulpit than in the professor's chair.

The present volume was prepared for the use of his own classes in the University, to meet a want which is likewise felt in the theological seminaries of this country. Besides the able treatises on Doctrinal Theology, of all schools, which are acceptable to our students, there is also needed a manual on Biblical Theology proper.* The existing German works on this branch, learned and admirable as some of them are, do not in all respects so well meet the demand as does this volume of Dr. Van Oosterzee. It is clear, simple, well arranged, and thoroughly imbued with the spirit of the New Testament writers. Its criticisms of other works, and its literary references will also be found of value. It has already been translated and published in this country by Dr. Day, in the *Theological Eclectic*. The present edition, printed from the English stereotype plates, will, it is hoped, increase its circulation and usefulness. It may safely be said, that every student of theology should have it at hand; and also that it will be of great use to all intelligent laymen interested in the study of the Sacred Scripture, especially in its doctrinal contents.

NEW YORK, Nov. 10, 1871.

---

* See an article on Biblical Theology with especial reference to the New Testament, by Rev. C. A. Briggs, American Presbyterian Review, 1870 Also an article in the same Review, 1870, by Rev. T. P. Westervelt, on Oosterzee's Theology of the New Testament.

AUTHOR'S PREFACE.

THE present handbook owes its origin to the personal need of the writer. Called, *inter alia*, to lecture on the Biblical Theology of the New Testament as a separate branch of theological science, I looked in vain for a manual which should in all respects correspond to my wishes. Taking into account the great wealth of the subject, and the limited time which could be devoted by my class to this important theological discipline, I felt impelled as early as possible to set my hand to the work, and to present my students with a book which should by no means render unnecessary a more complete analysis of the material therein treated of, but should rather incite thereto ; and should thus form, in some measure, the basis on which yet further to build.

From the nature of the case, therefore, much could be only hinted at which calls for additional oral information ; and, on the other hand, as far as possible, all had to be set aside which belongs to the domain of kindred theological science. In the choice, also, of literature to which the student is referred, I had regard less to completeness than to adaptation, and reserve to myself the right and the duty of adding thereto as occasion may demand. The "points for inquiry" at the end of each section are designed to serve, not as rigid bonds, but as hints leading to further discussion and interchange of thoughts. I hope in this way to have contributed something also towards the "self-culture" of those who think they can derive some profit from the study of my book. *That constant application to Holy Scripture itself must inseparably accompany the use of this handbook will be at once self-evident.* Only thus can it call forth a thorough acquaintance with the Scriptures, and prepare the way for the study of Systematic Theology.

Should this attempt answer the end in view, it is my intention to issue a similar compendium of Christian Dogmatics, and possibly also of Practical Theology—to both which subjects, no less than to Biblical Theology, I am called to devote my best endeavours. To the former and present members of my class, who have hitherto followed these lectures with interest, and not without profit, these pages bring with them my sincere and heartfelt salutations.

VAN OOSTERZEE.

Utrecht, Sept., 1867.

TRANSLATOR'S PREFACE.

BUT few words are necessary in introducing an English Edition of this work. That such a text-book for students was felt to be needed is apparent from its speedy reproduction in a German form (Barmen, 1869). Another reason also has weighed with the Translator. There are not a few, among those who make no claim to the title of Theological Students, for whom the Christian faith—no less than the Christian life—of the first age will always be a matter of supreme importance;—who believe, moreover, that independent research in the domain of New Testament doctrine is essential to the cultivation of genuine devotion;—and who will gladly avail themselves of every suitable means of learning somewhat more fully what is "the mind of the Spirit." For such, a trustworthy compendium of the teaching of the New Testament Scriptures themselves is well-nigh indispensable. In making use of the present volume to this end, the necessary labour of consulting the Scripture authorities will be abundantly repaid—not least in those cases where the bearing of a citation is not *at once* seen.

In the literature of the earlier part of the volume some of the Continental works have been referred to by their English titles, even where no translation exists: where a translation is extant, the fact has, as a rule, been indicated, except in the case of well-known writers, such as Neander. Readers who have an opportunity of consulting the work of Archbishop Trench on the Parables of our Lord, and the Bible Dictionaries of Drs. Smith and Kitto on the various Apostolic writers of the New Testament, will acquire thereby a considerable addition to the English literature of the subject.

For convenience of reference, there has been added to the English translation an index of subjects, and another of the principal Greek words cited in the volume.

M. J. E.

Stratford-on-Avon, Sept., 1870.

CONTENTS.

INTRODUCTION.

SECTION		PAGE
1.	Definition of the Science	1
2.	Its History	9
3.	Its Method, Main Division, and Requirement	21

FIRST PART.

OLD TESTAMENT BASIS.

4.	Mosaism	28
5.	Prophetism	37
6.	Judaism	47
7.	John the Baptist	57
8.	Result	60

SECOND PART.

THE THEOLOGY OF JESUS CHRIST.

9.	General Summary	61

FIRST DIVISION.

THE SYNOPTICAL GOSPELS.

SECTION		PAGE
10.	The Kingdom of God	68
11.	Its Founder	74
12.	The King of Kings	80
13.	The Subjects	87
14.	Salvation	98
15.	The Way of Salvation	109
16.	The Completion	118

SECOND DIVISION.

THE GOSPEL OF JOHN.

17.	Introduction	129
18.	The Son of God in the Flesh	135
19.	The Son of God in His relation to the Father	142
20.	The Son of God in His relation to the World	150
21.	The Son of God in relation to His Disciples	163
22.	The Son of God in relation to His Future	170

THIRD DIVISION.

HIGHER UNITY.

23.	Diversity and Harmony	175
24.	Result	186

THIRD PART.

THE THEOLOGY OF THE APOSTLES.

25.	General Survey	190

Contents. xi

FIRST DIVISION.

THE PETRINE THEOLOGY.

SECTION		PAGE
26.	SUMMARY	198
27.	PETER, AN APOSTLE OF JESUS CHRIST	206
28.	PETER, THE APOSTLE OF THE CIRCUMCISION	217
29.	PETER, THE APOSTLE OF HOPE	225
30.	THE SECOND EPISTLE OF PETER	233
31.	KINDRED TYPES OF DOCTRINE	241
32.	RESULT AND TRANSITION	251

SECOND DIVISION.

THE PAULINE THEOLOGY.

33.	GENERAL SURVEY	255

FIRST SUBDIVISION.

HUMANITY AND THE INDIVIDUAL MAN BEFORE AND OUT OF CHRIST.

34.	THE GENTILE AND JEWISH WORLD	265
35.	THE CAUSE OF THIS CONDITION	271
36.	ITS CONSEQUENCES	281

SECOND SUBDIVISION.

HUMANITY AND THE INDIVIDUAL MAN THROUGH AND IN CHRIST.

37.	THE PLAN OF SALVATION	286
38.	THE CHRIST	296
39.	THE WORK OF REDEMPTION	304
40.	THE WAY OF SALVATION	316
41.	THE CHURCH	324
42.	THE FUTURE	333
43.	KINDRED TYPES OF DOCTRINE	343
44.	RESULT AND TRANSITION	368

THIRD DIVISION.

THE JOHANNINE THEOLOGY.

SECTION		PAGE
45.	GENERAL SUMMARY	372

FIRST SUBDIVISION.

THE GOSPEL AND THE EPISTLES.

46.	THE WORLD OUT OF CHRIST	381
47.	THE APPEARING OF CHRIST	389
48.	LIFE IN CHRIST	398

SECOND SUBDIVISION.

THE APOCALYPSE.

49.	DIVERSITY AND HARMONY	406

FOURTH PART.

HIGHER UNITY.

50.	HARMONY OF THE APOSTLES WITH EACH OTHER	416
51.	HARMONY OF THE APOSTLES WITH THE LORD	427
52.	HARMONY OF THE LORD AND THE APOSTLES WITH THE SCRIPTURES OF THE OLD TESTAMENT	433

THE THEOLOGY OF THE NEW TESTAMENT.

INTRODUCTION.

SECTION I.

Definition of the Science.

THE Biblical Theology of the New Testament is that part of theological science which presents in a summary form the doctrine of the New Testament concerning God and Divine things, and expresses the same in systematic order. In its character, extent, and aim, it is distinguished from Christian dogmatics, and belongs to the domain of historic theology.

1. Theology is in general the science of God and of Divine things: according to a newer, but not, therefore, better definition, the science of religion. In the stricter sense, this word designates the science of God, in contradistinction from that of man, of sin, of Christ, etc. Theology, the name for the *locus de Deo* in dogmatics, as distinguished from anthropology, hamartology (doctrine of sin), Christology, etc. There is no religion of any importance which has not a more or less developed theology, as, for instance, the

theology of Mosaism, of Islamism, of Buddhism, etc.; yea, even philosophy has its theology, as well as its anthropology and cosmology. From this purely philosophic theology, the Christian, however, is distinguished: inasmuch as the former is the fruit of our own thought, matured by reflection and experience; the latter, on the other hand, is derived from a special Divine revelation, whose authentic document is the Holy Scripture. To this latter alone the words of Thomas Aquinas have their application—*a Deo docetur, Deum docet, et ad Deum ducit.*

2. The Biblical theology of the New Testament has to do with the ideas of God and Divine things which are presented in the New Testament. It investigates, in other words, the doctrine of the New Testament, without, at the same time, wishing to maintain that the New Testament presents a strictly defined system of doctrine, and much less that the essential characteristic of the Christian saving revelation consists exclusively or principally in its doctrine. If this is justly denied, it cannot be disputed that the New Testament really contains a doctrine of God and of Divine things. This doctrine the Biblical theology of the New Testament presents in a summary manner, contemplates each of its parts in itself and in connection with the others, and determines its place in history as a complete whole.

In the widest sense of the word, Biblical theology embraces the doctrine of Divine things, as contained in the Old Testament as well as in the New. It is known how close is the connection between the two,

Definition of the Science.

Novum testamentum in vetere latet: vetus e novo patet (Augustine). If, therefore, a perfect separation is scarcely conceivable, a certain distinction is yet possible, desirable, in some sense necessary ; and has, consequently, often been attempted, especially in later times, with the desired result.

3. The distinction between Biblical theology of the New Testament and Christian dogmatics—which are not seldom confounded to their common injury—begins already to be clear to us. Both parts of theological science have their peculiar character. That of Christian dogmatics is historico-philosophic ; that of the Biblical theology of the New Testament, on the contrary, is purely historic. The former investigates, not what the Christian Church in general, or one of its parts, acknowledges as truth, but, above all, what, in the domain of Christian faith, must really be regarded as truth. The Biblical theology of the New Testament, on the other hand, inquires only what is adduced as truth by the New Testament writers. From its stand-point, it has to do, not with the correctness, but with the contents of the ideas which it finds in the teaching of Jesus and the Apostles. *Elle ne démontre pas, elle raconte* (Reuss).*

It has in this another aim than that proposed by one who treats of systematic theology. While dogmatics seeks to develop the subject-matter of the

---

* Obscure and incorrect is the distinction of Schenkel (*Christliche Dogmatik*, vol. i. p. 380). "Its design is not to bring to light the truth of salvation, but only the reality of the Scripture history of salvation."

Christian faith, and to lay firm its foundations, Biblical theology, of the New Testament, has fulfilled its task when it has clearly presented what, in the New Testament, in contradistinction from other religious documentary authorities, is proclaimed as truth; although the question, with what right it is so proclaimed, is left to the sister science. If its aim is in so far a humbler one it has, on the other hand, a so much wider compass. Though, since the time of Calixtus (1634), dogmatics and ethics have been separated—with what right we here leave undecided—yet this separation is, in the domain of the Biblical theology of the New Testament, as little justifiable as desirable. A clear line of demarcation between the doctrine of salvation and the doctrine of life had no existence in the mind of Jesus and his Apostles. From the stand-point of the New Testament writers, faith and life are not only united, but one. Biblical theology has, consequently, not less to investigate the practical than the theoretical side of the New Testament teaching. On the other hand, it cannot have as its proper object to treat of the life of the Lord and his Apostles in addition to their doctrine, which is attempted, amongst others, by C. F. Schmid, in a work to which we shall shortly have occasion to refer.

While the Biblical theology of the New Testament has a much more objective character than Christian dogmatics, it can yet dispense with the help of the latter, although Christian dogmatics cannot possibly dispense with its help. It demands, therefore, in one who treats of it, not only that he should be a

Definition of the Science.

Christian philosopher, but also, above all, a good exegete and thorough historian. As for the hermeneute, so also for the Biblical theologian of the New Testament, the main question is, *What readest thou?* * It is on this account also better to designate our science by the name of Biblical theology than of Biblical Dogmatics of the New Testament. When we speak of the Biblical dogmatics of the New Testament, we naturally think of a complete system of ideas, so far as this can be deduced, as a whole, from the New Testament. Biblical theology, on the other hand, seeks to investigate, in a purely historical manner, the whole teaching (*leerbegrip*) of each single writer of the New Testament. Besides this, the word *dogma* reminds us almost involuntarily of the Church. The sayings of Jesus and of the Apostles, with which the Biblical theology of the New Testament has to do, have been just the elements from which the later dogmas have been derived, and by which they have been established.

4. The character of our science we have above indicated determines at the same time its place in the organic whole of the theological encyclopædia. If we distinguish between exegetical, historical, systematic, and practical theology, it will soon be seen that the Biblical theology of the New Testament takes its place at the head of the second of these, where it shines as "a focus of light in theological study" (Hagenbach). Thankfully this science receives

* Compare J. J. Doedes, "Hermeneutics of the New Testament Writings." (English translation.)

the indispensable services which exegesis renders to it, and in turn confers these services upon the following parts of historic theology, as well as of systematic and practical theology, and especially on the history of Christian doctrines, whose basis and initial point it is. On the other hand, it can leave the critical investigation of the history of those sources from whence it draws, to the so-called introductory science —Isagogics of the New Testament. Without doubt, Biblical theology may not leave unused the light kindled by the latter science as a help in its investigation. On disputed questions, which are of importance for his subject, it is to be expected of the Biblical theologian that he should express his opinion, support, and defend it; but a formal treatment of these questions, leading to a final decision, ought not to be expected of him in this capacity. The unceasing accumulation of material demands, above all in our days, a division of labour. The ideal of our science is attained if it presents a clear, well-arranged, complete, and comprehensive view of the doctrines contained in the writings of the New Testament, without troubling itself what is asserted, with or without justice, by criticism, concerning the origin, the connection, and the value of these books.

5. The importance of the investigation in which Biblical Theology is engaged, after what we have said, scarcely needs to be mentioned. Even from a purely historic point of view, it merits the attention of every one who treats of the history of humanity and of the kingdom of God upon earth. The ad-

vanced *Christian* justly attaches great value to an exact acquaintance with the answer given by the Lord and his Apostles to the highest questions of life. Especially must the *Christian theologian* learn to distinguish the teaching of Jesus and his Apostles from many other teachings. As a *Protestant*, he has, moreover, an interest in this investigation which is not felt by the Roman Catholic, or not felt in the same degree; and far from its being the case that in our time this investigation is rendered less important on account of the variously modified views of Holy Scripture, it is rather manifest of itself that—entirely apart from the justice of the modifications we have indicated—the very signs of the times most urgently impel us to its unwearied prosecution.

On the idea and character of our science, compare F. F. Fleck on *Biblical Theology as a Science in our Time*, in Rohr's "Prediger-Bibliothek," anno 1834; Schenkel, *The Problem of Biblical Theology, etc.*, in "Studien und Kritiken," 1852; the introduction to Lange's *Bible Work* ("Homiletical Commentaries," English Translation, Edinburgh); and, above all, the article of C. I. Nitzsch, in Herzog's "Real-Encyklopædie," vol. ii. p. 219 and following.

POINTS FOR INQUIRY.

CHARACTER and psychological basis of theological science in general.—Wherefore was the investigation of the Old and the New Testament theology at first combined and afterwards separated?—Criticism of some other definitions of our science, more or less different from our own.—Views in regard to its place in the Encyclopædia.—Wherefore does not the life of Jesus and his Apostles belong to its domain?—More exact statement and defence of its importance in itself, and in comparison with other branches of theological science.—From what cause is the low estimation of this science on many hands to be explained; and wherefore and how is this to be combated?

SECTION II.

Its History.

THE age of the Biblical theology of the New Testament, as an independent part of theological science, extends not far beyond the present century. It has passed through a long period of preparation, but has developed itself, in any considerable degree, only within a short time, and is now in a condition of promise and of life, which powerfully impels to its further cultivation.

1. Not without reason is it usual, in the introduction to any scientific investigation, to afford a sketch of its history. In this case, also, history proves itself "the light of truth, the witness of the times, the instructress of life." It makes us acquainted with that which has been already done within a given sphere, and on this account, also, with that which yet remains to be done. It shows how the science has gradually attained to an independent rank, affords the key to the explanation of its present con-

dition, and places us thus in a position further to build upon a foundation already laid.

2. Some one has justly termed the Biblical theology of the New Testament an "especially Protestant" science. It is so at least to this extent, that though the germ of this science was before present, it could only freely develop itself on the soil of Protestantism. The period before the Reformation may be designated the preparatory one. To this period belong the most important Fathers of the first centuries, who are more or less Biblical theologians. Especially does this honourable title belong to the coryphæi of the Alexandrine school. In some measure, the work *de testimoniis*, which is usually ascribed to Cyprian (*obiit* A.D. 258), may be adduced as an instance of independent research within this sphere, as well as also that of the African bishop, Junilius, *de partibus legis*, which belongs to the sixth century. That the Middle Ages were not favourable to works on Biblical theology is manifest from the nature of the case. As a rule, the question then was not—What is the teaching of Scripture? but—What is the teaching of the Church? They did not, however, entirely abstain from appealing to Scripture against those who differed from them; and the age before the Reformation prepared at the same time the way for a juster and more successful treatment of Biblical theology, especially that of the New Testament. The *Doctores ad Biblia* were expressly called to its explanation, and Luther's example shows with what zeal individuals among them entered upon this work. The

dogmatic masterpieces of the Reformation are at the same time the fruit of an earnest study of the Bible; although it was by no means entered upon from an historic standpoint, or with a purely scientific aim. Unfortunately, there arose in the seventeenth century a new scholasticism in place of the old, and the boundary line between Biblical theology and the dogmatics of the Church was more and more obliterated. Exegesis retired to the background, polemics came to the front. Even polemics, however, appealed to the so-called *dicta probantia*, which were expounded more or less according to the tenets of a particular school. The desire to find the truth of salvation as clearly and perfectly expressed as possible, even in those living under the Old Covenant, gave rise to very special investigations. Thus the theology of Job (1687), of Jeremiah (1696), even that of Elizabeth (1706), was treated with minute care. In an increasing degree—alongside of scholastico-dogmatic investigation—the necessity for Biblical exegesis (not yet purely historical) made itself felt, and the means thereto were supplied on various hands. In Strasburg, Sebastian Schmidt published his *Collegium Biblicum* (3rd edition, 1689); in Holland, Witsius and Vitringa called forth a purely Biblical school. Even the reaction of Pietism against orthodoxy affected favourably our science in its earliest stage; and during the whole eighteenth century there is manifested an increasing effort to throw off the scholastic yoke, and in the presentation of the Christian doctrine of faith and life, to return to Biblical simplicity. As types of this tendency, we may mention M. C. Heyman, *Versuch einer Bibl. Theol. in Tabellen* (4th edition, 1758); A. F. Busching, *Epitome Theologiæ, e solis litteris sacris concinnatæ* (1757), and by the same writer, *Gedanken von der Beschaffenheit und der Vorzug der Bibl. Dogm. Theol. vor der scolastischen* (1758); above all, D. G. F. Zachariæ, *Bibl. Theologie, oder Untersuchung des Bibl. Grundes der vornehmsten Theol. Lehren* (3rd edition, in five parts, 1786); and Storr, *Doctrinæ Christianæ e solis litt. SS. repetitæ Pars Theor.* (Stuttgard, 1793 and 1807). Their footsteps were followed, both within and without our country, at the end of the last century and the beginning of the present, by distinguished Biblical theologians of the supernaturalistic school.

3. Yet, however valuable all this is, the purely historical treatment of the Biblical theology of the New Testament is entirely a fruit of modern time, which brings forth ever more clearly the distinction between this and ecclesiastical or philosophical dogmatics. The idea that the Biblical theology of the New Testament must be treated as an independent part of historic science was first expressed with clear consciousness on the rationalistic side. This took place on the part of J. Ph. Gabler (Professor at Altorf) in the year 1787, in an academic discourse, *De justo discrimine Theol. Bibl. et Dogm.*, wherein he insisted that in the domain of the first-named science (Biblical theology) the doctrines of the different writers must be objectively investigated, distinguished from each other, and accurately arranged. His main thought

was further developed by his colleague, G. L. Bauer, who (1800-1802) published a *Biblical Theology of the New Testament*, in four parts, to which a fifth was promised. While this writer gave to his historic investigation an apologetico-practical tendency, an independent standpoint was taken by C. F. Ammon, in his *Outline of a purely Biblical Theology* (Erl. 1792), and his *Biblical Theology* (2nd edition, in three parts, 1801-1802). According to his view, Biblical theology should deal only with the "materials, fundamental ideas, and results of Biblical teaching, without troubling itself about the connection of the same, or weaving them into an artificial system." "This business," he says, "is reserved for the writer on dogmatics, who harmonises together these results." Whether the task of dogmatics is so simple as it would appear from these words, may remain for us at present a matter of indifference; it suffices that the historic character of our science has been intelligently expressed by Ammon. Yet more clearly is this done by G. P. C. Kayser, in his work, *Bibl. Theologie, oder Judaismus und Christianismus*, etc. (Erl. 1813-14); but especially by the Basle Professor, W. M. L. de Wette (died 1850), who has rendered this science most important services, less as concerns results than as concerns method. He placed Biblical dogmatics parallel with those of the Lutheran Church, in a certain respect opposite to them, and distinguished in the former better than had been before done between the ideas of Hebraism and those of Judaism, between the doctrine of Jesus and that of the Apostles. He asked, above all things, not whether he could harmonize his views with the Scripture teaching, but what the Scriptural conceptions were, how they were developed from each other, and beside each other, and in what connection they stood with the peculiar ideas of the time in which they were first uttered. Without doubt this work also has its weaker sides: Biblical theology is here too much Biblical dogmatics in the stricter sense of the word, and the peculiar philosophic standpoint of the author —he belonged to the school of Fries—had an overweening influence upon the historic view of his subject. This, however, does not prevent his having made, in some respects, gigantic progress in the good way, so that others with the desired success could further build upon the foundation he had laid. This was done also, although in a less happy form, by L. F. O. Baumgarten-Crusius, Professor in Jena, in his *Outlines of Biblical Theology* (1828); by L. D. Cramer, *Prelections upon the Biblical Theology of the New Testament*, brought out by Nabe, Leipzig, 1830; and on a much greater scale by D. V. Colln, Professor at Breslau, whose *Biblical Theology*, in two parts, was published after his death, in 1836, by Dr. D. Schulz.

It was, however, not only the wholly or half rationalistic school of theology which devoted itself with manifest preference to the prosecution of this part of the science; on the supernaturalistic side also its domain was cultivated by skilled hands. During the second quarter of the century, the theology of the Old Testament began to receive especial attention. The writings on this subject of Steudel (1840), Oehler

(1840), and especially of Havernick (1848), deserve to be mentioned with honour. As far as the New Testament is concerned, our science is especially under deep obligation to the ever-memorable Neander (died 1858). In the first part of his *Life of Jesus* (1st edition, 1837), he gave an historic summary of the doctrine of the Redeemer as derived from his parables, in which we cannot fail to recognise the master hand which had already analysed with rare tact the doctrinal teaching of the different apostolic writers, in his *Planting and Training of the Apostolic Church* (1st edition, 1832). He brought out the finer shades of thought in the peculiarity of each one, but at the same time pointed out the higher unity, and sought especially to show "how, notwithstanding all difference, there was an essential unity beneath, unless one is deceived by the form, and how the form in its diversity is easily explained." The weaker sides of Neander's treatment are avoided in one of the best works which we have here to mention, C. F. Schmid's *Bibl. Theol. des N. T.*, which, after his death, was edited by Dr. K. Weizsacker (1853), of which a new edition appeared in 1864. He presents the theology of the New Testament objectively and clearly, and penetrates with manifest sympathy into the organism of the different groups of doctrines, the treatment of which is preceded by a special biography of the Lord and His Apostles. If the latter is not to be commended (comp. § 1, 3), his work deserves the preference to the incomplete *Theology of the New Testament*, by Dr. G. L. Hahn, Leipzig, 1854. This treats only of the fundamental idea of God and the world, which underlies the teaching both of the Lord and His Apostles, without making a just distinction between the different doctrinal types, and brings out indeed very clearly the unity of the fore-mentioned ideas of God and the world, but without doing sufficient justice to the diversity of the doctrinal development in the writers of the New Testament. As far as the theology of the Apostles especially is concerned, we give the preference to H. Messner, *The Doctrine of the Apostles*, Berlin, 1856—a book here and there a little heavy in style, but rich in contents, and constructed on a good method; and especially G. V. Lechler, *The Apostolic and Post-Apostolic Age, with regard to Diversity and Unity in Doctrine and Life*, crowned in the year 1848 by the Teyler Society, and published in 1857 a second time, so greatly augmented and improved that it may almost be called a new work. The special literature of the Petrine, Pauline, and Johannine theology we shall cite in the proper place. That the treatment especially of the theology of Jesus must be considerably modified through the influence of the criticism of Strauss and the Tübingen school, was a natural consequence of the spirit of the time, and is manifest, besides, from many examples.

In general we must not suppose that even where the purely historical character of our science is acknowledged and defended, the theological and philosophical standpoint of the writer has been without great influence upon its treatment. How prejudicially the Hegelian philosophy has affected

Biblical theology we may perceive from the work of Vatke (1835), whose *à priori* construction of doctrine and history has been combated but not improved by Bruno Bauer, *The Religion of the Old Testament*, Berlin, 1838-39. As far as the New Testament is concerned, we should bestow a yet higher praise than we do upon the, in many respects, so excellent *Histoire de la Theol. Chrét. du Siècle Apostol.*, by E. Reuss, Strasburg, 1852 (latest edition 1864), if the clearness and completeness of the presentation were equalled by its strict objectivity. But in the grouping, here and there also in the treatment and appreciation of the materials, the author's considerable sympathy with the Tubingen construction of the earliest Church history is unmistakable, whilst his investigation, moreover, extends beyond the limits of the New Testament; which is not advantageous for the recognition of the entirely peculiar value of its contents. In a far greater degree, however, does this objection apply to the work of the head of the Tübingen school, Dr. F. C. Baur, in whose *Prelections on New Testament Theology*, published after his death by his son (1864), the well-known bright and dark sides of this school are, so to speak, concentrated. The whole rich material of New Testament theology Baur divides into three different periods, after he has first separately dealt with the teaching of Jesus. To the first of these he assigns the four Pauline epistles, acknowledged by him as genuine, together with the Apocalypse, and discusses their dogmatic contents. In the second follow the Epistle to the Hebrews, the

C

smaller epistles of Paul (with the exception of those to Timothy and Titus), and, further, the Epistles of Peter and James, the Synoptical Gospels and the Acts. In the third, finally, the doctrinal contents of the pastoral epistles and the Johannine writings, which, according to Baur, are by far the latest in the whole canon. Thus the whole conception and method rests upon a system of isagogics and criticism, to which no one will give the name of impartial. Yet more arbitrarily and with much less talent has this presentation of history been attempted from the same standpoint by L. Noack in his *Bibl. Theol., Introduction to the Old and New Testament*, Halle, 1853. From the Roman Catholic side an important contribution to our science has been made in Germany by J. A. B. Lutterbeck, *On the New Testament Doctrines; or, Investigations as to the Period of the Religious Change, the Stages preparatory to Christianity, and the first form of the same.* (Two parts, Mainz, 1852). It contains a treasure of material, although the author himself has published it only as a *Handbook of the Earliest History of Doctrines and Systematic Exegesis of the New Testament*, and although he leaves the doctrine of Jesus entirely untreated of, and, on the other hand, has taken up a great deal that does not properly belong to the subject.

As far as the literature of Holland is concerned, comparatively much has been done for the advancement of Biblical and Evangelical dogmatics (Muntingbe, Egeling, Heringa, Vinke), but as yet but little for the scientific and purely historic treatment of New Testament theology. From the standpoint of the Groningen school many an important contribution to the knowledge of the doctrines of Paul and his fellow-Apostles has been received in the early issues of *Waarheid in Liefde*. A copious compendium was afforded to his students by the Leyden professor, J. H. Scholten, in his *History of Christian Doctrine during the Period of the New Testament* (2nd edition), Leyden, 1858, in which the well-known clearness and acuteness of the author is just as little to be denied as the influence of his own dogmatic system upon the result. An important contribution to Biblical theology was made by Dr. A. H. Blom, in his treatise, *The Doctrine of the Messianic Kingdom among the First Christians, according to the Acts of the Apostles*, Dordr., 1863; a study in which, not in vain, the requirement of strict objectivity is made. In regard to *Eschatology*, an exact and thorough historic and exegetical investigation has been made by J. P. Briet (Two parts), Thiel, 1857, 1858.

4. At the end of our historic summary we see that, while it is by no means impossible to treat Biblical theology as an independent science, just as little is a new attempt at the development and completion of this science to be regarded as superfluous. It is further clear that the requirement of the science is so much the more fully met, in proportion as we keep before the eye its objective historic character; that, on the other hand, untimely admixture of one's own dogmatic and philosophic opinions can only tend to its

essential injury. During a succession of years, shipwreck has been made on one or other of these rocks alternately; either the unmistakable diversity of the doctrinal contents was sacrificed to the prosecution of an ideal unity, or the higher unity was sacrificed to a too strongly coloured diversity. The former of these especially was more prevalent at an earlier period, under the influence of ruling dogmatism; the latter more especially in our own time, under the influence of the criticism which gives the present tone. True wisdom demands that we avoid Scylla, and remain equally far from Charybdis. But this leads us to the following section.

Compare, on the subject treated of in this section, Reuss, *Histoire de la Théol. Chrét.*, pp. 13-28; Baur, *Vorlesungen uber neu-testamentliche Theologie*, p. 1-44.

POINTS FOR INQUIRY.

WHENCE is it that the Biblical theology of the New Testament is as yet a comparatively youthful science? What beneficial and what hurtful influence has the Tübingen school exerted upon its development? Is it possible and necessary to keep it free from the influence of a definite Christian philosophic system?

SECTION III.

Its Method, Main Division, and Requirement.

THE method of our investigation can, from the nature of the case, be no other than the genetic, chronologico-analytic. The main division of the material is determined by the peculiarity and mutual connection of the different doctrinal systems which are met with in the New Testament. If the treatment is to correspond to its object, it must be carried out in a truly scientific manner, but at the same time in a truly Christian spirit.

1. In every science the question as to the mode of proceeding is of primary importance. All the value of a result stands or falls with the legitimacy of the method by which it is obtained. As a part of historic theology, our science can obey no other laws than those which apply to every historic investigation. The method must, consequently, be a *genetic* one, that is, it must take into account not only the con-

tents, but also the manner of origination (genesis) of the different ideas. In this, historico-psychological exegesis, especially, will render good service. Further, it must be *chronological*. We find in the New Testament a series of writings and thoughts which, gradually formed, were not seldom developed under the opposing influence of one writer upon another; even the inner process of development of one and the same writer—*e g.*, that of Paul—was by no means immovably fixed during a succession of years. "History is the unfolding of life" (Schmid). Here, consequently, the well-known direction, *distingue tempora*, is to be carefully observed. Finally, *analytical* or disjunctive. We have to ask not at once after the doctrines of the Apostolic age *en bloc*, but after those of each of the different witnesses which meet us in the New Testament. It is true we have here also to do with a higher unity; but this becomes manifest only when the manifest diversity is first clearly presented. The synthesis has no value unless the analysis has been pure. "It is of analysis that we shall seek the light which shall lighten our path; of analysis, which teaches the historian to lose sight of himself, in order not to fail of his subject, which knows how to respect the particular character of each fact, of each idea that it meets, which recognises to each epoch, to each group, to each individuality even, however small, its right to appear to-day in the mirror of history, that which it once was in the reality of life" (Reuss).

2. The main division of the subject upon which we are entering is already, in principle, indicated by what we have said. First, we must separate *the theology of the Lord Jesus Christ and that of the Apostolic writers* from each other, and treat of the former before the latter. In dealing with the first, the difference between the utterances of the Lord in the *Synoptics* and those in the *Gospel of John* is at once evident. Also, the investigation of the Apostles' doctrine demands a similar threefold division. *Peter, Paul, John*, give—and indeed in this order — their successive testimony. Around these leading forms are grouped also others, who manifest more or less of spiritual affinity with them and their thoughts. Thus, to the Petrine theology belongs the doctrinal system of James and Jude; the Gospels of Matthew and Mark must also be arranged under this head. Around Paul are grouped his predecessor Stephen, his fellow-labourer Luke, and his spiritual kinsman the author of the Epistle to the Hebrews. John stands alone; but the John of the Fourth Gospel and of the Epistles, on the one hand, and the John of the Apocalypse, on the other hand, are sufficiently different for us to listen to the one only after the other has spoken.

In these two main divisions, the material for our investigation is comprehended, but not yet fully mastered. We cannot understand the teaching of the Lord and His Apostles so long as we have not—even though only in a general sense—learnt to know the ground out of which the plant grew.

A preparatory chapter must consequently precede the investigation of these, a chapter in which, indeed, not the whole theology of the Old Testament is treated of, but the religion from which Christianity sprang, the expectations it fulfilled, the condition, finally, the thoughts and wants of the age in which the Lord and His Apostles arose; in other words, Mosaism, Prophetism, and Judaism, as distinguished from an earlier Hebraism. We may best sum up the contents of this first, merely preparatory—but, nevertheless, indispensable—chapter, under the name of *Old Testament basis*. Upon this follows, as the *second* part, the theology of Jesus Christ; as a *third*, that of the Apostles, according to the plan above indicated. But is our investigation with this at an end? Just as little as the building whose foundations are laid, and whose walls are brought to the required height, but to which roof and gable are still wanting. In a *fourth*, or last part, must the synthesis of the completed analysis be attempted; in other words, the higher unity of the doctrine of the Apostles with each other, and with the Lord, must be spoken of. Only thus does the edifice of New Testament theology stand before our eyes as a compact whole. "Thus will New Testament theology have before it the task of developing the organic connection of New Testament doctrine" (Schmid). Only with this can we rest contented. And if now it is seen that none of the main parts before mentioned can either be left out or placed in other order, without the harmony being broken, then is at once made manifest the necessity as well as the justice of our main division.

3. The demand that the investigation to be instituted should be at the same time both scientific and Christian, will, as a whole, be contradicted by no one. Nevertheless, a word of further explanation will not be superfluous.

An investigation is *scientific* when it corresponds with the requirements of science in general, and of that science in particular to which it relates. "Science is a well-grounded and well-ordered knowledge, the fruit of just observation and philosophic induction" (Mulder). Theological science is consequently a well-grounded and well-ordered knowledge of God and Divine things, derived from those sources whence necessarily it must be drawn. This science in its examination receives light from faith in God and His revelation; but this faith, in place of fettering or obscuring the spirit of free investigation, rather calls it forth, and gives to its labour the most suitable direction. In regard to this investigation, also, the requirement is made that it should be thorough, exact, complete, impartial, and truth-loving. Impartiality, however, must not be conceived of a systematic denying or ignoring of all the principles upon which others proceed (freedom from prepossession), for this is neither necessary nor possible. It rather demands that, with candid mind and spirit, we hold ourselves open to every impression, and desire nothing but truth, whether it harmonises or not with our own favourite opinions. Such a love of truth, which becomes no one more than him who is treating of theological science, is naturally united with that moral earnestness which can by no means be wanting in an investigation like the present. To this extent, we may say that a truly scientific spirit is not merely a bent of the mind, but of the whole intellectual and moral life, so that, like eloquence, it may be called not only a gift, but a virtue.

Scientific investigation will at the same time be *Christian*, if it is, above all, begun and continued in a Christian spirit. Even in the examination of the doctrine of Jesus and the Apostles, we may not possibly forget what great importance the New Testament possesses for the religious and Christian life. The theologian who is also a Christian cannot possibly be untrue to his faith when he enters upon the domain of science. Nor is this by any means demanded: faith here also leads to a better recognition and knowledge, and the latter in turn puts us in a position better to believe (1 John v. 13.) Nevertheless, the Christian and the ecclesiastical standpoint must not here be regarded as entirely the same. The New Testament is here regarded and consulted purely as an historical document: the question whether it is still more than this, and in what relation it stands to the faith and life of the Christian, belongs exclusively to the domain of Christian dogmatics, and on this account is not here discussed. Then, also, must our investigation, secondly, be undertaken in a Christian spirit, that is, in the spirit of Christian humility, which is conscious of its limited capacity;

Its Method, Main Division, etc.

in the spirit of living faith, which impels so much the more powerfully to seek to fathom the mysteries of the kingdom of God; above all, in the spirit of ardent love for the Gospel, which easily and willingly enters into the spirit of the sacred writer. Here, also, sympathy is the indispensable condition of a deeper insight. Finally, the investigation must have a Christian aim: personal sanctification through the knowledge of the truth; the upbuilding of the kingdom of God in us and around us; and thereby, above all, the glorifying of Him for whom are all things, even in the domain of science.

Compare Schenkel, *Task of Biblical Theol.*, in *Studien und Kritiken*, 1852, i. p. 61 and following; Nitzsch, Article in Herzog's *Real-Encycl.* ii. p. 225.

POINTS FOR INQUIRY.

THE importance of method in the theological domain.—Criticism of some other modes of division and subdivision.—To what extent is an absolute impartiality in the investigation of our science indispensable, possible, desirable?—Is a purely historical investigation, such as is here attempted, consistent with the reverence we owe to Holy Scripture?

FIRST PART.

OLD TESTAMENT BASIS.

SECTION IV.
Mosaism.

MOSAISM is the religio-political institution which the Israelitish nation owes to Moses, and in consequence of which Israel has occupied an entirely unique position in the history of the development of the religious life of humanity. The main source of knowledge in regard to it is the Canonical Scripture of the Old Testament; its basis is a special revelation; its character, monotheistic; its form, theocratic; its worship, symbolico-typical; its design, purely moral; its standpoint, that of external authority, but, at the same time, of conscious preparation for a higher development.

1. The edifice of the New Testament theology reposes entirely upon an Old Testament basis. The Gospel is to be understood, neither in point of con-

tents or form, without a knowledge of prophetic Scripture; and this again leads back to Moses and the religion founded by him.*

2. That the Israelitish nation occupies an entirely unique place, particularly in the history of religion, cannot be ignored. In commerce and luxury it is surpassed by the Phœnicians, in art and science by the Greeks, in bravery by the Romans and other nations. In the religious domain, on the other hand, we meet in Israel with ideas, institutions, expectations, which we find nowhere else; historic forms, whose counterpart we elsewhere seek in vain; above all, a self-consciousness, which can only be the fruit of boundless arrogance, or of an inestimable privilege.† The objective and subjective height on which Israel stands is only to be explained by Mosaism.

3. For a just knowledge and appreciation of Mosaism, that of Moses himself is necessary. This is derived partly from profane sources — Egyptian, Grecian, Roman; partly from the sacred archives of the Old Testament, and above all of the Pentateuch. Not all, however, is of purely Mosaic origin which is called after the name of Moses; just as, also, not all is Christian which is associated with the name of Christ. It is the no less indisputable than important vocation of a thorough criticism to distinguish the originally Mosaic element from that which was later added, whether by way of development or through a process of degeneration.

* Comp. John iv. 22; 2 Tim. iii. 15.
† Deut. iv. 7; xxxiii. 29. Ps. lxxxix. 15; cxlvii. 19, 20.

4. Notwithstanding all that Moses has in common with other founders of religion in antiquity, his personality, his character, would remain absolutely inexplicable, unless he had been the interpreter and bearer of a special Divine revelation. The idea, the possibility, the reality, the characteristics of this special revelation, are brought out by the science of dogmatics. Biblical theology only attests the fact that Moses arose as an extraordinary messenger of God,* was recognised as such by his contemporaries and by posterity,† yea, even by Jesus and the Apostles,‡ and proved himself such, not only by signs and prophecy, but especially by the inner excellence of his religious teaching, which no one has yet succeeded in explaining upon purely natural principles. The Divine revelation granted to Moses, nevertheless, has its roots in an earlier one, and is the continuation of a golden thread of Divine promises, whose beginning is lost in hoary antiquity.§ Only from a supernaturalistic Christian standpoint can Mosaism be fully understood.

5. Mosaism shows from the beginning a strictly monotheistic character. It recognises Jehovah not only as the highest, but also as the only God,‖ beside whom to no creature in heaven or on earth may religious adoration be paid. If Israel in the wilderness and later was guilty of idolatry,¶ this took place in direct antagonism with the Mosaic principle, which

---

* Numb. xii. 6-8. † Deut. xxxiv. 10-12.
‡ Matt. xv. 3-6; Rom. iii. 2 § Exod. ii. 24, 25.
‖ Deut. vi. 4. ¶ Amos v. 25-27.

pronounces death upon this trangression. There is just as little ground for maintaining that this Mosaism arose out of an earlier Polytheism in the way of gradual development, as for explaining it out of the peculiarity of the Semitic race. "*Ce qui domine dans l'histoire des Juifs, ce n'est pas la race, mais la religion, deux choses distinctes, et qui ne s'expliquent pas mutuellement.*" (La Boulaye.) On the contrary, everything forces us to think of a personal revelation of God, in whatever form, given to the father of the nation, forgotten by his descendants in Egypt, renewed to Moses, and in Mosaism enriched with new elements. In consequence of this revelation, Israel knows the Lord—the Almighty Creator of heaven and earth—in His unity, majesty, spiritual nature, and His spotless holiness, united with compassion and faithfulness. This truth is here the axis around which all turns— "le dogme des dogmes." Its recognition raises Israel above all the nations of the earth, and is the unalterable condition of national and individual happiness. Nevertheless, the prospect of this latter does not, as a rule, extend farther than on this side the grave.*
However firmly the hope of individuals clings even in death to the Ever-living One, life and immortality have been first brought to light by the Gospel.†

6. The covenant which God, according to His promises, established with Israel through the mediation of Moses, becomes the basis of the *Theocracy*. The word is from Josephus (*contra* Apion. ii. 16); the thing itself is to be regarded neither as an imitation

* Exod. xx. 12. † 2 Tim. i. 10.

of other forms of religion—*e.g.*, Egyptian—nor as a merely natural fruit of a limited nationality of sentiment, nor as the involuntary consequence of reaction against heathenism. It was the work of the free and gracious choice of Him who, though He is Lord of the whole creation, made Israel more especially to be the people of His possession. The covenant-act of the theocracy thus founded was the law-giving at Sinai; its seat the sanctuary; its end—not the arising of the kingdom, by which it was only modified—but the destruction of the Israelitish state; its highest benefit finally was the appearing of Him who put an end to the wall of separation between Israel and the nations. Only when we have recognised this its theocratic character, is the history of Israel, and in connection with this, the ever higher revelation of the majesty of God, credible, and in a certain degree comprehensible.

7. As Covenant-God will God not only be acknowledged by Israel, but also be worshipped in a way well pleasing to Him. The ritual appointed by Moses displays a symbolico-typical character.* The outward forms are the visible expression of higher religious ideas; the ceremonies then present are at the same time shadows of future persons and things (*typi personales et reales*). Type and symbol is by no means the same thing. The symbol stands related to the idea, as its sensuous expression; the type to the antitype, as the shadow to the reality. The symbol shadows forth the invisible; the type repre-

* Coloss. ii. 17; Epistle to Hebrews, *passim*.

sents that which is as yet concealed. We see both united in the most important religious act—as of every religion, so also of Mosaism—the sacrifice. It is the symbol of voluntary consecration to God, and especially is the sin-offering a type of the perfect sacrifice of the New Covenant. "The notion of the typical is inseparable from that of a teleological development, in which the present is pregnant with the future" (Martensen). Rules for the further explanation of particulars are supplied by the symbolics and typology of the Old Testament.

8. If, consequently, the form of Mosaism is a lofty accommodation to the rude condition of the nation, its tendency is at the same time a purely moral one. The religious and moral element is here most intimately blended. The spotless holiness of the King of Israel becomes at the same time the highest ideal of the subject.[*] The lively feeling of one's own unholiness, the need for forgiveness of sin, delight in the grateful praise of God, is by the sacrificial ritual at once called forth and satisfied; and the spirit of love, compassion, humanity—notwithstanding the narrowest limitations of nationality—is cherished by a legislation which, even in the minutest particulars, manifests the design to unite together as closely as possible religion and life. Without justice has it been maintained that the Mosaic economy is founded merely upon legality, not upon morality, in the proper sense of the word, inasmuch as it regulates only external actions, no inner principles. Even the beginning of

[*] Levit. xix. 2.

the decalogue proves the contrary.* With all the experience of the terror of the Lord, the requirement of love to Him stands ever in the foreground;† and when Jesus sums up the whole law in this one precept, the genuinely Israelitish conscience testifies that He has interpreted it with perfect justice.‡ That which, regarded alone, would seem to stand in more or less of opposition to this strictly moral character of Mosaism,§ must be explained with the eye upon the whole, in the light of that age, and in connection with the special government of God.

9 To the law it was nevertheless impossible to work the fulfilment of its just demands in sinful man. Its stand-point was that of outward authority, like that of the pedagogue over unruly lads ‖ In Mosaism, man stands to God, not in the relation of a child to a father, but of a subject to his king, or of a transgressor to his judge. By far the greater number of commandments manifest, therefore, a prohibitory character;¶ and as the promise of life is attached to obedience, so also is the threatening of death made to transgression.** It is true, the love of God is here in principle manifested and recognised;†† but for the awakened conscience this is less prominent than His holiness and righteousness, which must ever impose new chastisements. Thus, then, is love to Him

---

* Exod. xx. 2.   † Deut. vi. 5.
‡ Mark xii 28-34.   § *e g* Exod. iii. 21, 22; 1 Sam. xv. 3.
‖ Gal. iv. 1, 2.   ¶ Coloss. ii. 21.
** Gal. iii. 10.
†† Exod. xxxiv. 6,7; Psalm ciii. 13; 1 Kings xix. 11-13.

Mosaism. 35

certainly demanded, but by no means wrought, by the law.* Mosaism, indeed, knows the promise of a regeneration of the heart ;† but the letter, as such, kills.‡ In this respect, the spirit and power of Mosaism is admirably symbolized in the bearing of the nation at Sinai.§

10. Thus regarded, Mosaism will be less a preparation for Christianity than an opposition thereto; since therein—that which here can be by no means overlooked—no place was left for higher development. But the same Divine revelation, which had founded Mosaism, had at the same time made provision for its development by means of prophetism.‖ Mosaism displays a particular colouring, but universalistic are the reminiscences of ancient promises, which it has preserved intact,¶ and the aspirations which its interpreters express from the highest stand-point of their religious development.** Thus it manifests in itself a harmonious unity; not, however, that of the completed building, but of the firm foundation upon which the edifice is to be further raised.

Compare, on the Theology of the Old Testament in general, the works cited in Section II. On the history of Israel and of the Old Testament, those of Hess, Kalkar, Kurtz [English Translation], Ewald [English Translation], Stanley. Also the Prelections of Da Costa, *over waarh en waardij der Schriften v. h. O. V.* Amst. 1844. Articles on Moses and Egypt, in

---
* Rom viii., 15.   † Deut. xxx. 6.   ‡ 2 Cor. iii. 6.
§ Exod. xx. 18-21.   ‖ Deut. xviii. 15-18.
¶ Gen. iii. 15 ; xlix. 10.   ** Numbers xi. 29 ; 1 Kings viii. 41-43.

Herzog. Auberlen: *Göttliche Offenbarung* (Divine Revelation.) Trip: *Ueb. die Theophanien d. A. T.*, in the works of the Society of the Hague, 1856. Dillmann: *Ueb. den Ursprung der A. T.-lichen Religion.* Giessen, 1865. Bahr: *Symbol. des Mos. Cult.*, Heidelb., 1837. Kurtz: *Mosaic Sacrifices.* Piccardt: *De legislat. Mos. indole morali*, Traj., 1839. Tholuck: *Das Alt. Test. im N. Test.* (two appendices to the Commentary on the Epistle to the Hebrews). Umbreit: *Das Evang. im A. T.*, in Studien and Kritiken, 1849. I.

POINTS FOR INQUIRY.

Diversity and connection of the Old and the New Testament.—Summary and criticism of the different views of Mosaism.—Is it possible to explain the origin of Monotheism in Israel in a purely natural way?—The hypothesis of stone-worship.—Harmony and diversity of the theocracy and the later hierarchy.—To what extent is Mosaism entirely original? (Spencer and Witsius.)—The different forms of special revelation.—The symbolical character, also, of other ancient religions.—How is the former over-estimate and the later neglect of typology to be explained?—Detailed indication of the symbolico-typical element in different kinds of sacrifices.—To what extent can the Mosaic legislation, as compared with others, serve as a proof of the Divine origin of Mosaism?—Mosaism and the Messianic expectations.

SECTION V.

Prophetism.

Prophetism, which is in its nature **not less** unique than the original Mosaism, and is just as little to be explained in a rationalistic or magical way, was at once the continuation and fulfilment of earlier revelation, and as such an inestimable blessing, not only for Israel, but also for the Gentile world. It prepared the way for the Gospel of the New Covenant, exercised considerable influence upon its contents and form, and raised its high value above all reasonable doubts.

1. As Moses had, as prophet, stood far above his contemporaries,* so also there arose after him, here and there, extraordinary men of God. Even in the time of the Judges we see single prophets arise,† although the period of unbroken prophecy begins only with Samuel. He appears to have been the founder of the so-called

* Numbers xii. 6-8. † Judges iv. 4; vi. 8.

schools of the prophets, which soon after came to a higher development under Elijah and Elisha. Their own relation towards Saul and David represents at the same time that of their successors towards later kings. As representatives of the theocracy, called by Jehovah himself, they arise out of different tribes and districts. They are by no means above the law, but maintain its authority, enforce its spiritual observance, and interpret God's deeds and purposes, into which they have a deeper insight than others. On this account, in more than one respect different from the priests, they bear the names of Messenger or Ambassador of God, (מַלְאַךְ יְה) Speaker, (נָבִיא) Seer, (רֹאֶה), and others of similar import. They teach the nation to understand the signs of the times, and even not seldom utter prophecies in the strict sense of the term, *i.e.*, definite proclamations of such events of the future as could not possibly be calculated in a natural way. Just as little as the predicting of the future is to be regarded as the highest vocation of the prophet, just so little will an impartial criticism exclude, *à priori*, from their activity the prophesying of those hidden things which stood in organic connection with the development of the kingdom of God. The assertion that the truths made known to the prophets in no case extended beyond the natural limits of human knowledge, is in irreconcilable conflict as well with the expressions of their own self-consciousness as with the facts themselves.

2. That the Israelitish Prophetism is an entirely unique phenomenon is seen if we regard it, on the

one hand, in itself, on the other hand, in comparison with heathen soothsaying *(mantik)*. Only on theistic soil can a plant like this flourish; only as a link in a chain of special Divine purposes of salvation can Prophetism be explained. Here, also, there is no choice between a supernatural conception and an unnatural representation thereof. He who explains Prophetism rationalistically forgets that the expression of the human feeling, and of the prophetic consciousness of the Seer, is often diametrically opposed;* and makes the whole theocracy, finally, a work of reflection and calculation, exceptionally favoured by the course of events. The Israelitish prophet sees more than others, because more has been communicated to him by God than to others. No doubt, the capacity for receiving this communication was present in the prophets in no ordinary degree; but the source of their personal certainty, as regards the present and the future, lay in a special revelation given to them, in preference to others, and in different ways. With the untenable theory of a merely magical or mechanical inspiration, the fact of this inspiration itself does not fall. Prophecy was the ripened fruit, not of a divination only, but of a revelation whose contents and form attached themselves to the individuality of the prophets and the condition of the moment, without, however, being explicable from these alone. " History supplies the occasion for prophecy, but not its measure."—(Delitzsch.) Genuine prophecy arises through the co-

* 1 Sam. xv. 11 ; xvi. 6, 7 ; 2 Sam. vii. 3-7.

operation of the Divine with the human factor, and builds upon the result of the past and present, in order thence to direct its glance to the mysteries of the future.

3. Prophetism stands in very close relation to Mosaism. It secures the observance of the precepts of the latter, which would else be constantly forgotten;* but developes at the same time its dogmatic contents, and adds to it essentially new elements. While Mosaism had proclaimed God's unity, Israel's prophets, at the same time, extolled His majesty in an unapproachable manner, and wielded the lash of satire against the folly of idolatry.† The idea of the Angel of the Covenant, and that of the Spirit of the Lord, manifests itself much more clearly in the word of the Prophets than in Moses.‡ The doctrine of Angels as well as of Demons, of which Mosaism possesses only slight traces, is, especially by the later prophets, developed powerfully and on many sides. Also, the expectation of resurrection and judgment after death, in regard to which Moses had been silent, is by some of them expressly mentioned.§ While even Mosaism in principle was purely moral, the prophetic word, above all, directs the attention to the spiritual nature of God's commandments,‖ and urges in opposition to a mechanical formalism and ceremonialism, the necessity for a spiritual consecra-

---

* Mal. iv. 4, 5. † Isaiah xl. and xliv.
‡ Isaiah lxiii. 9, 10.
§ Isaiah xxv. 6-9 xxvi. 19; Ezek. xxxvii. 1-14; Dan. xii. 2, 3.
‖ 1 Sam. xv. 22; Isaiah i. 11-18; Micah vi. 6-8.

Prophetism. 41

tion of self to God as the essence of the sacrificial ritual.* Finally, if Mosaism was adapted only for a particular nation; the prophets placed themselves upon the wall of separation, which they are not yet able to take away, and proclaim a kingdom of God which, proceeding from Jerusalem, embraces all nations,†—a golden age of the future, fairer than the heathen ever imagined it.‡

4. Messianic prophecy also, as well in the narrower as in the wider sense — in regard to the person and kingdom of the Messiah — may in a certain sense be regarded as an outgrowth from Mosaism. It is the continuation of a golden string of promises, with which the Pentateuch had already made the prophets and their contemporaries acquainted (*See* § IV. 10). The house of David, himself a prophet rejoicing in the loftiest prospect of the future,§ becomes the point around which gather the fairest expectations, shadowed forth in ever clearer outline. In the earlier prophets,|| Joel, Amos, Hosea, these are expressed in more general forms; but already, in Micah, and especially in Isaiah, the ardently-desired offspring of David is depicted in ever livelier colours.¶ To the description of his kingly glory, attaches that of his prophetic and high-priestly activity, especially in the last chapters of Isaiah.** If here, also, the posterity

---

* 1 Sam. xv. 22 ; Isaiah i. 11-18 ; Micah vi. 6-8.
† Isaiah ii. 4   ‡ Isaiah xi. 6-9.
§ 2 Sam. xxiii. 1-7 ; Matt. xxii. 43 ; Acts ii. 30.
|| Joel ii. 28-32 ; Amos ix. 11, 12 ; Hosea iii. 5.
¶ Micah iv. 5. ; Isaiah vii. 14 ; ix. 1-6 ; xi. 1-10.
** Isaiah xlii. and xlix. ; l. 4-11 ; lii. 13—liii. 12.

of David is not forgotten (lv. 3), yet it is especially the servant of the Lord, who brings salvation not only to Israel, but also to the Gentiles, who appears as suffering, the innocent for the guilty, and as the true spiritual Israel becomes at once the source of temporal and of spiritual blessing for all the nations of the world.* That, consequently, which has been already indicated before the captivity is, during this period, repeated, enriched with new traits. As it were out of the ruins of the destroyed Jerusalem, Jeremiah sees the throne of David arising in glorious brightness,† and sets forth at the same time all the spiritual glory which the new dispensation has above the old.‡ Ezekiel represents the Son of David under the beautiful image of a Cedar and of a Shepherd,§ and sees a stream of living water flowing out of the new temple.‖ Daniel stands as the world's prophet upon a height, whence in the stillness of the night he beholds how the image of the earthly monarchy is broken before his eyes, and sees the kingdom of heaven, symbolised under the form of a Son of man, coming upon the clouds of heaven. ¶ And also after the captivity, the same expectation of spiritual blessings manifests itself in variously modified forms, but in substance essentially the same. Haggai** looks for a revelation of God

* Comp. Oehler, *der Knecht Jehovah's im Deutero* (?) *Jesaiah*. Stuttgard, 1865
† Jer. xxiii. 5, 6.   ‡ Jer. xxxi. 31-34.
§ Ezek. xvii. 22-24; xxxiv. 23.   ‖ Ezek. xlvii. 1-12.
¶ Dan. c. vii.   ** Hagg. ii. 6-9.

even among the Gentiles, in consequence of which the latter glory of God's house far surpasses the former glory. Zechariah* sees the priestly and the kingly office united in the offspring of David, who comes in meekness to the wretched. Malachi,† who sees in Him the Angel of the Covenant, proclaims at the same time the second Elias as his forerunner. Each prophet towers above his predecessor: all together point to the One who is the end (final aim) of Law and Prophecy.

5. No wonder that such a Prophetism was inestimably beneficial for Israel. It was the continual channel of revelation, the bulwark of religion and, so to speak, the unswerving conscience of the Theocratic state. By means of Prophetism, Israel saw at once its past conserved, its present enlightened, its future assured. Thence it happens that the possession of prophets was regarded as a peculiar privilege,‡ their cessation bewailed as a national misfortune.§ Even for the Gentile nations, Prophetism was exceptionally beneficial. The activity of many prophets (Elisha, Jonah, Daniel) extended beyond the limits of the land of promise, with the definite effect of preparing for the founding of the kingdom of God on a wider scale. Above all, the Greek translation of the word of prophecy was exceedingly serviceable to this end.

6. Prophetism thus, both in Israel and in the Gentile world, prepared the way for the Gospel of

---

* Zech. vi. 12, 13; ix. 9.　　† Mal. iii. 1; iv. 5.
‡ Nehem. ix. 30; Amos ii. 11.　　§ Psalm lxxiv. 9.

the New Testament. Without doubt, it tended to preserve that Monotheism, without which a special revelation of spiritual blessings was not conceivable. It called forth and intensified the consciousness of sin, that the nation might so much the more ardently sigh for deliverance. It preserved alive hope, even when hope seemed to be in vain, and, as opposed to the terrors of the law, proclaimed the consolation of the promise. Even the whole personality—the work and the fate of the leading prophets—served as a foreshadowing of Him who was to be the crown and centre of all the revelations of God.*

7. For the writer on New Testament Theology, also, the study of the prophetic word of the Old Testament is of an importance which cannot be overlooked. Upon the contents and form of the first proclamation of the Gospel it exercised a many-sided influence. The Gospel appears as the fulfilment of prophetic expectations; and appeals, in proof of its Divinity, to prophetic utterances.†
In the mirror of this Scripture, the Lord beheld his own image, and in it have thousands recognised Him as the Christ. As well the description of His person, as the representation of His work in the New Testament, finds its key in the language and ritual of the Old. Yea, however great the difference between the form of the prophetic and the apostolic utterances, the influence of the former upon the latter

* Isaiah lxi. 1; Comp. Luke iv. 18, 19; Matt. xii. 40; xxiii. 37.
† Luke xxiv. 27; Acts xvii. 3; and many other places.

is in this respect also indisputable. The eschatology of the New Testament, for instance, is in great measure clothed in the language of the Old Testament prophets, and Old Testament voices find their more powerful echo therein. Leave prophetic Scripture unregarded, and apostolic Scripture will be, for you, partly unintelligible, partly incredible. Regard the latter in the light of the former, and its truth and divinity appear for you ever clearer. That it is, however, necessary to distinguish contents and form of prophecy in its explanation, and carefully to guard, on the one hand, against realistic misconception of Eastern imagery, on the other hand against a spiritualistic subtilising of the reality here proclaimed, scarcely needs to be mentioned. Definite rules for the interpretation of the word of prophecy are furnished by the hermeneutics of the Old Testament.

On Prophetism in general, compare—besides the monographs of A. Knobel (1838), F. B. Koster (1838), and H. Ewald (1840), and the Articles in Herzog— F. Delitzsch, *Bibl. Proph. Theol.*, &c., 1835; Tholuck, *Die Propheten und ihre Weissagung*, &c. Gotha, 1860; Hoffmann, *Weissagung und Erfullung.* Nordl., 1841; Hengstenberg, *Christology of the Old Test.* (English translation); J. J. van Oosterzee, *Christologie*, i. pp. 39-74, ii. pp. 543-554; Dusterdieck, *De Rei Propheticæ in V. T., quam Universæ tam Messianæ Naturâ Ethicâ.* Gott., 1852; Keil, *Introduction to the Old Test.* (English translation); the Roman Catholic Professor Haneberg, *Einleitung in die Heilige Schrift.* Regensburg, 1852. Pp. 243-309; Smith, *Prophecy a Preparation for Christ*, Bampton Lecture for 1869.

POINTS FOR INQUIRY.

How is the gift of prophecy described by the prophets themselves?—Is there ground for reposing confidence in these expressions of their self-consciousness?—History and characteristics of pseudo-prophetism.—The schools of the prophets.—The relation of the prophetic office to that of the priests and kings.—Organic connection and development of Messianic prophecy.—Ground and significance of the disappearing of the prophetic gift in Israel.—Peculiarity of the prophets of the Old Covenant as compared with those of the New.

SECTION VI.

Judaism.

THE original Hebraism, sustained and purified by the word of Moses and the prophets, does not by any means attain, in later Judaism, to a condition of normal development, but rather one of retrogression and deep degeneracy. In this light it presents itself to us on a glance at the religious condition, the ideas and requirements of the contemporaries of the Lord. Acquaintance with these is necessary, in order rightly to understand, and justly to appreciate, the utterances of Jesus and the Apostles, whether as to their contents or form.

1. Although it is certain that the word of the Lord and the Apostles attaches itself to that of Moses and the prophets, it is yet clear that this takes place, not without respect to given circumstances and definite requirements. A want of acquaintance with this fact renders the doctrine of the New Testament unintel-

ligible. A knowledge of Judaism, not less than of Hebraism, is for this reason not only important, but necessary.

2. By Judaism is understood the peculiar mode of thought of the Israelites (now called Jews) after the Babylonian captivity, in the moral and religious domain, and in all which is necessarily connected therewith. Not unhappily has it been characterised as "the unsuccessful attempt at the restoration of Hebraism, and the mingling of positive elements thereof with foreign doctrines of a mythologico-metaphysical character, in which is felt the influence of intellectual reflection without living inspiration—a chaos which awaits a new creation." (De Wette.) It is known to us partly from Biblical sources—the latest portions of the Old Testament, the Gospels, Acts, and several Epistles of the New Testament, to some extent also from the Septuagint; partly from non-Biblical sources—the Apocryphas and Pseudepigrapha of the Old Testament, the oldest Targums, the Talmud, the Jewish elements in the Sibylline books, the writings of Flavius Josephus, of Philo, and others.

3. The moral and religious condition of the Jews after the Babylonian captivity manifests, in more than one respect, a relatively good character. Idolatry has disappeared, the temple is restored, a number of synagogues and houses of prayer have arisen (Acts xv. 21), and the knowledge of the Holy Scriptures, there read in appointed order, has perceptibly increased. Collected into one volume, and prepared for wider circulation by means of the Alexandrine translation

(LXX.), the Old Testament is distinguished by a sharp line of separation from the apocryphal literature which arose at the same period, and carefully interpreted and preserved by the chiefs of Rabbinical learning. The wall of separation between Israel and the Gentile world is perceptibly lower, and a considerable number of proselytes, both of the gate and of righteousness, attaches itself to the once greatly despised Jews. The forms are in many respects excellent, and the Maccabæan heroic age shows that the ancient spirit is not yet entirely extinguished. The Messianic expectation, finally, is now more than ever known, wide-spread, and prized.

4. But, notwithstanding all this, this period bears traces of growing old. The religious life, impeded in its normal operation, on the one hand, by legalism, on the other by pride of works, manifests more of an intellectual and anxious than of a believing and joyous character; a narrow-minded exactness about trifles takes the place of former inspiration. False prophets do not arise at this period, but at the same time the voice of true ones is silent; the past is lauded, but the present does not attain to the former height. Side by side with the law, tradition comes into play (Matt. xv. 1-14); along with Mosaic ideas the influence of the Alexandrian, Persian, and other religious conceptions begins to be manifest; and whilst knowledge puffs up, love is forgotten. The schools of Hillel and Shammai divide the minds of men, and the sects which arise during this period contribute their measure to the degeneracy of Judaism.

5. The *Pharisees*, who arose as a sect about three centuries before Christ, and had gained many adherents among the people, especially among the women (Mark xii. 40), and had united the greater part of the Scribes under their banner, represented the conservative principle. However many parties there were among them, their people felt themselves one. They held that not only as Israelites were they separated (פָּרַשׁ) from the Gentiles, but also, as the pious, from the sinners among the Israelites. Their doctrine is distinguished by a highly-developed pneumatology, Christology, eschatology; their morals by formalism, rigorism, casuistry; their practice in the religious domain by zealotism (Matt. xxiii. 15), in the political by revolutionary movements which rendered them the dreaded antagonists of the Roman government.

The *Sadducees*, who opposed themselves to the others as righteous (צָדַק), unless it be preferred to derive their name from a certain *Zadok*, are related to the Pharisees in some measure as the Epicureans to the Stoics. Less numerous, but more influential than their opponents, they often make common cause with the court party (Mark iii. 6), and entertain in politics highly conservative principles, in religion exceedingly lax ones. By means of an entire ignoring of all higher destiny, they brought the doctrine of moral freedom so emphatically into the foreground, and that of future punishment, on the other, they placed so entirely in the background, that their whole mode of thought and life must stand in direct antagonism to that of their rivals. The charge of great immorality, however, has been no more proved than the assertion that of the Old Testament they accepted only the *Thora* (Pentateuch). Indisputable, on the other hand, is their rejection of angelology, and perfectly explicable is their increasing hostility to the gospel of the resurrection.* The *Essenes*, finally, who were known to us, not from the New Testament, but only from Philo's writing—*quod omnis probus liber*—and Josephus (compare also Pliny, H. N. v. 17), and are not to be confounded with the Therapeutæ, may be regarded as representatives of the practico-ascetic principle. They are, as it were, the hermits of Israel, and are distinguished from others by their contempt of earthly treasures, their prohibition of the oath, their laudation of celibacy, disapproval of bloody sacrifices, and their entire community of property. The difference between their mode of thought and that of John the Baptist, and above all of Jesus, is in itself great enough to render untenable the conjecture of an original affinity of the Gospel of the Kingdom with Essenism.

6. In the midst of the varying strife of these sects, we see the people becoming despised and degraded.† The religious class of the people consisted in great part of those who were poor ($\pi\tau\omega\chi o \iota$, אֶבְיוֹנִים) as well in earthly things as in much that passed for wisdom and piety.‡ To these lowly and simple ones belonged not only the Lord's relatives, but also the greater part of His friends and followers; while even among the

* Acts iv. 2; xxiii. 8. † Matt. ix. 36; comp. John vii. 49.
‡ Matt. v. 3; xi. 25.

despised Samaritans* persons of such a spirit were not altogether wanting. The hostility between the Samaritans and the Jews could only tend to increase the moral wretchedness.

7. The religious ideas of Judaism, developed in the midst of such circumstances, manifest a peculiar union of light and shade. The idea of God in many, although monotheistic, began in practice to bear more of a deistical (conceiving of God as apart from the world) than a theistical character; the service of God was less a common worship than service in the slavish sense of the word. No doubt the science of dogmatics, under the influence of foreign ideas, was in some points enriched. Angelology attained to further development,† and not less demonology, in connection with which, also, exorcism was practised (Matt. xii. 27). So, also, was eschatology, especially by the Pharisees, developed in plastic forms, however much in principle it was based upon single prophetic utterances (Dan. xii. 1-3). Finally, as regards morals, the great principles of Mosaism were explained and applied to existing circumstances by means of a great number of commands and prohibitions, but at the same time weakened in their effect, if not altogether contradicted ‡ Thus was the Jewish religion impoverished in the same proportion in which the doctrine of faith and morals was gradually diffused.

* John iv. 39-42.
† See, for ex., LXX. on Deut. xxxii. 2 : comp. Acts vii. 53; Gal. iii. 19 ; Heb. ii. 2.
‡ Matt. xxiii. 16-22.

Judaism. 53

8. More fully have we here to speak of the Messianic expectation during this period. The doubt whether such an expectation existed at all (B. Bauer) belongs to the curiosities of theological literature. Less easy than to prove its existence is it rightly to define its nature. Josephus knows it, but, for reasons easily to be explained, is silent in regard to it. Philo makes but a single allusion to it (*De Præm.* p. 924, *De Execrat.* c. ix.), and also the Apocryphas of the Old Testament contain only a few sporadic references.* More is to be learned from the so-called Book of Enoch, written probably a century before Christ; also the Fourth Book of Ezra, although of later origin, affords us an important source. Above all, we have to do with the ideas which are found here and there in the New Testament. From all these sources we learn that the expectation of the Messiah was widely diffused, but varied greatly in point of contents and value, and never appeared as a compact whole.

The whole history of the world is divided into two periods, the pre-Messianic and the Messianic.† The former is the period of conflict and misery; the latter that of peace and blessedness, brought about by the coming of the Messiah. The transition from the one period to the other is indicated under the name of *the last days*. With these coincides the beginning of the days of the Messiah, whose revelation is proclaimed by outward signs. They consist of days of great distress (ὠδῖνες), of the appearing of a particular star,‡

* See, for ex., 1 Macc. ii. 57; iv. 46; xiv. 41.
† αἰών οὗτος and ὁ μέλλων, עוֹלָם הַזֶּה and עוֹלָם הַבָּא.
‡ Matt. ii. 2.

of the rising of Elias or one of the other prophets to prepare the way of the Lord,* and above all, in the appearing of a mysterious evil being (the Antichrist, Armillus); while, also, the establishment of His kingdom is preceded by the battle with hostile world-powers (Gog and Magog.) After all this comes the Messiah, or rather He will be there without any one knowing from whence. This, at least, is the opinion of a part of the nation (John vii. 27), whilst the Scribes expect that He will come out of Bethlehem (Matt. ii. 4-6). He will be a man among and of men (*see* Justin Martyr, *Dial. cum Tryphone*, c. 49), sprung from the chosen family of David, and anointed with the Holy Spirit. It can no more be proved that the popular faith looked for a miraculous conception of the Messiah through the Holy Ghost, than that it ascribed to Him a superhuman nature and dignity. For the idea of a suffering and dying Messiah, there was also but little room; on the contrary, it was expected that the Christ would abide for ever (John xii. 34), and would set up His kingdom in Israel (Acts i. 6). Upon the question whether, with Judah and Benjamin, the other ten tribes would also share in this blessedness, opinions differed. In any case, however, they hoped from Messiah for a solution of all rankling controversies (John iv. 25), a knowledge of hidden things (John xvi. 30), especially, also, a number of astonishing miracles (Matt. xi. 2-6; John vii. 31); and in consequence of all this, a deliverance, conceived of by some as a more outward one, by others as more spiritual

* Mark ix. 12; John i. 21.

Judaism. 55

(Luke i. 74-75). He will at His coming awake the dead—the Israelites first—will triumph over the enmity of hell and of the heathen, and prepare for the world a salvation in which also the non-Israelite nations will share. Of this salvation Jerusalem will be the centre, the purified earth the theatre, and the restoration of all things the crown (παλιγγενεσία, ἀποκατάστασις πάντων).

9. The real want of the nation, in whose midst we meet such ideas of higher light and life, however unmistakeable, was by no means generally recognised, far less satisfied by existing things. The desire for outward deliverance far surpassed that for spiritual blessing. The latter, however, was not entirely wanting (Luke ii. 38 ᵇ), and could in any case be awakened. The appearing of the herald must to this end precede that of the Lord.

On the history and sources of knowledge for Judaism in general, compare De Wette, *Bibl. Dogm.*, sec. 76-82, and the literature there cited. A. Gfrorer, *das Jahrhundert des Heils*, 1838, II. Lutterbeck, *l. c.* i. p. 99. E. de Pressensé, *Religions before Christ* (English translation). Articles in Herzog's *Real-encycl.* C. E. van Kœtsveld, *de Phariseën, Sadduc. en Herod.*, the Hague, 1862. Pressensé, *Jesus-Christ* (p. 66 and following of English translation). On "The Fulness of the Time," see our *Leven van Jezus*, i. p. 265 and following.

POINTS FOR INQUIRY.

WHENCE is the difference between Judaism and Hebraism above all to be explained?—More exact criticism and mutual comparison of the sources.—Jewish Apocalyptics.—The Alexandrine philosophy in relation to Judaism.—What is to be ascertained with sufficient certainty as to the origin, character, and mutual relation of the different sects?—The relation between Essenism and Pythagorism.—Origin, peculiarity, Messianic expectation of the Samaritans.—Proselytism and the Diaspora.—Which are, as a whole, the bright and the dark sides of the Messianic expectation of this period? —What remains of genuine Hebraism are still to be **observed in Judaism?**

SECTION VII.

John the Baptist.

In the arising and work of this forerunner of the Lord, Mosaism approaches its goal, prophetism attains its point of culmination, and Judaism receives a salutary restraint.

1. The Biblical theology of the New Testament can neither treat of the history of John the Baptist, nor set forth the loftiness of his character. It is satisfied with indicating in general the position which belongs to him as an indispensable link in the chain of doctrinal development.

2. If Mosaism has as its object, by means of the law, to lead to the knowledge of sin, and thus to awaken the longing for redemption, the voice of the second Elias sounds forth for no other end. As standing above the earlier men of God and nearest to Jesus, he merits the name of the greatest of the prophets (Luke vii. 29). Entirely new revelations he does not proclaim, but once more powerfully lays hold of the

old, and brings them into direct connection with a person already present (Luke xvi. 16). His whole manifestation and work is *one* voice (Luke iii. 4); his word, as it were, the powerful *finale* of the prophetic symphony. But for this very reason, he exerted upon Judaism a wholesome restraint. He assails all self-righteousness in its vital point, and brings about in the nation a sharp but salutary separation (κρίσις)

3. The significance of John is to be sought, above all, in his testimony as to the person and work of the Messiah. In examining the contents of this testimony we must distinguish between the period before, and that after, the baptism of the Lord. The least ambiguous and most powerful utterances are heard towards the end of his course (Acts xiii. 25). In the beginning it is especially noticeable how the form of his Messianic expectation attaches itself to his own mission, and at the same time bears a strongly Old Testament character. While he himself baptises, he proclaims another baptizer, who, however, comes forth endowed with the gifts of the Holy Ghost; a Messiah who arises in Israel, not simply as a Deliverer, but as a Judge. He points out the insufficiency of descent from Abraham without, however, speaking of the calling of the Gentiles. After this proclamation of the Messiah in general, he begins from the time of the Lord's baptism in Jordan, to point to Him definitely as the promised Messiah. His heavenly descent (John i. 15), and His expiatory work, conceived of in the most universal sense (John i. 29), now come clearly into the foreground; and even his last testimony declares the

wholly unique greatness of Christ, and the peculiarity of his own relation to Him as his forerunner. (John iii. 27-36).

4. This testimony of John the Baptist is especially important on account of the peculiarity of the source whence it flows. It was the fruit of careful training, accurate investigation of the Scripture, special revelation of God, and personal contemplation of Jesus. Yet more high becomes its value, when we observe how far he stood above the thoughts and wishes of his contemporaries; and, above all, how high the estimate entertained of him by the Lord himself.* Nevertheless, compared with the teaching of the Lord and His Apostles, is the testimony of John the Baptist relatively poor, and not essentially raised above the stand-point of the Old Testament.

Compare the different works on the Gospel History. The article on "John," by Guder, in Herzog's *R. E.*, and literature there cited.

POINTS FOR INQUIRY.

THE time of the arising of John the Baptist (Luke iii. 1, 2).—Contents and value of the testimony of Josephus concerning John.--Connection of the circumstances of the life of John with his mission.—His relation to the Old Testament and to the New.—Diversity and harmony of the Gospel narratives concerning his Messianic testimony.—What is the sense of John i. 15-29?—Of Matt. xi. 3?—The disciples of John.—The eternal significance of John's appearing.

* Matt. xi. 7-15; John v. 35.

SECTION VIII.

Result.

MOSAISM and Prophetism contain the germ and starting-point for the testimony of the truth, which was given by the Lord and His Apostles, and is contained in the Holy Scriptures of the New Testament. In Judaism we find nothing by which the personality of the Lord and the contents of His Gospel can be explained in a merely natural way.

"L'opposition radicale qui existait entre les deux mouvements religieux, ressort avec evidence de leur resultat definitif. L'enseignement du Christ aboutit à l'Evangile et celui des Rabbins au Talmud. D'un côté, nous avons une vivante histoire qui est toute pénetrée d'un esprit nouveau, sans formules arrêtées, et sans rituel; d'un autre côté un corps de traditions enchevêtrées, une réglementation de toutes les formes de la piété poussée jusqu'aux détails les plus minutieux."

E. DE PRESSENSÉ.

SECOND PART.

THE THEOLOGY OF JESUS CHRIST

SECTION IX.
General Summary.

The investigation of the theology of Jesus Christ proposes, as its object, to become acquainted with the contents of our Lord's teaching given during His life upon earth—concerning God and Divine things, as it is communicated to us more especially in the four canonical Gospels. For the just appreciation thereof it is necessary, above all, to bring into its true light the peculiar character, source, and form of this teaching, and its relation as well to that of the Old Testament as to that of the Apostles and their fellow-labourers.

1. Although our Lord Jesus Christ cannot, by any means, be said to have appeared on earth merely, or

even principally, in order to proclaim to men a new doctrine, and although He has set forth no peculiar system of doctrine, yet, according to His own declaration, He came into the world to testify to the truth (John xviii. 37). He did this by His personal manifestation (John xiv. 6-9), but also by his word, and the light which is shed thereby upon God and Divine things. The examination of the theology of the Lord Jesus Christ has especially to do with the latter of these.

2. The Biblical theology of Jesus Christ investigates exclusively—without entering upon any other domain—what the Lord taught concerning God and Divine things. It represents the contents and connection of His ideas of God and man, and the mutual relation of both, as presented by Him during his life on earth, whether in mere hints or in more explicit declarations. Though, in a certain sense, the word of the prophets (1 Peter i. 11), as well as that of the Apostles (Luke x. 16), is to be regarded as His, we confine our attention for the present especially to the latter.

3. Besides what we know from the four Gospels, there is not wanting opportunity of gleaning something additional concerning the Lord's doctrine. Tradition makes us acquainted with some so-called unwritten sayings; the Acts of the Apostles, and the Epistles also, contain single contributions.* Nevertheless, the four Gospels remain the principal source; and New Testament theology has not to wait for the

* Acts xx. 35; 1 John i. 5; 1 John iv. 21.

last word of isagogics on the questions yet unsettled in regard to the New Testament canon, before attaching to the communications of the Gospel the very highest value. It may do so the more freely, since even those critics—who dispute, for instance, the genuineness of the first Gospel in its present form—yet regard the discourses (*Logia*) of the Lord found therein as being, on the whole, a faithful expression of His spirit. At the present stage of critical investigation, however, the fourth Gospel demands a separate examination. (Compare Sec. III., 2.)

4. In order to place ourselves at the true standpoint we must, above all, have regard to the peculiar character of the Lord's teaching, as it is contained in the Gospels. As, in general, the whole may be known from its parts, so do the parts in turn receive light from the rightly-comprehended spirit of the whole. It is not enough to say that the doctrine of Jesus shows a high *religious* character; this it has in common with that of many others; and the history of our own time shows clearly enough to what a wretched use the word *religious* is sometimes put. In the doctrine of the Lord a distinctly *soteriological* character must be acknowledged; in other words, all that the Lord proclaims concerning God and man, concerning sin and grace, concerning the present and the future life, especially all that He testifies concerning himself, stands, more or less, in immediate connection with that *salvation* which he has come to reveal and to bestow. It is not so much religious truth in general, as in an especial sense, the truth as it regards salva-

tion, which has been brought to light by Him. For this very reason is it possible to present the teaching of the Lord, with all its riches, *as a whole;* because, from beginning to end, it reveals the character of the Gospel (Luke iv. 16-22; comp. John vi. 68).

5. In inquiring as to the source whence Jesus himself drew the truth proclaimed by Him, that which he owes to nature, and to the Scriptures of the Old Testament, can in no case be lightly estimated. And just as little must His education by Mary, His manifold contact with the spirit of His age, and its most important representatives, and His sorrowful life-experience, be excluded. The personality of Jesus was, nevertheless, more than everything else, the true source of His doctrine, which on this very account is, in the highest sense of the word, to be called *His*, and bears from beginning to end the impress of the most perfect originality. This statement is contradicted only in appearance by the Lord's own words at the Feast of Tabernacles (John vii. 16). At all times He proclaims what He has himself seen in communion with the Father (John xii. 44-50); and testifies of the truth because and as, He bears it in himself; His knowledge of God and of man displays no discursive character, but rather an intuitive one; it is not born of logical demonstration, or of sporadic observation (observation of isolated facts), but of inner contemplation.

6. As the substance, so, also, is the form of the Lord's teaching determined by His personality. Without the formalism of the school, or any display of

rabbinical learning (John vii. 15), He delivers His discourses, as the occasion arises, in a form which, while thoroughly popular, is never plebeian, and in which the tone of the speaker ever varies with the nature of his subject, and the necessity of his hearer. By that expression of higher authority with which He teaches, He is distinguished not only from the Scribes of His day, but also from the prophets of the Old Testament;* and, by the grace of His words, even the most unsusceptible spirit is touched.† Although here and there, irony is not wanting,‡ the undertone is ever love, sorrow, and holy severity; and never is a spirit of trenchant sarcasm apparent. Both the parabolical form of His teaching in the three first Gospels, and the pregnant and paradoxical nature of many an expression in the fourth Gospel, adds to the impressiveness of the discourse. In short, nowhere is more perfect harmony between substance and form to be found than in the teaching of the Lord. The highest truth and freedom is here united with the highest beauty; a beauty, nevertheless, not of a sensuous, but of a moral and sacred character. Every material that He touches becomes gold in His hands.

7. Although the teaching of the Lord is, in point of form and substance, intensely original, it does not stand alone, but in a clearly determined relation to that which precedes and follows. It is, as it were, the

---

* Matt. v.—vii.   † Luke iv. 22; John vii. 46.
‡ Mark vii. 9 (consult the Greek Text upon this and the following citation); Luke xi. 41.

golden middle-link in a connected chain of very different and yet not contradictory teaching. The word of Moses and the prophets is in such wise taken up, fulfilled, and completed by Jesus, that even that which is old receives, in His hands, an entirely new appearance, and that which is new appears to be properly only the ripened germ of the old. Even when he does not immediately adduce the word of prophecy, it is yet the clear mirror in which He sees reflected the image of himself and the kingdom of God. Never does he make use of the Apocryphas of the Old Testament; but even when He is on the point of departure, He directs the eye of His disciples to the Law, the Prophets, and the Psalms.* According to the Synoptics, therefore, as well as John, His word stands to that of the Old Testament in a relation of conscious dependence.

For the Apostolic proclamation, on the other hand, this word forms a brief, clear, and powerful text; and we shall afterwards see that the essential elements of the various doctrines have their root in single expressions of the Lord, or truly stand in connection therewith. His teaching is the light which breaks forth in theirs, as it were in different colours. We proceed at once to contemplate the splendour of this light.

Compare on the main points treated of in this summary: F. A. Krummacher, *uber den Geist und die Form der Ev. Geschichte*, Leipzig, 1805 (an old, but by no means unserviceable book). Reuss, *Histoire*

---

* Luke xxiv. 44; compare Matt. xxiii. 35.

de la Theol. Chrét. du Siècle Apostolique, Strasburg, 1852. Schmid, *Bibl. Theol. des N. T.* Our *Life of Jesus* (new edition). i. 433 and foll.; ii. 343 and foll.; with the literature there cited. C. E. van Koetsveld, *De Gelijkenissen van den Zaligm.* I. General Introduction. Trench, on the Parables. F. Delitzsch, *Jesus und Hillel.*

POINTS FOR INQUIRY.

WHICH theological schools of earlier or later times have attached to the teaching of Jesus, as such, a too one-sided value?—Which have underrated its value?—Relationship in this respect between the former rationalism and the modern naturalism.—What belongs, and what does not belong, to the domain of the ἀλήθεια of which Jesus testifies?—Different value of the *dicta* ἄγραφα.—Wherefore does the proclamation of Jesus bear the name of *the Gospel* of the kingdom?—What is that which is properly new in the proclamation of Jesus, as distinguished from other men of God?—The typico-symbolical character of the first proclamation of Jesus at Nazareth (Luke iv. 16-22).—What is the sense and force of John vii. 15-16?—Was Jesus a Rabbi?—Personality in connection with subjectivity, temperament, and character.—Comparison of the parables of Jesus with those of the Rabbis, especially as regards the form.—Agreement and difference of the doctrine of Jesus with that of Moses and the prophets.—Wherefore do the Apostles, both in the Acts and the Epistles, so seldom refer to the words **of the Lord?**

FIRST DIVISION.

THE SYNOPTICAL GOSPELS.

SECTION X.

The Kingdom of God.

No IDEA comes so markedly into the foreground in the teaching of the Lord, according to the three first Gospels, as that of the kingdom of God or kingdom of heaven, which had been of old foretold by the prophets, and was expected by the contemporaries of Jesus. The Gospel which He proclaims is the Gospel of the kingdom ; and the kingdom itself is a religious-moral institution, which—boundless in extent and everlasting in duration—in its design to unite, sanctify, and save humanity, embraces heaven and earth.

1. In the contemplation of the doctrine of the Lord, according to the Synoptics, we must proceed from the

The Kingdom of God. 69

foundation-thought by which, above all others, it is ruled. It is that of the Kingdom of God (in Mark and Luke) or of heaven (usually, in Matthew), which is also termed the kingdom of His Father,* of the Father of the righteous,† or of the Son of man.‡ "L'idée fondamentale, qui se reproduit à chaque instant dans l'enseignement de Jésus, est celle du royaume de Dieu" (Reuss). As John, so does He also, even at His first appearing, § proceed from this thought, and links thus His proclamation with the expectations of the Old Testament.‖ This expectation was, indeed, of so universal and so favourite a character among His contemporaries, that He did not, any more than John, find it necessary to explain what He meant by this term. We must derive from His teaching itself the conception of the kingdom; which is found only a few times in the words of the Apostles (compare, however, 2 Peter i. 11; Rev. i. 9; Acts i. 6, xiv. 22), but so much the more frequently in His own. The Gospel of the kingdom He proclaims as a revealed mystery.¶ From the different single traits the image of the whole will thus unfold itself before our eyes.

2. Thus much becomes, then, at once clear:—The kingdom is (*a*) *something new*. Since it *drew near* only in the fulness of time (Matt. iv. 17), it was not before found upon earth. It is consequently not merely the continuation of the former thread, but the

---

* Matt. xxvi. 29.   † Matt. xiii. 43.   ‡ Matt. xvi. 28.
§ Mar. i. 15.; compare Matt. ix. 35.
‖ Ps. xxii. 28; Obadiah v. 21; compare also Wisdom x. 10.
¶ Matt. xiii. 11.

commencement of an order of things not before seen.*
It is, nevertheless, at the same time (*b*) *something
essentially present.* When He comes, it appears with
Him—it is already in the midst of those who are asking when it shall appear.† It is by no means to be
identified with everlasting salvation—in the latter it
attains to completion, but it is found in principle even
here—and though it is not of the earth, yet it is
founded (though not with outward signs or display)
upon the earth. It is, at the same time, (*c*) *something
spiritual*, belonging to a higher sphere of life than
this visible creation. The privileges, duties, and expectations of its subjects are, if not exclusively, at
least pre-eminently, of a spiritual nature. What is to
be the rule of this kingdom ‡ stands in direct antagonism with that which ordinarily prevails in other
kingdoms ; the king discountenances all useless interference in the domain of civil right. § Even with the
idea of the Christian Church, that of the kingdom of
God, must not be confounded. The Church ‖ is only
the inadequate outward form of the kingdom of God ¶
—the kingdom of God, itself a spiritual communion,
to become a member of which, without a spiritual

* Luke x. 23, 24 ; compare Matt. xxvi. 28, † Luke xvii. 20, 21.
‡ Matt. xx. 25-28 ; compare Luke xxii. 24-27. § Luke xii 13, 14.
[‖ The ordinary use of the term "Church," as co-extensive with the whole number of those who make an outward profession of Christianity in the world, would seem, however (cf. Eph. v. 25-27), to be unknown to the New Testament writers. The kingdom of God, on the other hand, until its glorious manifestation, includes the outward Church, which is *in*, but not necessarily *of* it ; compare Matt. xiii. 41.]
¶ Matt. xiii. 24-30 ; v. 47—50.

The Kingdom of God. 71

change, is impossible.* As such, it is also, as far as its extent is concerned, (*d*) *something unlimited*. Much more even than the old prophets is the Lord† raised above all contracted nationality of spirit, and has proclaimed—not merely at the end of His course, but from the beginning—the universality of the kingdom of God.‡ Isolated expressions, which seem to breathe another spirit,§ are to be explained by special circumstances, and are greatly outweighed by others.‖ No wonder, then, that the kingdom of God is (*e*) *without end*, bounded neither by time nor space. Moses and the prophets ever point forward to better days; but Jesus knows nothing higher than the kingdom founded by Him, predicts for His cause a complete triumph,¶ and promises to abide for ever with His own.** But although this kingdom is destined for eternity, it, nevertheless, developes itself in time. The kingdom of God is, on that account, (*f*) *something growing*, which, from small beginnings, developes itself outwardly in accordance with its spiritual nature, with the most surprising success.†† Therefore must His servants pray and labour.‡‡ It may, indeed, be taken from him who unthankfully despises it.§§ Where, however, it is sought and found, it is (*g*) *something incomparably glorious and blessed*,‖‖ a salvation for the loss of which nothing can compensate,¶¶ and whose

* Matt. xviii. 3. † Compare Isaiah ii. 2-4.
‡ Matt. v. 13, 14; viii. 11, 12. § Matt. x. 5; xv. 24.
‖ Matt. xxviii. 19; Luke xxiv. 47; Acts i. 8.
¶ Matt. xxiv. 14; xxvi. 13. ** Matt. xxviii. 20.
†† Matt. xiii. 31-33; Mark iv. 26-29. ‡‡ Matt. vi. 9; ix. 37-38.
§§ Matt. xxi. 43. ‖‖ Matt. xiii. 44-46; xxii. 2. ¶¶ Luke xiii. 25-30.

possession is, as the pledge of all other blessings,* above all things desirable.

If we unite all these features, the correctness of the description given of the kingdom of God at the head of this section will become apparent. It is, then, as such, diametrically opposed to the kingdom of darkness,† and, rightly considered, is nothing else than the perfected theocracy already indicated in the Old Testament, but now freed from all impeding fetters, and raised far above all the ideals of antiquity. "The kingdom of God, as the kingdom of Christ, the combining of the glorification of God with the salvation of the children of God, is clearly distinguished from all religious ideas of the future in heathenism, Judaism, or Mahometanism" (Lange). The foundation-thought of the doctrine of Jesus yet awaits its fulfilment, but this fulfilment approaches. That the kingdom of God shall remain no mere vision, is assured to us in the person of its Founder.

Compare, on the idea of the kingdom of God, our *Life of Jesus*, with the literature there adduced, i. 461 and following. Already Hess has furnished a treatise on the *Doctrine of the Kingdom of God*, in which he shows how prominent a place this idea occupies in Holy Scripture, especially in the teaching of the Lord. It is surprising, therefore, that Schmid, in the work cited (i. p. 324), assigns to it the third place in his treatment of the doctrine of Jesus. Much better Neander, who, in his *Life of Jesus*, derives a whole

* Matt. vi. 33.   † Matt. xii. 26-28.

"system of truths" from the parables of the kingdom of God.*

POINTS FOR INQUIRY.

WHAT distinction is to be observed between John the Baptist and Jesus in regard to the preaching of the kingdom of God?—Wherefore does the Lord call it a μυστήριον, Mark iv. 11?—Nature, aim, and connection of the parables in Matt. xiii.—The different shades in which the same foundation-thought is expressed in these parables.—What is the sense of Luke xvii. 20, 21?—What of Matt. xi. 12, 13?— Is the opinion well founded that the idea of the kingdom has gradually undergone a modification in the teaching of the Lord?—Wherefore does not this idea come into greater prominence in the teaching of the Apostles?

* On the light in which the kingdom of God is regarded by the Jewish rabbis, see Schoettgen or Lightfoot.

SECTION XI.

Its Founder.

THE Founder of the kingdom of God is, according to the testimony of Jesus, no other than Himself, the Christ, the Son of the living God, who, as such, is not only a true and faultless man, but also partaker of a superhuman nature and dignity, to which no creature in heaven or earth can lay claim.

1. The kingdom of God, which the most excellent of His nation expected,* was not merely proclaimed by Jesus, but actually founded by Him, on earth. He points—partly in figurative, partly in more concrete language—to himself as being come to give that which has been fruitlessly sought apart from Him. He is the Heir of the vineyard,† the Bridegroom to whose wedding feast the guests are called,‡ the King who

---

* Luke xiii. 51.   † Matt. xxi. 38.   ‡ Matt. xxii. 2.

disposes sovereignly of the weal and woe of His subjects.* It is true He nowhere declares, "I am the Messiah." He is, especially in the first part of His public ministry, even opposed to the open proclamation of His Messianic dignity.† But yet He manifests himself clearly enough as really being the Messiah,‡ and rejoices when a testimony is given of Him in this respect, § and finally regards an enforced silence concerning this truth as inconceivable. ‖ Thus He attaches himself to the Messianic expectation of His time; but will fulfil it, not in the sense of Judaism, but of the Old Testament prophets, especially of those prophets who spoke not only of the glorified, but also of the suffering Christ (Luke xviii. 31).

2. In a peculiar manner the consciousness of His Messiahship is expressed in the name *Son of man*, which Jesus employs exclusively of himself, in contradistinction from every other. It is nothing else than the allegorical designation of the Messiah in His lowly appearance on earth, derived from the vision of the prophet (Dan. vii. 13, 14). He who chooses for himself this appellation, implies that he is conscious of being originally more than man, and, inasmuch as He has come as man among men, of living in a condition of temporary humiliation. On this account His witnesses, with few exceptions (Acts vii. 56; Rev. i. 13; xiv. 14), no longer employ this name in regard to their Master, after He has passed from the life of humiliation to that of exaltation. Expressions like

* Matt. xxv. 34. † Mark i. 34. ‡ Matt. xi. 4, 5.
§ Matt. xvi. 13-17. ‖ Luke xix. 38-40.

Matt. xii. 8, xiii. 41, and xvi. 28, would indeed sound strange if He who employs them had chosen the name Son of man merely to represent himself "comme pauvre enfant d'Adam, et comme objet de la prédilection divine" (Colani).

3. The question, how and by what means this consciousness was developed, is one less for the Biblical theology of the New Testament than for the biography of Christ. The former only establishes the fact that this consciousness was present with the Lord from the beginning of His ministry, upon which it has impressed a definite form. "Jesus had early the consciousness of His Messiahship, as early as the days of John" (Keim). The account given, Matt. xvi. 13-17, is misinterpreted and misapplied so soon as it is made to teach, that before this conversation Jesus had not deeply felt and clearly indicated His Messiahship (Colani). Expressions like Matt. v. 11, 12; vii. 21-23; x. 32, 33, 37-42; xii. 6-8, and not less narratives like Luke iv. 16-22; vii. 18-23, for an impartial judgment, decisively prove the contrary. The increasing clearness and power with which the Lord speaks of His Messiahship towards the end of His life, is not the consequence of an inner process of development, but the consequence of the changing relations in connection with the plan of His work.

4. Although He is consequently distinguished from every other man, He is far from feeling that He is only in appearance united with mankind; on the contrary, He lays manifest stress upon the fact of His **true** humanity. He holds himself bound, without

limitation, by the rule that man shall not live by bread alone ; * ascribes to himself body, † soul, ‡ and spirit, § and compares himself with other men. ǁ Even as the Son of David He attaches a definite significance to this His human descent. ¶ Only in one respect does He feel and show himself as man distinguished from other men, in that He, the lowly one, never ascribes to himself imperfection, distinguishes himself clearly from those who are evil,** calls the obedient children of God His kinsmen,†† presents himself as the physician in regard to the morally sick.‡‡ Although He constantly forgives sins,§§ He never confesses any, not even at His baptism by John.ǁǁ He well knows that He can be tempted,¶¶ but never does weakness with Him lead to a fall, or temptation to sin. God alone He calls good,*** but, at the same time, shows that He himself is good, in this respect also, that He does not arrogate to himself this title of honour.

5. That which the Synoptics reveal to us of the consciousness of Christ is not, however, exhausted by all that has been said. True and holy man, He yet feels himself exalted above all creatures in heaven and earth. He places himself not merely above kings and prophets,††† but also above angels ;‡‡‡ and speaks ever of "my" Father, never in conjunction with others, of

---

* Matt. iv. 4. † Luke xxiv. 39. ‡ Matt. xxvi. 38.
§ Luke xxiii. 46. ǁ Matt. xii. 41, 42. ¶ Matt. xxii. 42.
** Luke xi. 13. †† Matt. xii. 50. ‡‡ Matt. ix. 12.
§§ Matt. ix. 2. ǁǁ Matt. iii. 15.
¶¶ Matt. xvi. 23 ; xxvi. 41 ; compare Mark xii. 15.
*** Matt. xix. 17. ††† Matt. xiii. 17.
‡‡‡ Matt. xiii. 41 ; xxvi. 54 ; Mark xiii. 32.

"our" Father. Even in the expression, "the Son of man *is come*,"* there shines through the words the consciousness of a former existence; but yet more strongly does the consciousness of Divine dignity appear in the forgiveness of sins,† and in declaring and promising many other things which, on the lips of the most religious man, would sound as absolute blasphemy.‡ Most clearly of all is this seen in more than one of His parables. § Full of this consciousness, He calls himself greater than the temple, ‖ the wisdom of God, ¶ the Lord of David;** predicts for His words an everlasting duration,†† and promises to His people an enjoyment of His presence far above all limits of time and space.‡‡ To the Father, indeed, He feels himself subordinate, as well in power §§ as in knowledge. ‖‖ With reverence and thankfulness He looks up to Him in prayer and thanksgiving. The relation between Him and the Father is, nevertheless, so entirely unique that it remains absolutely unfathomable to the finite understanding. ¶¶ He who speaks like Christ knows and feels himself not merely a child of God in the moral sense of the word, but also a son of God in the supernatural sense of the word; who is of heavenly origin, and has appeared on earth to fulfil the Divine counsel. Only when, in the most arbitrary manner, the originality of

---

* Luke xix. 10. † Matt. ix. 2.
‡ *See*, for example, Matt. x. 32-38, as compared with xxii. 37, 38.
§ Matt. xxi. 37; xxii. 2; Luke xix. 12. ‖ Matt. xii. 6.
¶ Luke xi. 49. ** Matt. xxii. 45. †† Matt. xxiv. 35.
‡‡ Matt. xviii. 20; xxviii. 20. §§ Matt. xx. 23; Acts i. 7.
‖‖ Mark xiii. 32. ¶¶ Matt. xi. 27; compare Luke x. 22.

all the cited texts has been disputed, and their sense diluted, can it be maintained with any show of reason that the synoptical Christ is, according to his own expressions, nothing but an excellent man who has been anointed with the Holy Spirit.

Compare what we have said in our *Life of Jesus*, ii. p. 475-477; *Christology*, ii. p. 40-55, and the literature there cited; Colani, *Jesus Christ et les croyances Messianiques de son temps*, Paris, 1864. On the supernatural character of Christ, the German article of Schneckenburger, *On the Divinity of Christ according to the Synoptical Gospel*, Studien und Kritiken, 1829, ii.; the Dutch work of Jonker, *Inquiry as to the relation in which Jesus, according to the three first Gospels, was conscious of standing towards God*, Utrecht, 1864.

POINTS FOR INQUIRY.

REVIEW and criticism of the principal opinions as to the significance and design of the name Son of man (Colani, Hoekstra, &c).—To what extent is a progress to be observed in the utterances of the Lord, as to His Messianic dignity? —Historic and psychological significance of that which occurred at Cæsarea Philippi Matt. xvi. 13-17).—Relation of name Messiah to that of Son of God.—Genuineness, sense, and force of the expressions (Matt. xi. 27; Luke x. 22.—Wherefore does not the Lord, in the synoptical Gospels, bring His superhuman nature and dignity yet more clearly into the foreground?

SECTION XII.

𝔗𝔥𝔢 𝔎𝔦𝔫𝔤 𝔬𝔣 𝔎𝔦𝔫𝔤𝔰.

THE dominion which the Lord possesses in the kingdom of God, He has received not of himself, but of the Father. This Father He proclaims as the only Faithful One, the personal and living God, who operates unceasingly, who especially reveals himself to men through the Son, and through the Holy Ghost works in them all that is truly good. The purity and dignity of this idea of God shows at the same time that He who expressed it spoke not too highly of himself.

1. However exalted the position the Lord assigns to himself, He feels himself in His deepest nature dependent upon the Father. The power which He possesses is a power conferred upon Him,* and the first place in the kingdom of God falls to no one

* Matt. xxviii. 18.

The King of Kings. 81

except as it is prepared of the Father.* The Father is consequently above the Son,† reveals Him in the heart,‡ and always hears His prayers.§ On His side, the Son desires nothing more ardently than that the will of the Father should be done,|| and reveals this Father, who alone, in consequence of His revelation, is known.¶ The Lord proceeds everywhere on the pre-supposition that man can be led, not, indeed, to a perfect knowledge of God, but yet to a pure and sufficient one.

2. Never do we obtain from the Christ of the Synoptical Gospels a sharply-defined description of the Divine nature. Tacitly He builds yet further upon the ideas of the Old Testament, in which He thereby recognises their truth; least of all does He wish to *prove* the existence of God. He sees God in all things, and shows Him to others in every work of His hands. He pre-supposes the unity** of the Godhead, and not less the personal nature of God, in consequence of which He is exalted above the whole creation, and above every single one of its parts, not only as the highest power, but also as the self-conscious and independent will.

3. Although the Lord frequently, especially in the presence of a mixed company, mentions God simply as God,†† He is accustomed to speak to His disciples of this God as the Father. In this, and by no means merely in the recognition of the sovereignty of God,

---

* Matt. xx. 23.   † Mark xiv. 36.   ‡ Matt. xvi. 17.
§ Matt. xxvi. 53. || Matt. xxvi. 39.   ¶ Matt. xi. 27.
** Matt. iv. 10; xix. 17.   †† Luke xviii. 7; comp. Matt. xix. 17.

although this, also, is acknowledged,* is indicated the peculiarity of His conception of God. When He names the name of Father, He describes above all His own relation to God ; but, at the same time also, the point of view from which His disciples are to regard the Highest Being. That God is the Father of all, inasmuch as He has created all, Jesus would certainly not have denied; but, in so general a sense, this appellation is never employed by Him. He indicates thereby, not so much a natural, as a moral and spiritual relationship, whose immediate consequence is fellowship with, and resemblance to God. However fatherly the disposition which God cherishes even towards the lost sinner (Luke xv. 11-32), they only are called children of God, who, in love and purity, bear in themselves the image of the Father, † and, as such, are opposed to the children of the Evil One.‡

4. Jesus ascribes to God no other attributes than those already ascribed to Him in the Old Testament ; but, whilst there, the holiness of God comes into the foreground, here love is the most prominent, the centre of Divine perfection, on account of which He presents Him for the imitation of men.§ The three principal forms of love, compassion,|| long-suffering,¶ and grace,** are all mentioned in the teaching of the Lord. No wonder that this God is spoken of as the fountain of all good gifts (Luke xi. 13).

5. The God of Jesus Christ is just as little the God

* Matt. xi. 25. † Matt. v. 9, 45, 48. ‡ Matt. xiii. 38.
§ Matt. v. 48 ; Luke vi. 36. || Luke vi. 36. ¶ Luke xviii. 7.
** Luke xviii. 13.

The King of Kings.

of Deism as the God of Pantheism. He does not cease to stand in immediate relation to that which He has made. He knows exactly the wants of all, and is able to satisfy them ; * *His knowledge* and *His power* embrace even that which is least.† His government is so boundless, and, at the same time, so faultless, that it may indeed be carped at, but cannot be improved (Matt. xx. 13-15). While He rewards the least good,‡ He also chastises the bad according to the most equitable law ;§ and shows at the same time, by the manifestation of this righteous government of the world, that He hears the unceasing prayer of faith.∥ This prayer is not merely of beneficial effect upon the petitioner himself, but is also ordained of God¶ as a means of obtaining help in all distress ; it is not even necessary to make Him acquainted therewith in many words.**

6. If God is in this manner known as Father, it is because it has pleased Him as such to reveal himself. He has done so, and still does so. in nature,†† in the history of humanity,‡‡ and especially of Israel, §§ but, above all, in the sending of His Son.∥∥ This revelation, which is designed for all, is, nevertheless, only inwardly contemplated and received where there is present a particular state of mind and spirit.¶¶ Where this is

---

* Matt. vi. 8 ; xix. 26.   † Matt. x. 29, 30 ; xviii. 14.
‡ Matt. x. 41, 42.
§ Luke xii. 47, 48.   ∥ Luke xviii. 1-8.   ¶ Luke xi. 5-8.
** Matt. vi. 6-8.   †† Matt. vi. 25-34.   ‡‡ Matt. xix. 4-6.
§§ Matt. xxi. 33, 34.   ∥∥ Matt. xxi. 37.
¶¶ Matt. v. 8 ; xi. 25 ; xvi. 17.

found, we attain to a knowledge of God and of His will, such as is denied to the wise of this world.*

7. As the Father reveals himself in the Son, so also does He work that which is good in man through the Holy Spirit, who is, therefore, represented as the sum of all good gifts.† But few hints does the Lord give as to the nature and operation of this Spirit. He declares that the Spirit dwells in Him,‡ promises Him also to His Apostles, especially for their strengthening ;§ promises this Spirit also in answer to the prayer of all who seek salvation ;|| while, on the other hand, the sin against Him alone is not forgiven.¶ The Divine nature of the Holy Spirit is clearly enough indicated by Him where, in the institution of Christian baptism, He links together baptism into the name of the Spirit with that into the name of the Father and the Son (Matt. xxviii. 19).

8. From the foregoing it will be seen how infinitely high the Lord's conception of God stands above that of heathen, or even of Jewish antiquity. Neither in the most renowned philosophers of antiquity, nor in Moses and the prophets, do we meet such a presentation of God's fatherly love as in the Gospel of the kingdom. It is true, God is spoken of in the Old Testament as the Father of the nation of Israel.** Especially is His compassion upon them that fear Him,†† and upon the unfortunate,‡‡ compared with that of a father

---

* Luke x. 21. † Matt. vii. 11 ; Luke xi. 13. ‡ Matt. xii. 28.
§ Matt. x. 19, 20. || Matt. vii. 11. ¶ Matt. xii. 32.
** Deut. xxxii. 5 ; Isaiah lxiii. 16 ; Mal. i. 6.
†† Ps. ciii. 13. ‡‡ Ps. lxviii. 5.

towards his children; but never is this name given to Him in regard to those who are not of Israel, never is such a fulness of love expressed by this name as on the Lord's own lips. More sublime descriptions of the majesty of God than those which are to be found in the Old Testament even He has not given; but a deeper, more spiritual, and more exalted conception of God's nature and mind than His, will be sought in vain. And, besides, it is so pre-eminently practical, that one can here speak just as little of the teaching of divinity as of theology, but only of His teaching of religion and of life.

9. Christ's conception of God shows, at the same time, with what truth He testified of His own superhuman origin and dignity (*See* Sec. xi. 5). Only to the Son can it be given to take such deep glances into the heart of the Father. Neither the Semitic race, nor the natural beauty of Nazareth (Rénan), nor the teaching of any human school, but only the personality of the Lord himself explains to us the mystery of His conception of God. Not because this man has the deepest religious feeling does God become in Him and through Him most manifest; but because God was in Him as in no other, can His conception of God be the highest and purest. Though there remain unsolved enigmas even here, yet "it belongs to the humility and strength of science to acknowledge that there are also mysteries in it which it has not fathomed" (Tischendorf).

Compare Schmid, *Bibl. Théol. of New Testament*, p. 126 and following; Reuss, *Hist. de la Theol. Chrét.*

p. 237 and following ; Lassen, *Jud. in Palest. at time of Christ*, p. 248 and following; Wittichen, *Idea of God as the Father*, Gott., 1865.

POINTS FOR INQUIRY.

HARMONY and difference between the Lord's conception of God and that of the Old Testament.—Its elevation above that of Judaism.—To what extent is the right of natural theology acknowledged by Jesus?—In what respect does His conception of God surpass that of the most illustrious sages of antiquity?—Can the personality of the Holy Spirit be deduced from the Lord's words in the Synoptics?—Does His conception of God bear a Unitarian, or a Trinitarian character?—Criticism of the **naturalistic explanations as to the origin of this idea of God.**

SECTION XIII.

The Subjects.

As the holy angels are servants, and the spirits of darkness opponents of the kingdom of heaven, so are men called to be subjects of the same. What the Lord testifies, concerning the nature and natural endowments of men, shows that they are capable of receiving this kingdom; what He declares concerning the sin and wretchedness of humanity, shows clearly its need of the salvation of the kingdom of God.

1. Although the kingdom of God has been founded on earth, it does not find on earth its principal servants. Even the prayer (Matt. vi. 10) which the Lord prescribes for His disciples, proves that, in this respect also, He designs to form the earth anew, after the model of heaven. He pre-supposes, in fact, that the angels stand in a very special relation to this kingdom of God. Repeatedly He describes them, not as momentary personifications of the blind powers of

nature, but as personal, immaterial, sinless, immortal beings,* who form together a heavenly family, before whose face the Father rejoices over the salvation of the lost.† Especially do they feel an interest in the weak and the little ones;‡ they stand beside the believer in death,§ and minister above all to the Son of man, both in His sufferings,‖ and in the revelation of His glory.¶ But, however great their knowledge and holiness,** they stand to the kingdom of God in no other relation than that of honoured and trusted servants. That each of the citizens of this kingdom has his individual guardian angel, is not taught in Matt. xviii. 10; and just as little does the word of Jesus justify any superstitious adoration of angels. His angelology contains no magical elements, like the Apocryphas of the Old Testament—as, for instance, the Book of Tobit — but bears a purely religious and moral character.

2. Also concerning the evil—*i.e.*, fallen—angels, the Lord expresses himself in equally unambiguous language. Nowhere does He speak of an eternal principle of evil, but repeatedly of a personal power which is opposed to the kingdom of God. Not the evil (thing) but the Evil One, is the enemy, to be delivered from whom the Lord teaches His disciples to pray.†† He calls him Beelzebub,‡‡ Satan,§§ and, in general, the enemy,‖‖ who sows the evil seed.¶¶ He is the

---

* Luke xx. 34-36.   † Luke xv. 7, 10.   ‡ Matt. xviii. 10.
§ Luke xvi. 22.   ‖ Matt. xxvi. 54.   ¶ Matt. xiii. 41.
** Matt. xxiv 36; Luke ix. 26.   †† Matt. vi. 13.   ‡‡ Matt. xxii. 27.
§§ Luke xxii. 31.   ‖‖ Luke x. 19.   ¶¶ Matt xiii. 39

true Destroyer,* for whom in turn an everlasting destruction† is prepared. It is true he is frustrated in his ineffectual endeavours by the protecting prayer of the Lord,‡ who already witnesses his humiliation from afar.§ At the present time, however, he is the author of all misery, even that of the body; ‖ the cause, at the same time, of that mysterious sickness which is ascribed to demoniacal operation.¶ There is no solitary proof that the Lord, in these and such like expressions, accommodated His language contrary to His own conviction, to the limited ideas of his contemporaries. Much is even in irreconcilable antagonism with this assertion. He regards the expulsion of demons as one essential part of His life's work** (which He also commits to His disciples),†† and beholds in the night of His suffering the powers of darkness, as in serried ranks, drawn up against Him in hostile array.‡‡ Only an arbitrary exegesis can attach a smaller degree of significance to such expressions than is required by the unity of the discourse and the spirit of the time. But an impartial criticism will not shrink from the obligation to distinguish between the main thought expressed in such declarations, and the peculiar form in which (in adaptation to the mode of thought then prevalent) it is expressed. Compare, for example, Luke xi. 24-27.

3. We stand on firmer ground when we begin to investigate the answer of the Lord to the oft-repeated

---

* Matt. x. 28 ; cf. Rev. ix 11. † Matt. xxv. 41. ‡ Luke xxii. 32.
 § Luke x. 18. ‖ Luke xiii. 16. ¶ Matt xvii. 21.
** Luke xiii. 32. †† Luke ix. 1 ; x. 19. ‡‡ Luke xxii. 53.

question, "What is man?" We see at once that He does not think lightly of the individual man, or of humanity. The very opposite is manifest from His observing the play of children,* His accepting the children's song of praise,† His estimate of the child-like character.‡ Only once do we read of His being displeased with anything, and that was when the children were denied approach to Him ; § and, almost as though it were by way of compensation, He immediately proclaims His kingdom theirs. Wrongly has it been asserted from such expressions (Schenkel) that redemption is not needful for all, since children are already members of the heavenly kingdom. Were that the case, the mothers ought to have sought, not a blessing, but a crown, for their children ; and the Lord would have contradicted that which He elsewhere (*e.g.*, Matt. xv. 19) speaks of the universal corruption of humanity. But it is clear He finds in children a receptiveness for His kingdom which, among adults, He so often seeks for in vain ; and it is equally clear that He proceeds from that ideal conception of the marriage union (Matt. xix. 4-6) which far transcends the view taken by his contemporaries.

4. Upon man's nature and receptiveness for the kingdom of God, Christ, by His testimony, puts the highest honour. Man is more than the lily, or the flower of the grass,|| more than the sparrow or sheep,¶ than the ox or ass.** Like all these he is a creature

* Matt. xi. 16, 17.   † Matt. xxi. 16 ; compare Ps. viii. 2.
‡ Matt. xviii. 3, 4.   § Mark x. 14. || Matt. vi. 25, 32.
¶ Matt. x. 29-31 ; xii. 12.   ** Luke xiv. 5.

of God,* but at the same time highly exalted above them, called to the kingdom of God,† called to love God, and to become like Him.‡

In this *man* the Lord distinguishes between body and soul, flesh and spirit.§ Enough, the centre of the human personality is for Him the heart; which may be not only without feeling, but also without understanding,‖ and thereout come all perverted thoughts.¶ The *word* conscience never occurs in His teaching, but that He estimated the *thing* at its true value is plain from His teaching concerning the inner eye of man (Matt. vi. 22-23). Noteworthy also in this respect is the parable of the land which, because it is earth and not stone, brings forth of itself ($αὐτομάτη$) the fruit of the seed sown (Mark iv. 28). There is consequently in man a receptiveness for that which is Divine; and this becomes a spontaneity when, with the use of suitable means, all that hinders the operation of the Gospel is taken away from the heart. On this ground the Lord awakens men to reflection,** and consideration of what and how they hear.†† He appeals to their natural understanding and feeling,‡‡ and requires that they should judge according to reason.§§ Nevertheless, He places the heart in man above the intellect,‖‖ and speaks on that account expressly of the good treasure of the heart, from which the good is to be brought.¶¶

* Matt. xix. 4.   † Luke xii. 32.   ‡ Matt. v. 48.
§ Matt. x. 28; xxvi. 41.   ‖ Luke xxiv. 25.   ¶ Matt. xv. 19.
** Matt. xi. 15; xiii. 14.   †† Mark iv. 24; Luke viii. 18.
‡‡ Matt. xxi. 31; Luke xi. 5-8.   §§ Luke xii. 56, 57.
‖‖ Matt. v. 3, 8.   ¶¶ Luke vi. 45.

Not by that which man knows, but by that which, properly speaking, he wills, is his inner worth determined. Yea, he has the perilous capacity for choosing between life and death ;[*] with which freedom entrusted to him is entailed a tremendous responsibility.[†]

Without doubt man is created for something higher than this world. Though his soul may perish, it can never be slain ;[‡] and the doctrine of the Sadducees is on this very account a monstrous folly.[§] The losing of life leads precisely to its preservation in the higher sense of the word ;[||] and for the believer the pledge of his everlasting existence is given in his personal communion with the ever-living God.[¶]

5. Man is, however, not only on account of his high position, *capable of* receiving the kingdom of God ; he also stands in the highest degree *in need* thereof. He is a sinner before God, and wretched in his own eyes. Whoever asserts that the Christ of the Synoptics takes an estimate of sin in point of depth below that of many of His Apostles, has listened very superficially to His utterances on this subject. While Paul contemplates sin in the light of his own experience, Christ contemplates it in the light of the law, and of His own unsullied perfection.

The universal prevalence of sin is rather presupposed by the Lord than taught by Him. He distinguishes, it is true, between the moral condition of different men ;[**] but nowhere is there any evidence

---
[*] Matt. vii. 13, 14. [†] Matt. xxiii. 37. [‡] Luke xii. 4, 5 ; xvi. 19-26.
[§] Matt. xxii. 29. [||] Matt. x. 39 ; xvi. 25.
[¶] Matt. xxii. 30 ; Luke xx. 38. [**] Matt. v. 45 ; Luke viii. 4-15.

that He ever regarded any one of them as sinless. The honourable and good heart * is no absolutely pure one, but an upright and well-disposed one, which is on this very account prepared to receive the seed of the word. He addresses His contemporaries as evil, as contradistinguished from the holy Father;† and regards them as the sick who need the physician.‡ The *whole*, whom He opposes to these, are in His estimation just as little worthy of this name as those ninety-and-nine just ones §—who need not conversion —are perfectly just. Even for His sincere disciples He regards prayer for the forgiveness of offences as an abiding necessity;‖ and beside the lost son in the parable stands no perfectly obedient one; but an unloving brother, whose self-righteousness is yet more repulsive than the unrighteousness of the other. No man is unconditionally good,¶ and therefore it is demanded of all men, without exception, that they should become changed in mind.**

7. The source of sin is psychologically to be sought in the heart;†† more definitely in the weakness of the flesh, which, therefore, even for the disciples of the Lord has a dangerous side. ‡‡ Metaphysically it is to be traced to the Evil One, that subtle agent of wickedness§§ who constantly seeks to lead man to destruction.‖‖ Everyone is exposed to temptation, and will fall into its snare without watchfulness

---

* Luke viii. 15. † Luke xi. 13. ‡ Matt. ix. 13.
§ Luke xv. 7, οὐ χρείαν ἔχουσι μετανοίας. ‖ Matt. vi. 12.
¶ Matt. xix. 17. ** Mark i. 15. †† Matt. xv. 19.
‡‡ Matt. xxvi. 41. §§ Matt. xiii. 39. ‖‖ Luke xxii. 31.

and prayer. Temptation (πειρασμός) and offence (σκάνδαλον) are in this teaching correlative terms, and signify that which leads man to sinful acts, and renders him, through obstinate continuance in evil, a child of the Wicked One (Matt. xiii. 38).

8. It is true, the nature of sin is never expressly defined by Jesus : the word ἁμαρτία signifies in the Synoptical Gospels the sinful act, never the sinful principle. That, nevertheless, the existence of this latter is recognised in its full significance, is manifest from Matt. xv. 19; compare v. 28. The impulse in which it manifests itself is, *per se*, unrighteousness and lawlessness ;* whilst its different forms bear the name of transgressions (παραπτώματα). In an admirable manner does the Lord describe the process of development of the sinful principle under the image of the Prodigal Son. At first he is only alienated in heart from the father; then, also, he outwardly departs from him; and by a false craving for freedom he is seduced from one degree of evil to another, and in consequence thereof is plunged in deepest wretchedness.

9. That sin makes man miserable lies in the nature of the case. Under its dominion he becomes a sinner (ἁμαρτωλός), who as such stands no higher than the despised publican. The unity of his inner life gives place to the most melancholy discord.† Yea, his life itself becomes another death.‡ In this condition the sinner, left to himself, sinks into ever deeper misery. He falls into a state of blindness, which may indeed

* ἀνομία, Matt. vii. 23 ; xiii 41 ; compare 1 John iii 4.
† Matt. vi. 24.   ‡ Luke xv. 24 ; compare ix. 60.

The Subjects. 95

be pleaded as an excuse,* but which is in itself culpable. It leads, spite of the most powerful warnings,† to a condition of obduracy; and this attains its highest degree in that determined enmity against known truth which is the terrible expression of the one absolutely unpardonable sin.‡

10. No wonder that on this account sin is threatened with so much the more tremendous a chastisement, in proportion as the transgressor was more highly privileged.§ For sin necessarily involves guilt, satisfaction for which from the stand-point of the law can be demanded with perfect justice; but the expiation of which is so entirely impossible to the sinner, that nothing is left for him but to sue for forgiveness.‖ Forgiveness is therefore to be regarded essentially as a gracious remitting of merited chastisement; and where this forgiveness is not conferred the transgressor has to fear the most terrible consequences. Under different figurative expressions the Lord shows us how this chastisement is inflicted in eternity,¶ and how with all gradation it will be faultlessly just.** Nothing, on the other hand, warrants us in the expectation that these chastisements themselves will some day find an end. The mentioning of the deep gulf,†† and the closed door,‡‡ gives cause rather to fear the opposite; and though we should be able to infer from

---

* Luke xxiii. 34. † Luke viii. 8; viii. 10; viii. 18.
‡ Matt. xii. 31, 32. § Matt. xi. 20-24; Luke xii. 47, 48.
‖ Matt. xviii. 25-27; Luke vii. 42; xii. 59; xviii. 13.
¶ Mark ix. 43-49. ** Luke xvi. 19-25. †† Luke xvi. 26.
‡‡ Matt. xxv. 10; Luke xiii. 25

Matt. xii. 32—what however is, not without reason, doubted—the possibility of the forgiveness of many sins in the future; yet the terrible sentence upon one sin remains in any case in its undiminished force.

11. Thus is the sinner, so far as in him lies, hopelessly,* but yet not irrecoverably lost.† The lost piece of money can be restored, the wandering sheep brought back—but never of its own strength. The objective necessity for redemption which cannot be overlooked, must become subjectively understood and felt.‡ The self-righteousness, in which this is denied, renders only the more culpable; and hypocrisy is the only sin against which the gracious Jesus shows himself inexorably severe.

On the subject of Demonology, see our *Life of Jesus*, Part ii. p. 140, and following, and the literature there adduced. On the sin against the Holy Ghost, *Life of Jesus*, ii. 330 and following. On the Anthropology and Hamartology of the Lord as a whole—see *Reuss, Histoire de da Theol. Chrét. du Siècle Apostol.* i. p. 195 and following. Schmid, *Biblical Theology of the New Test.*, i. p. 230, etc. Professor Scholten, in his *Geschied. der Chr. Godgeleerdheid*, remarkably enough, passes over this entire point in silence.

POINTS FOR INQUIRY.

THE traces of Demonology in Judaism.—Are the utterances of Jesus concerning the kingdom and power of darkness the

---

* Luke xix. 10.   † Matt. xix. 25, 26.   ‡ Luke xviii. 14

fruit of accommodation?—Of personal error?—Or of the knowledge of a mysterious reality?—In what respect does the Anthropology of Jesus stand above that of Moses and the prophets?—To what extent can the high position He assigns to children be harmonized with the hypothesis of a universal corruption through sin?—What does Luke xv. 11-16 teach concerning the history of the development of sin?— Does the teaching of the Lord according to the Synoptics not contain the slightest traces of the doctrine of the ἀποκατάστασις?—Does His indication of the sin against the Holy Ghost receive further illustration from other texts of the New Testament?

SECTION XIV

Salvation.

The blessedness of the kingdom of God—although preparation was made for it under the legal economy of the Old Testament, to which the Lord stands in a very definite relation—was first actually manifested and brought to light in and through Him. It consists in the enjoyment of temporal and spiritual blessings, which begin here and are completed in the future. The earthly manifestation, the active life, the redeeming death, and the heavenly glory of Jesus Christ, have together the definite aim of bringing this salvation unto all.

1. In order for ever to make an end to the dominion of sin and misery (Sec. 13) Christ arose with the Gospel of the kingdom (Mark i. 15). Although, however, He proclaims the Gospel as something relatively new, this novelty, in His estimation, exists not in the

Salvation.

thing itself. We have already (Sec. ix. 7) had occasion to observe the contrary; but this is the place in which to direct our attention to the relation in which the Lord places His word and work to the Old Testament, especially to Mosaism and the prophetic teachings.

2. The sacred Scriptures of Israel form in His eyes a collection of priceless worth. He appeals continually and exclusively to the utterances of the Law, of the Prophets, and of the Psalms. Yea, for the whole canon of the Old Testament He gives a by no means ambiguous testimony.* "It is written" is the rule for His own faith, and His own conduct; and thrice does the Book of Deuteronomy afford Him a weapon against the kingdom of darkness.† He teaches, moreover, that the same rule is binding on His contemporaries;‡ and regards it as utterly inconceivable that the Scripture should not be fulfilled.§ The word of Scripture possesses assuredly a teleologic significance;‖ and His own relation to the Scripture He expresses in the words "not to destroy (dissolve), but to fulfil."¶

3. It is not difficult to determine the relation in which the Lord stands to the prophetic part of Scripture. The whole Old Testament economy of salvation He regards as one continual preparation for His coming;** but especially in the words of the prophets does He see

---

* Matt. xxiii 35; Luke xxiv. 44.   † Matt. iv. 4-10.
‡ Luke x. 26; xvi. 29-31; Matt. xix. 8.
§ Matt. xxvi. 54; Luke xxii. 37.   ‖ Luke xvi. 16.
¶ Matt. v. 17.   ** Matt. xxi. 33-37.

direct references to His person and work,* and even to His forerunner;† and finds these references also in those places where without His guidance we should not have expected them (*e.g.* Matt. xxi. 42). Evidently He regards the word of prophecy from the typico-symbolical stand-point, and demands that His disciples also should do so (Luke xxiv. 25-27).

4. Less easy is it to determine the relation in which the Lord stands to the law. Thus much is at once clear, that He feels himself in spirit raised above its letter,‡ and bows by a voluntary subjection of himself, to its various precepts. That necessity, however, can release from its obligation,§ is by no means overlooked by Him. Least of all does He show any reverence for human tradition, which He strictly distinguishes from the precepts of the Divine law.‖ These last are binding upon himself and upon His disciples, without, however, its appearing that He attaches less significance to the ceremonial requirements of Moses, than to the moral precepts.¶ It is nowhere found that He either himself ever transgressed any original precept of the law, or suffered his disciples so to do. In the great antitheses of the Sermon on the Mount (Matt. v. 21-44), He combats indeed the later additions, but not the original requirements of the law. He expressly censures those who neglect the weightiest matters of the law; but requires that also the lightest should not be disregarded.** From those

* Luke iv. 18-19; xviii. 31. † Mark ix. 13.
‡ Matt. xii. 6; xvii. 27. § Mark ii. 21-28. ‖ Matt. xv. 9.
¶ Compare Luke ii. 41-43; Mark i. 44; Matt xxvi. 18.
** Matt. xxiii. 23.

of His contemporaries who retain in spirit the legal stand-point He demands constantly a strict observance of the law.* The multitude are required to act according to the words of the Scribes;† and His disciples are called, for the immediate future at least, to observe the Sabbath-commandment.‡ Thus also, towards the end of His public life, He confirms that which He had said at the beginning thereof,§ concerning the inviolable sacredness of the law.

On the other hand, it is seen that Jesus regarded the permanent union of the Old and the New as impossible, yea, destructive (Matt. ix. 15-17). He foresaw and predicted a time in which the old form should be broken through by the new spirit; and certainly, when He asserted the city and temple would fall, He could not have expected that after this time the Israelitish form of worship, according to the letter of the law, would continue to maintain its sway. But with profound wisdom He leaves the letter untouched, so long as the spirit which He feels living in himself had not passed over to His disciples, and waits calmly (in the full consciousness that a new covenant would be brought in by Himself)|| for the highest blessing promised under the old covenant.¶ Thus, in the con-

* Matt. xix. 18; compare also that which is added to Luke vi. 5 in codex D. *See* Tischendorf or Alford. ("On the same day seeing one working on the Sabbath, He said to him: Man, if thou knowest what thou art doing thou art blessed; but if not thou art accursed, and a transgressor of the law.")
† Matt. xxiii. 3.   ‡ Matt. xxiv. 20.   § Matt. v. 18.
|| Matt. xxvi. 28.   ¶ Jer. xxxi. 31-34.

sciousness of the Lord, the fulfilling of the law blends together in a higher union with the end of the dominion of the letter. Law and prophets must both serve to proclaim, and prepare the way for, the salvation He came to bring.

5. The salvation assured in Him to the subjects of the kingdom of God is by no means of an exclusively spiritual kind. The meek one shall inherit the earth, the faithful servant receives wide-extended dominion and reward.* Yet this outward blessing comes only after the attainment of the inner, with which we have above all to do. As well negatively as positively, this blessedness is described by the Lord in the fairest colours. Those who inherit the kingdom of God escape thereby all the misery which arises from being lost; they are for ever preserved.† Their sins are forgiven them,‡ and in consequence thereof they enjoy a calm repose elsewhere sought in vain.§ This enjoyment is modified according to the different condition of those for whom it is designed. To the blind is promised sight, to the captives liberty, to the mourning consolation, to the hungry satisfaction, to the oppressed a rich compensation for all that has here been suffered for the sake of Christ. It cannot, however, be ignored that the central point in the prospect of salvation, as opened up by the Christ of the Synoptics, lies not in the present, but in the future life. To the everlasting life His own eye (as well as the eye of His

---

* Matt. v. 5; xix. 28; xxv. 21. † Luke xix. 10.
‡ Luke vii. 50; xviii. 14. § Matt. xi. 28.

Salvation. 103

contemporaries) is ever directed; and this life is conceived of as a condition beyond the grave. It is conferred on the return of the Lord in His glory upon him who has complied with the appointed conditions, and as such, puts for ever an end to earthly distress; while at the same time it makes the redeemed of the New Testament partakers of that joy of which the patriarchs of the old covenant had already tasted.*

6. The question remains to be answered, what the Lord according to His own teaching has done, is doing, or will do, to confer upon the world this unspeakable blessedness. Even His coming into the world, to which He did not originally belong, has for its object to receive a kingdom, and to seek the lost ones as subjects of that kingdom.† He came forth,‡ therefore, especially to the lost sheep of the house of Israel,§ and the whole labour of His life was consecrated to this great end. As a sower He enters upon the field of the world; and calls Himself the Teacher of His disciples.‖ Even His miracles must serve to make known that the kingdom of God is come near,¶ and to reveal Him as the Christ.** He certainly does not favour an unhealthly craving after the miraculous, regards false miracles as possible, and forbids the untimely proclamation of His own ;†† but, on the other hand, He recals His miracles to the mind of His disciples,‡‡ and pronounces inexcusable the

* Matt. viii. 11, 12.   † Luke xix. 10, 12.   ‡ Mark i. 38.
§ Matt. xv. 24.   ‖ Matt. xxiii. 8 ; compare xxvi. 55
¶ Matt. xii 28.   ** Matt xi. 4, 5.
†† Matt. viii. 4 ; xvi. 1-4 ; xxiv. 24.   ‡‡ Mark viii. 19-21

rejection of a word confirmed by such deeds.* Certainly a proof that the working of miracles constituted in His opinion no such subordinate element in His earthly activity as it has since been the fashion with unbelief to assert.

7. It is, however, especially His suffering and dying that He brings into immediate relation with the communication of the blessings of the kingdom of God. No purely historic criticism will dispute that the Lord prophesied beforehand his sufferings and death. It is true there is, according to the unanimous account of the Synoptics, a point in His history† after which these references come more distinctly into the foreground; but even before this there were by no means wanting allusions, figurative indeed, but not the less remarkable.‡ The more nearly the earthly life of Jesus approaches its end, the more clear do they become;§ and terminate finally in a clear indication of the time and the way and manner of His death,‖ united at a comparatively early period with the promise of His resurrection.¶ That the disciples understood not this saying** explains the more easily their after-forgetfulness of it. At the same time, this account (compare Mark ix. 32) shows that the prophecy itself was not afterwards fabricated *ex eventu*. The point of view from which the Lord regards this suffering and death is from beginning to end the same.

---

* Matt. xi. 20-24. † Matt. xvi. 21-23.
‡ Matt. ix. 15; xvi. 24, 25.
§ Luke xii. 50; xiii. 33; compare Matt. xvii. 22, 23; xx. 18, 19.
‖ Matt. xxvi. 2. ¶ Matt. xvi. 21. ** Mark ix. 9, 10.

Salvation.

It belongs to that which is of God.* He must be put to death that the Scripture may be fulfilled.† We can here just as little think of a purely moral necessity as from the well-known parable of the ungrateful husbandmen (Matt. xxi. 37) we can deduce the conclusion—God really expected the world would reverence His Son. The end for which His dying was so absolutely necessary is often expressly declared. He has come to serve ;‡ and this serving attains its highest point in the voluntary surrender of His soul as a ransom for many. Not some simply, but many, are thereby delivered from the destruction of which they must otherwise have remained the prey. His blood is shed for many for the remission of sins (Matt. xxvi. 28) ; *i. e.*, that there may be for them forgiveness of sins. Although only Matthew adduces these words, we are not justified (with Baur) in regarding them as unhistoric ; since, apart from the additional words, "for the remission of sins," the idea expressed thereby is already essentially present in speaking of the blood of the New Covenant.§ That the Lord regarded His death at the same time in the light of a propitiatory sacrifice is clear from the account given by Luke of the Last Supper, as compared with the general contents of Isa. liii., which are here manifestly present to the mind of Jesus.‖ The question—repeated notwithstanding all these declarations of Jesus—" whether there has not been in the

---

* Matt. xvi. 23. † Luke xxii. 37.
‡ Matt. xx. 28 ; Mark ix. 45. § Compare Exod. xxiv. 8.
‖ Luke xxii. 37 ; compare also Luke xxiii. 31.

course of time more put into them than they originally contained" (Baur), is to be expected from a certain well-known stand-point; but only calls forth on the other side the charge of a *parti pris*. So much, at least, is certain—that Jesus' own words nowhere contain anything which is in contradiction with His utterances concerning the object and fruit of His death. That, in Matt. ix. 2 and xviii. 35, forgiveness of sins is spoken of without the immediate mention of His death, is at that time, and under those circumstances, easily conceivable. Equally may we admit that the parable of the Prodigal Son contains pure and glorious truth, without seeking to find in it the whole of the truth concerning propitiation; which could be revealed only later. And never must it be forgotten that Jesus, for wise reasons, was accustomed to speak but little of His death.

8. Far from the work of the Lord, by which He prepares for the world the highest blessings, coming to an end with His death, rather does His heavenly glory stand in the closest connection —as with His own humiliation, so also with the completion of His plan of salvation.* On this account He professes himself King,† and ceases not after His exaltation to stand in personal relationship with His own.‡

That in this promise more than a mere moral power must be intended, is evident from the assurance that all power is given Him *in heaven also* (Matt. xxviii. 18).

* Luke xxiv. 26.   † Matt. xxv. 40.   ‡ Matt. xviii. 20; xxviii. 20.

Salvation.

This power He manifests in ever greater measure, and this revelation He speaks of as a coming in glory. This coming begins even with His life on earth, makes progress before the eyes of all during the lifetime of some of the Apostles—especially in the destruction of Jerusalem*—and will be seen in its full perfection only in the completion of the ages, the indications of which correspond with those of the downfall of Jerusalem (Matt. xxiv. and xxv). It is as when a stone is cast into the water, it describes ever larger circles, until the last loses itself in the wide expanse.

On the relation of the Lord to the Old Testament in general, and to the Mosaic law in particular, *see* Lechler, *das A. T. in den Reden Jesu*, Studien und Kritiken, 1854, I. E. J. Meyer, *uber das Verhaltniss Jesu und seiner Junger zum Mos. Gesetz.* Dr. Ph. S. van Ronkel, *Specimen J. C. doctrinam exhibens de V. T. libris*, Traj. 1860. Comp. J. E. R. Kauffer, *de bibl. ζωῆς αἰώνιου notione*, Dresd., 1838. J. Riet., *de leer van Jezus aang. de ζωὴ αἰώνιος*, Utr., 1864. C. A. Hasert, *Ueber die Vorhersagungen J. von seinem Tode und seiner Auferst.*, Berl., 1839. A. Ritzschl, *die Neutestam. Aussagen uber den Heilswerth des Todes Jesu*, in the Jahrb. fur deutsche Theol., 1863, ii.

* Matt. xvi. 28; xxvi. 63, 64.

POINTS FOR INQUIRY.

To what extent does He place himself upon the same level with the servants of God of the Old Testament, and to what extent above them?—Is the conjecture that the prediction of His death and resurrection may have been modified *ex eventu* critically well-founded?—May we assume that He has spoken more on this point than the Evangelists relate?—Can we understand in the same sense all His utterances with regard to His "coming?"

SECTION XV.

The Way of Salvation.

ALTHOUGH all are called to the blessedness of the kingdom of God, it can be partaken of by the sinner only through penitence, faith, and that renewal of heart which is manifest in the bearing of the whole life. All who tread this path form together a spiritual community, which on account of its peculiar constitution—but, above all, on account of its character and tendency—stands far above every other; and is destined to extend itself, and to endure unto the end of the world.

1. Since the kingdom of God is primarily designed for all (Sec. x. 2), so must also—according to the teaching of the Lord—all be invited thereto. Although His personal mission extended only to Israel,[*] and

[*] Matt. xv. 24.

His Gospel was first brought to this nation;* yet He foresaw, desired, and required the early removal of the wall of separation. Christian universalism has its origin, not in Paul (Tübingen school), but in Jesus himself, as we know Him from the Synoptical Gospels. The more Israel rejects the message of the kingdom, the more does He dwell on the calling of the Gentiles.† Many indeed are already called, and all must be so; all bear the name of called to whom in reality the invitation of the kingdom of God has come, whether they have accepted the same or not. They who accept it are by far the lesser number, and bear the name of the chosen.‡ God himself has brought them to the enjoyment of this privilege;§ while he, on the other hand, who has experienced, in connection with himself, the labour of seeking love, and yet fails to attain to this blessedness, must ascribe to himself the loss thereof.||

2. Such a chosen partaker of the blessings of salvation will he only be who has undergone a great change; and this is, according to the view of the Lord, necessary for all—even for His Apostles.¶ Neither with His forerunner (Luke iii. 8), nor with himself, does a merely external descent from Abraham suffice, in order to become a citizen of the kingdom of God. He demands an inner change of mind ($\mu\epsilon\tau\acute{a}\nu\text{o}\iota\text{a}$) with an outward returning ($\dot{\epsilon}\pi\iota\sigma\tau\rho\text{o}\phi\acute{\eta}$) to the way of life.** But whilst the demand of John is especially

* Luke xxiv. 47. † Luke xiv. 16-24. ‡ Matt. xxii. 14.
§ Matt. xi. 25, 26; xvi. 17. || Matt. xxiii. 37 ¶ Matt. xviii. 3.
** Luke xvii. 4.

The Way of Salvation.

directed to the outward life of morality,* Jesus directs His eye especially to the inner life. The true starting-point in conversion He points out with admirable precision under the figure of the Prodigal Son, who begins to come to himself.† Instead of the Pharisaic principle, *from without inwards*, that of Jesus is *from within outwards*.‡ Upon the inward state of the heart depends with Him not only much, but all.§ Only where this is shown to be right has the outward reparation for the misdeed value in His eyes.∥

So high does the demand for conversion stand with Him, that it must ever be proclaimed in immediate connection with the promise of the forgiveness of sins ;¶ because, while never affording a title to the enjoyment of forgiveness, it is the indispensable condition thereof.

3. With equally great emphasis does Jesus demand the presence of faith ($\pi i \sigma \tau \iota s$) which stands in the closest connection with conversion. He understands thereby not merely a barren consent of the understanding, but rather a confiding acceptance of that which, upon good evidence, we may regard as truth. Whilst He speaks of believing John the Baptist** ($a\dot{v}\tau\hat{\omega}$), He speaks of a believing *in* himself†† ($\epsilon\dot{\iota}s\ \dot{\epsilon}\mu\dot{\epsilon}$), which expresses a closer relationship. The object of the faith demanded by Him is, in general *the Gospel*,‡‡ or in a wider sense all that the prophets have declared,§§ or (in its

---

* Luke iii. 10-14.   † Luke xv. 17.   ‡ Luke xi. 39-41.
§ Matt. xii. 33-35.   ∥ Luke xix. 8, 9.   ¶ Luke xxiv. 47.
** Matt. xxi 25, 32.   †† Matt. xviii. 6 ; Mark ix. 42.
‡‡ Mark i. 15.   §§ Luke xxiv. 25.

highest development) God.* But since He is conscious of being himself the centre of the Gospel of God, He demands not only faith in His word, but also in His own person.† Upon this faith He makes dependent not only the working of His miraculous deeds,‡ but also participation in the kingdom of God.§ In His estimation faith is certainly the highest element in man's moral life—the only one of which we read that, either by its high development or by its entire absence, it called forth the wonder of the Lord.‖ It is not strange, therefore, that faith has here the greatest promise attached to it,¶ yea that He desires above all to find faith upon the earth at His return (Luke xviii. 8).

4. As this faith is at first a coming to Christ,** so does it manifest itself in a continued following of Him. This following is, however, impossible without perfect self-denial; and if this is to have any significance, it must be a voluntary, daily-renewed, and constant practice.†† This demand, so peculiar and original in form, has no less an object than the spiritual delivering up to death of all that hinders our entirely consecrating ourselves to the cause of the Lord, without shrinking even from that which is most arduous.‡‡ The Lord consequently demands deep and earnest consideration before we begin to follow Him;§§ but after we have once taken the decisive step, then, also,

---

* Mark xi. 22.   † πιστευόντων εἰς ἐμὲ. Mark xviii. 6.
‡ Matt. ix. 2.   § Mark xvi. 16.   ‖ Mark vi. 5; Luke vii. 10.
¶ Matt. xvii. 20.   ** Matt. xi. 28.   †† Luke ix. 23.
‡‡ Mark ix. 43-50; Luke xiv. 26, 27.   §§ Luke xiv. 28-31.

a self-surrender and stedfast fidelity which ventures the uttermost in order to win that which is best.*

5. He, therefore, who first comes *to* Christ, and then follows *after* Him, naturally walks henceforth in a different path from that in which he has hitherto walked. Upon the subject of the kingdom of God is manifestly imposed the obligation to faithful effort : not in order to repose, but to toil and to win, is he called into the service of his Lord.† In this activity, his maxim must ever be—Conscientious fidelity united with continual watchfulness in regard to an ever-uncertain future.‡ Consistently herewith Christ urgently enjoins upon him persevering prayer,§ a holy solicitude, which eventually renders possible, and even easy, a becoming freedom from anxiety.‖ But the spirit of the children of the kingdom must especially manifest itself in their conduct towards others, and towards each other. Whilst they, as far as possible, live at peace among themselves,¶ yea, seek their true greatness in fulfilling the offices of ministering love,** they are called to show forth love to all††—even to the enemy‡‡—and to make manifest that they are in this respect under the guidance of another spirit than that of the world; yea, even than that of the Old Testament.§§ Only thus do they approach that moral perfection which must be the object of all their endeavour (Matt. v. 48).

* Matt. xix. 29, 30 ; xxiv. 13. † Matt. vii. 21 ; xxi. 28 ; xxv. 14.
‡ Luke xii. 35, 36, 46.   § Matt. xxvi. 41 ; Luke xviii. 1-18.
‖ Matt. vi. 25-34.   ¶ Mark ix. 50.   ** Matt. xx. 25-28.
†† Luke x. 25-37.   ‡‡ Matt. v. 44.   §§ Luke ix. 55.

6. It is impossible that those who are animated with such a spirit should remain permanently alone. They form a spiritual community, of which we cannot for a moment doubt that it is in accordance with the mind of the Lord. It is true His utterances do not tell us that He willed a Church in the sense in which this word is afterwards used. The word itself (ἐκκλησία) occurs only twice* in the Synoptics; and in the latter case (Matt. xviii. 17), it seems to be used only in general to denote the assembly of His disciples (קָהָל, *convocata societas*, used also of the Synagogue). Without our impugning, with Reuss, the historic fidelity of the former (Matt. xvi. 18), it is at once evident that there was present before the mind of the Lord an ideal which would be realized only in the future. If, therefore, He leaves to the Spirit, who shall later guide His disciples, to call into being the form which shall unite them and all believers together; yet does the King of the kingdom of God evidently concern himself with the community of His subjects as a thing of the highest importance. He assuredly did not design to prepare the highest blessings of salvation merely for a greater or lesser number among them, but for all His disciples. This is evident even from the parable of the wedding-feast and the many guests, the vineyard with its different labourers, the household with its various grades of servants. Therefore does He educate His disciples not singly, but together, united into a little community. Even in regard to the spirit in which they are henceforth to be united, He lays

* Matt. xvi. 18; xviii. 17.

down certain immutable principles. Fasting cannot be imposed on them,* the oath must be superfluous amongst them,† common prayer is an important duty,‡ and equally so the mutual oversight of love, as opposed to the outcry of error.§ Self-exaltation is as distinctly forbidden as strife;|| and with unwearied readiness to forgive,¶ must be united the greatest caution in the judgment of others.**

7. Having respect to the abiding communion of His people, the Lord has appointed two sacred rites, which are of great significance for His kingdom. By the ever new proclamation of His death in the supper of the Lord,†† He will unite them permanently to himself and to each other. By baptism He designs to separate all believers from the heathen and Jewish world, and to unite them in the confession of the Father, the Son, and the Holy Ghost.‡‡ If, as it is asserted (Strauss), the latest criticism of the Gospels is "pretty much of accord" that the baptismal formula arose with the final revision of the first Gospel, then the said criticism will have to hasten to reconsider its hasty verdict. He who has no dogmatic reasons for so doing, finds just as little cause for doubting the historic character of the baptismal formula, as of the institution of the Lord's Supper.

8. The Church thus chosen out, and united according to the will of the Lord, extends itself and main-

---

* Matt. ix. 14, 15.   † Matt. v. 33, 37.   ‡ Matt. xviii. 18-20.
§ Matt. xviii. 15-17. || Matt. xxiii. 8-12.   ¶ Matt. xviii. 23-35.
** Matt. vii. 1-6   †† Matt xxvi. 26-28.
‡‡ Matt. xxviii. 19; Mark xvi. 16.

tains its existence to the end. Already (Sec. x. 2) we have learnt to recognise the fundamental law of this increasing development; here it must only be further observed that it takes place (in harmony with the will of Jesus) by purely spiritual means, especially through the proclamation of the Gospel.* The triumph of His kingdom, and the continued existence of His Church—not possible without the severest conflict†— was predicted by the Lord, not merely as possible or probable, but as beyond doubt certain.‡ It has its reason in the immovable nature of the foundation which upholds the rising edifice (xvi. 18); and its pledge of success in the constant presence of the Saviour,§ who went away in order to remain, but *also* —in order to return.

Compare Reuss, *Histoire*, i. p. 192. Schmid, *Bibl. Theol.*, i. p. 299 and following. Dr. J. P. Stricker, Diss. Theol. *de mutatione homini secundum Jesu et App. doctrinam subeunda*, H. C., 1845. G. C. N. Matthaeï, *Jesu Christi doctrina de jure jurando*, Hal., 1847. Dr. J. P. Köstlin, *der Glaube, sein Wesen, Grund, und Gegenstand*, Gotha, 1859. Dr. J. I. Doedes, *De leer van het Avm*. Utrecht. 1847, p. 50, and following.

* Matt. xxiv. 14. † Matt. x. 34-36; Luke xii. 49-51.
‡ Matt. xvi. 18. § Matt. xxviii. 20.

POINTS FOR INQUIRY.

Is the conception of the κλῆσις with the Synoptical Christ perfectly the same as that which obtains with Paul?—What is to be learnt concerning the true nature of the μετάνοια from Luke xv. 17., *seq.?*—Diversity and higher unity of the object of faith.—The peculiar mode of presenting self-denial (Luke ix. 23).—The relation of the subjects of the kingdom of God to each other and to civil society.—To what extent can Christ, according to His own teaching, be regarded as the Founder of the Christian Church?—Comparison of the institution of baptism as given by the Lord, with the baptism of John.—Form and significance of the institution of the Lord's Supper.

SECTION XVI.

The Completion.

The blessedness of the subjects of the kingdom of God outlasts death, but attains its culmination only with the coming of the Lord, by which the glory of the King is manifested, and the tried fidelity of His subjects is recompensed with the full reward of grace. This coming is heralded by signs which leave a deep impression, is accompanied by mighty revolutions in the cosmical and ethical domain, and brings about that final separation of good and bad which puts an irrevocable end to the present dispensation of the world.

1. Although it is a certain fact that the true subject of the kingdom of God is even here unspeakably blessed,* yet it cannot be denied that this happiness

* Matt. v. 3-10; Luke x. 23, 24.

The Completion.

is continually interrupted or troubled. The entrance into the kingdom costs a conflict, the following on demands sacrifice.* The eye, therefore, naturally turns to the other side of the grave, and a very essential want would remain unsatisfied, had the Lord left unanswered the question as to the completion of the kingdom of God.

2. While man is, as such, immortal,† the believer is introduced after death into a blissful state of existence. The Lord, it is true, in a single instance, compares death to a sleep (Luke viii. 52, *b*.); but this does not prove that He conceives of a sleep of the soul. On the contrary, He describes believers of the Old Testament as living to God in the fullest sense of the word ;‡ and indicates§ that not merely the personality, but also the self-consciousness and memory, outlive temporal death. The kingdom of the departed ($ᾅδης$, שׁאוֹל) is for Him no place of immovable stillness and perfect equality (Job iii. 17-19), but the scene of a terrible contrast, which manifests itself immediately after death. While the transgressor is cast into hell (gehenna), the believer is carried immediately into Abraham's bosom (a figure, however, that is not employed as descriptive of the state of believers *after* the Lord's resurrection), there to be refreshed and consoled.‖ The supposition of a particular locality

---

* Luke xiii. 24 ; xiv. 26.

† To perish ($ἀπόλλυσθαι$) has not the idea of ceasing personally to exist.

‡ Luke xx. 38, *b*; compare Matt. viii. 11.

§ Luke xvi. 19-31.

‖ Luke xvi. 22.

underlies the mention of everlasting tabernacles,* into which those who have arrived earlier at their journey's end receive the friends who have benefited them, and is involved in the idea of the paradise which He promises to the penitent malefactor.† Both must be sought in the kingdom of the departed, and be regarded as the scene of a blessedness which begins immediately after death, but is completed only with the return of the Lord. The idea of the return of the Lord (ἡ Παρουσία) comes out so unambiguously and forcibly in His discourses, according to the Synoptics, that the attempt to declare by a stroke of the pen all expressions bearing thereupon to be spurious (Colani) can only be characterised as a not merely highly arbitrary, but well-nigh desperate mode of procedure. The universal expectation of the Apostolic age upon this point would be altogether incomprehensible if it had not the slightest point of support in his own utterances. And just as little can we suppose that the eschatological discourses of the Lord have been essentially modified and filled up in consequence of the destruction of Jerusalem. Only *before* this event could the downfall of the Jewish State and the end of the world be so intimately allied, as is, as a rule, the case in these discourses. And highly rash ought the assertion to be considered that Jesus—so far as He really delivered these discourses—was for once deceived in regard to future events. It is not yet the evening of the world; and we must earnestly contest the

* Luke xvi. 9. † Luke xxiii. 43.

The Completion. 121

assumption that if the Lord had seen in the expectation of His disciples only the fruit of a national prejudice, He would have expressed himself thus fully and emphatically upon this point. The exegetical investigation of His words must show to what extent, and wherefore, He associates the last times with the desolation of Jerusalem. Thus much, however, is certain, that He promises in the most positive manner He will yet appear again, after His lowly appearing on earth, for the manifestation of His glory ; and that thereby an end will be put to the present order of things.

3. The return will take place unexpectedly ;* but not without previous warning. It is announced by signs partly of an alarming, partly of a gladdening nature. To the latter belongs the universal proclamation of the Gospel, to the former the arising of false prophets—and the seduction from the truth therewith connected—war and pestilence, famine and earthquake, oppression, disunion, and wide-spread corruption in the domain of morals.† These are, in a word, the birth-pangs ($ἀρχὴ$ $ὠδίνων$) of that Messianic age which even the contemporaries of the Lord expected.

4. Now follows the appearing of the Son of man himself, heralded by that of His sign in heaven,‡ and accompanied by terrible events in the natural and moral world.§ The powers of heaven are shaken, the form of this world is changed. We are as little justified in understanding the expressions of the Lord

* Luke xii. 39, 40. † Matt. xxiv. 4-14. ‡ Matt. xxiv. 30.
§ Matt. xxiv. 29.

(with respect to this great end) in the literal sense, as we are justified in the name of the results of the so-called modern scientific view of the world in denying their truth. The form in which these changes are presented evidently approximates to the figurative representations of the ancient prophets; the main substance of the prophecy, however, is comprehended in the great idea that the worlds of nature and of man, each after its own manner, shall also have part in the manifestation of the future glory.

5. Only with this great final decision is the resurrection of the dead to be looked for—an event which the Lord in the Synoptical Gospels mentions but rarely and in passing; which, however, He represents as a collective event, and one deciding the everlasting portion of each individual. His conversation with the Sadducees (Matt. xxii. 23-33) has indeed been understood as promising an individual resurrection immediately after death; but as this, simply taken in connection with the ideas of His day, is in itself improbable, so does a more close examination of the argument Luke xx. 33-38 * show that He represents the resurrection as belonging to the events of an age yet future, and which coincides with the end of the world. Besides this the Lord speaks of a resurrection of the just † (a resurrection *from* the dead) as for all of them a simultaneous event. What, therefore, He speaks of the state of the blessed, that they are as the angels (Matt. xxii. 30), seems especially to be spoken of

* Compare Mark xii. 23-27.
† Luke xiv. 14; xx. 35; ἀνάστασις ἐκ νεκρῶν.

The Completion. 123

their condition of happiness after the completion of all things. The desire to find in the Lord's teaching a conception which seems to us more acceptable, must not lead us into wresting the original sense and clear purport of His prophetic word.

6. Simultaneously with the *Parousia* is the Messianic judgment to be expected, of which, in the Synoptics, He speaks much more than of the resurrection. Never does He represent himself as only a witness in this judgment, much less as belonging to the number of those called to its bar; but ever does He present himself as the Judge of the future, from whose decision no appeal to a higher court is conceivable. As such, He appears in His heavenly glory, calls all the nations of the earth to judgment, passes sentence according to the standard of that faith which works by love, and decides in regard to a weal or woe which shall find no end.* The angels make preparation for the execution of the sentence passed upon His enemies, and are active in carrying it out.† Only when this has been accomplished, will begin the time of the regeneration, that is of the entire renewal of the natural and spiritual creation.‡

7. It is here the place to speak generally of the reward which the Lord promises His faithful servant. The attempt has often been made to banish out of His words every thought of reward, or to forge--- out of that which is said in this respect in the discourses of the Lord—a weapon against the purity of His moral teaching. The one and the other without

* Matt. xxv. 31-46.   † Matt. xiii. 39-42.   ‡ Matt. xix. 28.

justice. Without sanctioning, or appealing to, a mercenary spirit, the Lord promises to the disciple who has made any sacrifice for His sake, or has wrought for Him, a true reward; that is, a proportionate recompense.* This reward is determined by very different laws than human ones—laws which are faultless—and a glance at the recompense may serve as an encouragement in the labour of love.† But the reward of the work is not on this account by any means the crowning of merit. The Lord proclaims on the contrary, with equal distinctness, the fact that all is conferred of grace, as that nothing is done in vain; that, consequently, the labourer has never the right to demand an especial reward. Luke xvii. 7-10 teaches this so strongly as to render unnecessary any other proof. The doctrine of reward is in a word here proclaimed, not from the legal, but the evangelical stand-point; and by it is an answer given not so much to the question, " What is really merited ?" as " What is graciously conferred ?" The principle of the labour can be only love and obedience, but the glance at the reward must serve to His followers as a counterpoise to so much that depresses. (Matt. v. 11, 12.)

8. After what has been said it is not difficult to show in what, according to the constant teaching of the Lord in the Synoptical Gospels, the future reward properly consists. The faithful servant receives an honour which compensates for all the reproach and all the conflict of earth. He is served by the Lord himself (Luke xii. 36, 37), is honoured with high com-

* Matt. xix. 29—xx. 16. † Matt. x. 40-42.

mendation, and is introduced to that position which he is capable of filling; he is made partaker of a joy which is as described under the most attractive figures, and is as full as it is unfading; and sees himself called to a work which gives him fresh opportunity of serving as an ornament and blessing in the now perfected kingdom of God.* Special distinction and dominion is promised to those who have occupied a prominent place of service and suffering in the kingdom of God; but even the slightest labour of love shall not fail of its proportionate reward. And all this blessing is in eternity enjoyed in unbroken mutual fellowship. He who transports himself into the future, and distinguishes with spiritual tact the image from the reality, will think twice before he characterizes the eschatology of the Synoptical Christ as "grossièrement matérialiste" (Reuss).

9. While the children of the kingdom, on the one hand, attain to their complete salvation; on the other hand, the time of final decision for the children of darkness also approaches. They become manifest as such, are separated from the righteous, and receive a just retribution. It may be true that the word rendered *eternal* or *everlasting* (αἰώνιος), does not contain in itself the idea of endless duration; yet the great antithesis with which the Lord closes His instruction, Matt. xxv. 46, does not admit of the supposition that at last even the ripened tares will be gathered into the good sheaf, and that, consequently,

* Luke xii. 36, 37; Luke xix. 15-19: compare Matt. xxv. 14-30.

the completed kingdom of God will include all without exception. Moreover, the terrible word spoken concerning Judas* renders necessary the contrary supposition, as also does the fearful doom pronounced upon the man who wilfully becomes a stumbling-block for others.† If it is thought that the opposite can be justified from the parable of the leaven (Matt. xiii. 33), the distinction between the domain of physical necessity and that of moral freedom is in this case entirely overlooked; and if such view seems harsh, it should be remembered that, according to other teachings of Christ,‡ the law of a responsibility proportioned to the advantages received is by no means lost sight of in the retribution of the future.

10. It cannot be denied that the Lord throughout His teaching, as well as in His last eschatological discourses, represents His coming as very near at hand. This was the natural consequence of the prophetic form of conception, in which the difference of time and space falls into the background, the exhortation to watchfulness and active labour receiving greater force from reference to the near, unexpected, and decisive future. Yet there are not wanting clear indications that for Jesus himself the destruction of Jerusalem and the final judgment of the world were by no means identical.§ But it is a great question

---

* Matt. xxvi. 24. † Matt. xviii. 6.
‡ See, for example, Luke xii. 47, 48.
§ Observe the words, "Immediately after the tribulation of those days," Matt. xxiv. 29; the "long time" of Matt. xxv. 19; the supposition of the servant, Luke xii. 45; as also the "Times of the Gentiles," Luke xxi. 24.

whether the capacity of the Apostles for understanding Him would at that time have admitted of any more explicit declaration. In any case it was less the exact fixing of the *time* than the living presentation of the *fact* of His coming manifestation which was, in the Lord's judgment, the main point. The repeated reference to this fact was immediately connected with the consolation and sanctification of His people, on which account it was insisted on by Him from the beginning to the end ; and perhaps the thought of His coming would bring to their mind a precept which, according to an ancient tradition, He once gave them, and which also will stand us in good stead in the investigation of these and all His words : " *Become approved money-changers* (*i.e.*, skilled in discerning the true riches).

Compare our *Life of Jesus*, new edition, iii. p. 104, and following. J. P. Briet, *de Eschatol. rede des H.*, in the *Nieuwe Jaarbb.*, v. 214, and following. Dr. E. H. van Leeuwen, Diss., *Jesu doctrinam de resurrect. mort. exhibens.*, Traj., 1859.

POINTS FOR INQUIRY.

FROM what cause has the Lord so closely connected His description of the last times with the destruction of Jerusalem ?—In what respect does this description coincide with the Jewish eschatology of His days, and in what does it deviate therefrom ?—The difficulties which meet us as well in the literal as in the allegorical interpretation of these His prophecies.—Is the assertion well-founded that, if Matt. xxiv.

and xxv. are genuine, Jesus was deceived?—Are there to be found, in the teachings of the Synoptical Christ, traces of the doctrine of a twofold resurrection?—Criticism of the objections against the interpreting of Matt. xxv. 31-40, as a description of the last judgment.—The doctrine of the millennial kingdom before the forum of the Synoptical Christ.

SECOND DIVISION.

THE GOSPEL OF JOHN.

SECTION XVII.

Introduction.

THE words of Jesus in the Fourth Gospel bear a character so peculiar to this Gospel that a separate treatment (above all in our time) is not only desirable, but necessary. In this it is of importance to distinguish as much as possible the utterances of the Johannine Christ from those of the Christian John. In the contemplation of the former, the theology of the New Testament must proceed from the main ideas by which the discourses of the Lord in this Gospel are governed.

1. We cannot pass over to the consideration of the teaching of the Lord in the Fourth Gospel, without a

previous word of introduction. The separate chapter devoted to this investigation must justify itself above all things by a reference to the peculiar character of the utterances of Christ here recorded. Even without in general entering into a consideration of the differences between the Fourth Gospel and the three others, it is seen at once that here, even when we hear the Lord himself speak, we are moving in an entirely different circle of thoughts. Not only is the theatre upon which we here meet Him, the form of His discourses, and the impression which is thereby made, different; but even the substance, compared with that of the Synoptical Gospels, offers important points of distinction. *There* the kingdom of heaven is presented, *here* it is the King himself; *there* the human, *here* the Divine side of the person of the Redeemer; *there* the blessedness of salvation on the other side the grave is brought into the foreground, *here* the blessedness on this side. Simultaneous treatment of the one and the other has for this reason, amongst others, its peculiar difficulty; for if one would show the harmony between the first three and the Fourth Gospel, this proof attains its value only after the frank acknowledgment of the diversities on either side.

2. This separation, desirable in itself, is at the present stage of the question as to John's Gospel doubly necessary. Never was the genuineness and credibility of this Gospel so bitterly assailed as now. The Biblical theology of the New Testament cannot indeed directly become mixed up with an investigation which belongs to the domain of Isagogics and

Biblical criticism; but it is able, in passing, to cast some weight into the scale, in so far as it investigates whether the doctrine of the Lord which is contained in the Gospel of John harmonises with His other utterances or not. If the accounts are seen to be in *this* respect—not to speak of any other—in irreconcilable contradiction, we find ourselves compelled to make a choice. If, on the other hand, the difference can be satisfactorily explained and solved, it follows that from this armoury, at least, no weapon with which to assail the Fourth Gospel can be brought forth.

3. There is still found, nevertheless, a considerable difficulty, even if we accept the genuineness of the Fourth Gospel, and in general its historical fidelity. There remains the question as to whether we are listening to Jesus as He truly *spoke*, or not rather as John—who not seldom reports with great freedom—*represents Him as speaking*.

The latter is asserted by many; and we cannot ignore the fact that when we compare the Gospel and the Epistles, we often find in the case of the Baptist, of the Lord himself, and the Apostle the same ideas expressed in the same, or at least similar, forms. Nevertheless, we must take care that no weapon against the trustworthiness of John's Gospel be forged out of that which, rightly regarded, serves as a proof of its genuineness. If John was truly the bosom friend of Jesus, and, more than others, penetrated with the spirit of the Messiah, it is conceivable that he evermore formed his style of language after that of the Lord; and is, on the contrary, entirely inconceivable that he should have placed in his Master's lips words of which he must know only too well that they were never spoken by Him.

Even if we admit that he transcribed the words of *the Word* (which, moreover, were spoken in another language), under a higher guidance, with Apostolic freedom, we can with less hesitation regard these as Jesus' own words, inasmuch as it is manifest that between the style of John himself and that of Jesus as recorded by John, a difference—not great indeed, but still clearly appreciable—is to be found. Thus John in his Prologue speaks of the Logos, but the Johannine Christ never gives himself this name. If the latter here designates himself as the Son of man, the Apostle in his testimony of his Master never employs this title. Jesus in this Gospel terms His disciples His brethren and friends; John avoids this appellation; Jesus speaks of His kingdom and that of God, but John, where he is himself speaking, does not mention this kingdom. As *Paraclete* the Holy Ghost* is promised by Jesus; by John the glorified Christ† himself is so designated; and while Jesus here speaks of God as a Spirit,‡ John proclaims Him only as Light and Love.§

Such peculiarities might be yet further adduced; and they could not be explained if John had without scruple put his own ideas into the Master's lips. If here and there it may be doubted whether the

* John xiv. 16, 17.   † 1 John ii. 2.   ‡ John iv. 24.
§ 1 John i. 5; iv. 16.

Introduction. 133

Apostle is himself speaking, or whether he is reporting the discourses of the Lord (*e.g.*, John iii. 16-21; compare iii. 31-36), yet the boundary-line is, for the most part, sufficiently distinct; and if the *form* of the citation belongs in part to the Evangelist, the fidelity with which its essential *contents* have been preserved can be successfully maintained. For the above reasons we hold it possible and necessary duly to distinguish between the doctrine of John and the doctrine of Christ, as recorded by John; and here to speak exclusively of the latter.

4. As in the contemplation of the utterances of Christ according to the Synoptics, so also here is it of the last importance to observe the central-thought by which the Lord's words, as presented by John, are dominated, in order thereby to gain light upon the separate parts. Only we must see to it that we do not confound the main idea of the Gospel itself with the main idea in the utterances of Christ which are preserved to us in the Gospel. The science of Isagogics investigates the main idea of the Gospel, by way of analysis; the main idea of Christ's utterances, on the other hand, is derived by Biblical theology from the total impression made by the words of the Lord herein recorded, as contradistinguished from the utterances of others. And then, certainly, it cannot be denied that these words bear in the highest sense a Christo-centric character; that, in other words, His own person and His own work is the great centre around which all moves. In a certain degree this was also to be observed in the discourses of the Synoptics,

but what was there an element of the Gospel of the kingdom has here manifestly become the main theme. We must consequently not begin with the question what the Lord proclaims concerning His kingdom in general, concerning the Father, or mankind; but what He teaches concerning himself, in relation to all these; and at length arrive at the point from which we can answer the question, how far such utterances really admit of reconciliation with those we have listened to in the former division of our subject.

On the Johannine question in general, compare—besides the *Introduction to the New Testament* of Guericke and Bleek (English translation, Edinburgh)—the excellent commentary of Godet; our work, *The Gospel of John* (English translation), and the literature there cited. Dr. C. J. Riggenbach, *die Zeugnisse fur das Evang. Joh.*, Bas., 1866. Godet: *Examen des principales questions critiques soulevées de nos jours au sujet du 4$^{me.}$ Evang.*, Paris, 1865.

POINTS FOR INQUIRY.

SINCE what time has the investigation of the doctrine of Jesus, as given by John, been conducted separately from that of the doctrine of Jesus, as given by the Synoptics?—Can the distinction between the doctrine of the Johannine Christ and that of the Christian John be fully sustained?—To what extent, and on what grounds, can we speak of a verbally accurate report of the utterances of the Lord by the Apostle John?—The remarks of the Evangelist himself, as compared with his citation of the words of the Lord.—Can one here properly speak of a doctrinal system?

SECTION XVIII.

The Son of God in the Flesh.

THE self-consciousness which expresses itself in the Fourth Gospel is that of God's own Son, who appeared among men as true and holy man, to be Israel's Messiah and the Saviour of the world; who, nevertheless, even during His sojourn upon earth, ceased not to stand in an entirely unique personal relationship to the heavenly world.

1. For the right understanding and appreciation of the Johannine Christ the question above all important is, "What self-consciousness does Jesus, properly speaking, express in the *I* which lays claim to a dignity so unique?" To this question—partly under the influence of subjective dogmatic ideas or wishes—different answers have been given. But whoever approaches the subject without prejudice and listens attentively, comparing that which the Lord speaks of himself in the third person with that which He speaks in the first, cannot long remain in uncertainty. As the

Fourth Gospel begins with the Divine origin of the Lord, the first and second, on the other hand, with His human birth, so also is the relationship of the words and discourses of Jesus in these Gospels. In the Synoptics they rise to the unveiling of His Divine dignity; in John they proceed from the assumption of this truth as a starting-point. Just as little as the *I*, which here expresses itself, is that of simple humanity, is here the Messianic consciousness of the Lord, even as the Son of God, conceived of as standing without any definite relation to humanity. Throughout it is the expression of the consciousness of the Son of God, *as incarnate in human nature*.

2. That the Lord, especially in the Fourth Gospel very often terms himself the Son, the Son of God, once also, the only-begotten Son,* is well-known. Of what kind this His relation is, according to His own words, must now be investigated. It is enough to remark, in passing, that in any case a supernatural relationship, a personality of more than earthly origin is indicated by this designation. This is manifest not merely from the fact that in John the Lord employs this appellation in reference to no other than himself, but also from the fact that as such He ascribes to himself a personal pre-existence even before His coming into the world, such as is attributed to no other.† The arbitrary way in which it has been

* John iii. 16.
† Compare, amongst others, cap. vi. 62; viii. 58; xvi. 28; xvii. 5, 24.

The Son of God in the Flesh.

sought to reject some of these texts as interpolations, is just as little to be defended as that of doing violence to their sense by explaining them of an ideal (impersonal) pre-existence. If anyone refuses to believe the expressions of the Lord's self-consciousness, let him at least not mutilate them by making them say something different from what—according to an impartial and unprejudiced exegesis—He really did say. The same self-consciousness, moreover, underlies those words in which He declares that for a particular end was He born, was sent, came forth from the Father,* and came into the world. At the same time it may be seriously doubted whether the Lord would ever have allowed himself to be saluted by a disciple as "My Lord and my God,"† if he had not had within himself the unvarying consciousness of superhuman origin and dignity.

3. But so far from its being the case that He, who knew how much He was more than man, was in his own estimation man only in appearance, He, on the contrary, terms himself a man who speaks the truth,‡ and repeatedly employs in regard to himself § the designation *Son of man*.‖ He speaks of His

---

* John x. 10; xviii. 37.   † John xx. 28.   ‡ John viii. 40.
§ John i. 52; iii. 14; v. 27.
‖ Explanatory of the human development of Jesus, and His need for the baptism of the Spirit to qualify Him for His Messianic work, the author elsewhere says, "Even in the flower-bud lies concealed the organism and power necessary for unfolding to a glorious flower; nevertheless, though it is already beginning to swell, it only opens its fragrant cup when a fostering sunbeam from heaven descends upon it." In like manner, once incarnate in human nature, "He could then (at His baptism), and later, be refreshed and strengthened, when a voice from

coming into the world,* shows the most tender solicitude for His mother,† makes express mention of His flesh and blood,‡ finds a question necessary for His guidance,§ and declares that His soul (ψυχή) is troubled.‖ Even upon the cross He complains of thirst,¶ and after His resurrection He bids Thomas place the hand in His side, and on the prints of the nails.** The criticism which, after such strong testimonies, calls the Christ of John a docetic Christ—because, in addition to these indications of humanity, He also proclaims higher things of himself—assumes what has first to be proved, that it is impossible to be more than man, and at the same time truly man.

4. Just as little can we doubt that the Lord, according to this Gospel, regards himself as absolutely pure and sinless. It is true, He can experience the power of temptation ;†† but the Prince of this world has nothing in Him.‡‡ Negatively He expresses this consciousness in the question He asks of the Jews (John viii. 46, *b*), which, so far as it is not the fruit of pride or self-deception, must be the expression of objective truth: positively it is shown in many a word in which He, who seeks not His own honour (John vii. 18), gives testimony of a morally normal

---

heaven solemnly declared Him the Son of God's good-pleasure ; and could receive from an angel (in His conflict in Gethsemane) that strengthening which the God-man, in His anguish of soul, might not forego." *Das Bild Christi nach der Schrift.* III. part of the author's *Christology* (German edition, p. 152).

* John xviii. 37. † John xix. 26. ‡ John vi. 54. § John xi. 34.
‖ John xii. 27. ¶ John xix. 28. ** John xx. 27.
†† John vi. 15 ; xii. 27. ‡‡ John xiv. 30.

relationship of himself towards God,* which is not for a moment interrupted or clouded. He does not, therefore, seek or find His place "among those who develop more highly the ideal of humanity" (Strauss), but places himself, without any assumption or any ambiguity, above all who have ever lived before Him, or will live after Him.†

5. As true and faultless man, the Lord expressly declares He has appeared on earth as Israel's Messiah and Deliverer. His relation to the world must be treated of hereafter. So far as concerns Israel, Jesus manifestly presents himself at an early period as the Messiah, and receives homage as such,‡ yea, makes salvation dependent on His recognition or rejection as such § Far from contradicting the multitude when they understand the name *Son of man* in the sense of the Messiah,‖ He, on the contrary, approves of it ; and while He denies before Pilate that His kingdom is of this world (ἐκ), He does not deny that He is a King. He repeatedly appeals to that which the Scripture testifies concerning Him,¶ and presents himself on the last evening of His life, as the Sent One, by way of pre-eminence, faultless before the Father.** He feels and manifests himself, consequently, as an historical person, to whom even Moses had pointed forward,†† and who had appeared for a time on earth, for the accomplishment of a definite work.

---

* John iv. 34 ; viii. 29 ; xi. 9 ; xv. 9 ; xvii. 4.   † John iii. 6.
‡ See John i. 52 ; iii. 14 ; iv. 26 ; and others.   § John viii. 24.
‖ John xii. 34, 35.   ¶ John xiii. 18 ; xv. 26.
** John xvii. 3, 4.   †† John v. 46.

6. Although He lives personally as man on earth, He feels himself, nevertheless, in heaven.* He was there not merely before His birth—He remained and remains there by virtue of His higher nature, after His coming upon earth. That which He speaks He has (in most intimate communion with the Father) heard and seen of the Father himself.† He is not merely conscious of His pre-mundane life, but also retains it, with that modification which the appearing in a true and holy humanity, necessarily brings with it. Having proceeded from the Father, He returned straightway to His immediate communion;‡ and yet ceases not during the interval of His earthly life to be in the Father, of Him to learn, and by Him to be loved. In His consciousness, therefore, is there a human and a Divine factor, originally distinct, then blended into a higher unity, in which the reality of the one sacrifices nothing to the reality of the other. Criticism has yet to prove its right to declare the existence of such a consciousness *à priori* impossible. That nothing less than this is expressed in the the Fourth Gospel, is (as a result of exegetical investigation) for the Biblical theologian a certainty.

Compare on that here treated of, in general, our *Christologie*, ii., 72, and following. F. W. Gess, *die Lehre von der Person Christi*, Basel, 1856, p. 134, and following. Weissacker, *uber das Johann. Selbstzeugniss Christi*, Jahrb. fur deutschen Theol., 1857, 1862. (Exegetical argumentation against the hypostatical pre-existence.) Astié, *Explication de l'Evang. selon*

* John iii. 13.   † John viii. 38; xii. 49, 50.   ‡ John xvi. 28.

St. Jean, etc., Gen. 1864, *passim*. W. Beyschlag, *die Christologie des N. T.*, Berlin, 1866, pp. 65-108. Excellent materials for combating the rationalistic interpretation of the Lord's words are furnished by Professor Scholten, *het Evang. van Joh.* Leiden, 1861. On the true humanity of the Lord, see F. Bonifas, *sur l'humanité de J. C. d'après l'Ev. de St. Jean*, in the Bulletin Théologique of the *Revue Chrét.*, 1864.

POINTS FOR INQUIRY.

It is of great importance to distinguish the expressions of the self-consciousness of the Central Person of the Fourth Gospel.—The different phases of modern criticism, as they are reflected in its treatment of John vi. 62, viii. 58, xvii. 5, and such like texts.—What peculiarities mark the Lord's expressions concerning His Messianic dignity in the Fourth Gospel?—Is not the name Son of God occasionally used by Jesus in its purely theocratic sense (John x. 33-38)? —Can John xvii. 3, be regarded as Christ's own word?

SECTION XIX.

The Son of God in His Relation to the Father.

As Son of God the Lord declares that He has ever been, and ever remains the object of the Father's love, and the sharer of His nature, majesty, and work; who has in the Father the foundation and goal of His life, manifests His name in the most perfect way, and in consequence thereof is able to lay claim to a homage and reverence such as cannot, without blasphemy, be rendered to any created being.

1. Although in the Fourth Gospel the name *Son of God* is occasionally used in the theocratic sense as a synonym of the name Messiah,[*] yet the Lord himself employs it, as a rule, in the metaphysical sense, to indicate in what relation He stands, by virtue of His nature and being, to the Father, in consequence of which He, as distinguished from every other, is the only begotten Son.[†] The expressions of His self-

---

[*] John i. 50, and elsewhere.   [†] John iii. 16.

consciousness are on this point of so much the more importance in proportion as they are the more lofty and manifold. Thus much is at once clear, that they indicate a relation into which He did not enter only after His human birth, but which dates from "before the foundation of the world."* Without doubt one would seek in vain in this expression our philosophic idea of eternity; but equally certain is it that every beginning of existence, in and with time, is thereby most decisively excluded.† The existence of the Son is an eternal existence. Never does He speak of a period in which He was not, or had not begun to exist. And what He always was and is, He remains also during His life on earth. The reality of His humanity has altered nothing in the essential character of His Sonship.

2. As Son, the Lord declares himself the object of the Father's highest love;‡ in consequence of which the Father, as in an eternal present, shows Him all that He does. This love is as unchangeable as Himself, and is returned by the Son with the intensest fervour.§ Although, consequently, the Father is and remains other than the Son, yet both—on account of their perfect communion of life—are essentially one; here there is found a unity of power, which again is not conceivable without a unity of nature and of being.‖

* John xvii. 5, 24.   † Compare Ps. xc. 2.
‡ John v. 20.   § John xiv. 31; xvii. 24.
‖ John x. 30. Calvin, on this place, remarks, "*Non disputat h. l. de unitate substantiæ*," but expresses himself insufficiently when he adds, "*sed de consensu quem cum Patre habet.*" That here we must think of oneness of *power*, from which *oneness of being* proceeds as a necessity,

When the Jews accuse Him, on the ground of such like utterances, of making himself equal with God (John v. 18), He does not deny this, but adds further explanation (v. 19-23), by which He sheds light upon His former utterances without in any degree weakening their force.

3. In consequence of this unity of nature and majesty, there exists between the Father and the Son a common action. The Lord expressly asserts this where He defends himself against the charge of Sabbath desecration.* It is especially the Divine work of the calling forth to life, and the holding of judgment which is committed by the Father to the Son.† While all life proceeds from the Father,‡ He awakens and calls it forth by the Son, both in the natural and the spiritual sense of the word. While God is judge (Ps. lxxv. 7), He judges no one and nothing without the Son. The characteristics of Divinity which are necessary to fulfil such a task, the Lord unreservedly claims for himself. He has authority over all flesh,§ and shows in all His words an acquaintance with that of which He speaks, far above all human knowledge;∥ yea, He can with confidence say, "Father, I will."¶

4. The will of the Son will, nevertheless, not for a

---

we have already remarked. *Christology*, ii. p. 76; compare our *Life of Jesus*, ii. p. 681.

* John v. 17. "Quæ conclusio stare non potest, nisi equalitas personarum Patris et Filii statuatur, ut recte Patres adversus Arianos hoc loco docuerunt."—BEZA.

†John v. 21-29.   ‡ 1 Sam. ii. 6; Deut xxxii. 39.   § John xvii. 2.
∥ John xii. 50, and other places.   ¶ John xvii. 24.

The Son of God in His Relation to the Father.

single moment act without that of the Father. In the Father, on the contrary, He has the foundation and aim of His life. As Son, He has received life of the Father, and lives through Him.* Just because He is the Son it is impossible for Him to do anything of himself, that is, out of the sphere of communion with the Father;† but because He is, as Son, partaker of the nature of the Father, He does, without exception, that which He sees the Father do. As Son, He declares himself dependent on the Father, speaks of the Father—not merely in respect of His human nature, but in respect of His nature as God-man‡—as greater than himself, and makes the seeking, not of His own, but of the Father's honour, the end of His life ;§ while He in turn looks to the Father to maintain the honour of the Son, and to glorify Him.‖

5. On earth the Son glorifies the Father, in that He reveals Him in a way in which He had never before been revealed. To this end He had been sanctified ¶— *i.e.*, set apart by the Father before His incarnation, and was later sealed by Him**—*i.e.*, endowed with the infallible marks of His calling. In what manner He fulfilled His commission we shall hereafter see. It is here the place to regard the conception of God which beams through the discourses of the Johannine Christ. Beams through—for it is at once evident that the Lord in this Gospel does not, any more than in the Synoptics, give a formal answer to the question, "What is God?" The name of Father is certainly

---

* John v. 26 ; vi. 57.   † John v. 19.   ‡ John xiv. 28.
§ John vii. 18.   ‖ John xvii. 1.   ¶ John x. 36.   ** John vi. 27.

no actual description of the nature of God, but of the relation in which God stands to Jesus, and through Him to His disciples. And however lofty the idea, "God is *spirit*,"* it is only the clear and pregnant expression of a truth of which, under the Old Testament, at least a prescience and indication was given.† Also the mention of God as—in opposition to the false gods of heathendom—the Only True One,‡ who has life in himself,§ is a repetition of that which has been taught in the Old Testament; and the attributes of the Divine nature, *e.g.*, holiness, righteousness, eternity, which He here adduces by name,|| have been already celebrated in the Psalms. Where, however, He speaks of the completed task of His life,¶ He declares with manifest emphasis that He has revealed the name of *the Father* unto men; and this word gives us a significant hint. He indicates that this name—the expression of the true nature of God—was before hidden (*i.e.*, not entirely unknown, but not known in its full lustre); but is now brought to light, because He has appeared, who, without boasting, could say, "He that hath seen me, hath seen the Father."** The Son consequently manifests the Father not so much by the word, which He speaks in harmony with other men of God, as rather that by His person, His manifestation in the flesh, is the satisfaction of the desire, "Show us the Father." As Son of God, He is at the same time the highest revelation of God.

6. As the highest revelation of the Father, in whose

---

* John iv. 24. † Exod. xxxiii. 18-23. ‡ John xvii. 3. § John v. 26.
|| John xvii. 11, 24, 25. ¶ John xvii. 6. ** John xiv. 9.

nature, majesty, and operation He has shared from eternity, the Son of God likewise laid claim to a homage and reverence* which, without idolatry, cannot be rendered to any creature. No doubt, to honour (τιμᾶν) is not the same as to adore (προσκυνεῖν); but the former expression (as the more general) includes the other as the more special form of homage, a homage which the Son could not possibly decline, since He truly desired to be honoured even as the Father (καθὼς).† On this account the demand for faith in Him and in God is most intimately united;‡ and He expressly declares that it is impossible to honour the Father and to reject the Son;§ the worship rendered to Him by the man born blind He receives, on the other hand, with approbation.∥

7. After all that has been said we cannot but admit that the Lord in John recognises no essential distinction between himself and the Godhead, except that which is inseparable from the personal relationship of the Son to the Father. He does not express himself figuratively on this point—as the Evangelist when he speaks (John i. 18) of the Son "in the bosom of the Father"—but as literally as possible. He is in the Father, and the Father in Him. All that which is the Father's, is therefore also His.¶ He is from above,** —an expression which, besides Him, no one (not even John the Baptist) uses of himself.†† He, and He alone, has seen the Father.‡‡ He came down

---

* John v. 23. † Compare John xx. 28. ‡ John xiv. 1.
§ John xv. 23; John xvi. 3. ∥ John ix. 38. ¶ John xvii. 10.
** John viii. 23. †† John iii. 31. ‡‡ John vi. 46.

from heaven:* that is, not that He is of heavenly nature, and, *therefore*, to that extent of heavenly origin.; but the converse is true—of heavenly origin, and in consequence thereof of heavenly nature. In a word, although He nowhere calls himself God, He claims not to be esteemed less than God, and the only distinction between himself and Him whom He at the same time calls upon in prayer is, finally, that the one is the Father and the other is the Son of His love, other than the Father, but yet of the same nature. In vain is the attempt made to gainsay this result by pointing to a few isolated expressions—such as John x. 34-36, xvii. 3, xvii. 20, 21—which seem to lend countenance to a feebler view. They cannot be thus taken in their isolation, but must be looked at in connection with other utterances of the Lord. And, even taken alone, they do not prove that which it has been sought to derive from them. In the first of these instances (John x. 34-36) the Lord's design is not—from the fact that, in lofty condescension to the lower stand-point of His hearers, He observes that persons clothed with theocratic authority often receive the name of gods—by any means to indicate that only in this figurative sense has He called himself the Son of God ; but He manifestly rises from the lower to the higher. In John xvii. 3, the Father is addressed as the only true God, not to the exclusion of all right of the Son to this title (compare vv. 5 and 10); but in distinction of the Father from the Son, who here speaks in the definite character of the Father's Am-

* John vi. 33, 38.

bassador. When, however, He declares that in the knowledge of himself, no less than of the Father, is everlasting life, He must have regarded himself as something more than a mere creature. Finally, from John xvii. 21, 22, it by no means follows that the Lord is speaking of a purely moral, and not rather a metaphysical union between himself and the Father. The whole juxtaposition belongs not to this circle of ideas; the Lord wills only that His disciples should be as intimately united among themselves as He is with the Father. The latter relation is for Him the prototype, of which He wills that they should become the copy. "*Illa unitas est ex natura, haec ex gratia; igitur illi haec similis est, non aequalis*" (Bengel). The empirical criticism which, while it understands the expressions of the loftiest self-consciousness in no feebler sense than that originally designed, on this very account regards them as unhistorical and incredible, remains still in principle at the lower standpoint of the Jews (John v. 18; x. 33).

Compare our *Christologie*, ii. p. 72 cet. Reuss, *l. c.*, ii. p. 360. Schmid, *l. c.*, i. p. 160 cet. Frommann, *Johann. Lehrbegriff*, p. 360 cet.

POINTS FOR INQUIRY.

Did the Jews really misunderstand the Lord, or not, when they asserted that He esteemed himself equal with God?—Does the Christology of Arianism find any support in the utterances of the Johannine Christ?—Do these utterances of the Lord favour the view which subordinates the Son to the Father?—What is the sense of John viii. 38?—What of John xvii. 21-23?

SECTION XX.

The Son of God in His Relation to the World.

THE name of the Father is revealed by the Son in a world which through sin and its Ruler is brought under the dominion of darkness, but receives of God in Christ new light and life. By His appearing and whole work, but especially by His sufferings and death, He communicates this light and life. Nevertheless, personally to enjoy this benefit, a faith of the heart is indispensable—a faith which is demanded on sufficient grounds, yet for moral reasons is by no means found present in all.

1. While the relation of the Son to the Father has existed from all eternity, His relation to the world had its beginning at a definite period of time. Concerning His relation to the world before His incarnation, the Lord—even in John—speaks nothing. But the more powerfully does He express himself in regard to that which, after His appearing in the world, **He purposes and works. Nevertheless, before we**

The Son of God in His Relation to the World.

direct our attention to this work, it is necessary from His own mouth to become acquainted with its theatre.

2. While we hear the Lord frequently in John, as in the other Evangelists, speak of "the world" (κόσμος), this word cannot be always understood in the same sense. The idea thereby expressed has a physical and a moral side. In the former sense it must be understood when, for instance, He says that He came into the world and again leaves the world;[*] in the latter when He testifies of His disciples that they are not of the world, even as He is not of the world.[†] In the former case the *world* is the same as the *earth*—this sublunary visible world, as it is emphatically opposed to the invisible and the higher; the world of men,[‡] in a word, apart from the relation of its inhabitants to God. The conception of the *world* attains an ethical side[§] only when this word, from the connected whole of the discourse, signifies the masses of men who have revolted from God, and who are not merely ungodly but anti-godly. Since, however, the Lord is conscious, not only as the Heavenly One of being distinguished from all that is earthly, but also as the Holy One of being distinguished from all that is impure, and declares that all that is born of flesh is flesh; it is no wonder that the conception of world is here constantly employed in an unfavourable sense.

3. In this world, however, sin (ἁμαρτία) bears sway; and this sin is not a weakness but a terrible power,

[*] John xvi. 28.   [†] John xvii. 14.   [‡] John viii. 12.
[§] So, *e.g.*, John iii. 17; xiv. 19; xv. 19.

which subdues the world to itself, and renders it worthy of the everlasting judgment.* The universality of sin is pre-supposed by the Lord where He speaks of His coming *into* and His being indispensable *for* the world : it is moreover expressly placed in the foreground in the conversation of the Lord concerning the new birth.† The birth of the flesh, in which all have part, is not only insufficient to bring them into the kingdom of God, but, on the contrary, renders them, without a new birth of the Spirit, even unfit for this kingdom. Here, as well as in Matt. xxvi. 41, the word flesh ($\sigma \acute{a} \rho \xi$) in its opposition to spirit, has not only a physical, but also an ethical significance. The flesh is in the natural man the leading and commanding power. The judging according to the flesh‡ leads therefore necessarily to error ; and is the more hurtful on this very account that those thus blinded think they are yet able to see.§

Sin, where it holds its sway over man, makes him at the same time its slave ;|| and this slave walks in a darkness which, according to the constant usage of the Fourth Gospel, is the symbol of the deepest misery.¶ The sinner fails of the true light, because the true life is wanting to him ; he finds himself in a condition of spiritual death, from which he can be awakened only by the word of might of the Son of God, but from which he must necessarily be awakened.** It is true, sin has its stages or degrees,†† but never

---

* John iii. 17.   † John iii. 5-8.   ‡ John viii. 15.
§ John ix. 41. || John viii. 34.   ¶ John xii. 35.
** John v. 25.   †† John xix. 11.

The Son of God in His Relation to the World. 153

is it excusable. It reaches its point of culmination in the transgression of rejecting Christ, in comparison with the guilt of which all other becomes almost as nothing;* and which is nothing less than a terrible manifestation of blind hatred towards God.† No wonder that it is punished in the most terrible manner. While the Christ of John is not inclined to see in particular misfortunes the chastisement for particular sins;‡ yet the general fact is clearly taught by Him, that the sinful world is already under a judgment which, if it is not averted, must inevitably end in perdition (John v. 24, 29).

4. But whence this dominion of death and of sin in the world? The Lord speaks of the Prince of the World (ὁ ἄρχων τοῦ κόσμου) as an enemy of God and His kingdom. He does not speak of individuals especially possessed by Satan—miracles in regard to persons labouring from this kind of malady do not present themselves in the Fourth Gospel—but the world in its defection from God appears in His eye as the great possessed one, held captive by this tyrant, and who must be healed by Him.§ His life, and especially His suffering unto death, is one long warfare against this enemy, out of which He comes forth triumphant ‖ Even against the disciples does this same power lie in wait;¶ but especially do the hostile Jews show by their deeds that they are allied to the Devil,** who was a murderer from the beginning.

---

* John xv. 22-25. † John xv. 23. ‡ John ix. 3.
§ John xii. 32 : compare Luke x. 18. ‖ John xiv. 30.
¶ John xvii. 15. ** John viii. 44.

Clearly the Lord is not here alluding to the first fratricide (1 John iii. 12), but to the history of the fall (Gen. iii). To the question, "Whence, then, sin in the Evil One?" He answers simply that Satan rests not (οὐχ ἕστηκεν) in the truth, because there is no truth in him. Not truth, but the lie, in his element; on this account he is both a liar and a murderer from the beginning—*i.e.*, from the beginning of the history of sin in humanity. That the devil was created evil the Lord does not assert, any more than that He can be called a fallen angel; and for the simple reason that He is here speaking of the origin of sin *in humanity*, not in the spirit world. He who infers from this silence that the Lord favoured the principle of dualism—in other words, that He represented the Wicked One as the eternal self-existent principle of evil—proceeds further than the letter, or the spirit, of this mysterious utterance of the Lord permits.

5. Although, however, every one who serves sin, at the same time upholds the kingdom of darkness; yet all men do not stand in absolutely the same relation to this kingdom. On the contrary, the Lord recognises —apart from the relation in which they stand to Him —two different classes of men. There are those who naturally see, and become blind; and blind ones desirous of healing, who become seeing;* those who, by virtue of the principle dwelling in them, do evil, and those who do the truth † and hear God's word, because they are of God;‡ who wish to do His will,§

* John ix. 39-41. † John iii. 20, 21. ‡ John viii. 47.
§ John vii. 17.

and inwardly have heard and learnt of Him.* For such lovers of light, *the* light has only to show itself, and they will at once recognise and follow it. For others, on the contrary, it is morally impossible to distinguish the truth, because, in consequence of the prevalence of perverted principle, the susceptibility for truth has become extinguished. They *cannot* believe,† and on this account *will not* come to Christ: they belong not to His sheep.‡ They do not love Christ, because (in the moral sense of the word) not God, but the Devil, is their father.§

6. The cause of this radical difference lies not—according to the teaching of the Lord—in God; for His purpose is to save the world,‖ into which, and for which, He sent His Son. Neither does the cause lie in any inevitable necessity of nature, for never does He favour the principle of a dualistic view; and He could not possibly rebuke unbelief as strongly as He does, if it were only men's misfortune, not their fault. How could He, for instance, say (as in John xv. 22), "but now they have no excuse for their sin," if they had not been personally responsible for sin? It will consequently be in the spirit of His teaching if we ascribe to Him the conviction which we find expressed by Him in the Synoptical Gospels also—that the *not willing* is a work of freedom, and the *not being able* a consequence of the abuse of freedom; and that, on the other hand, where faith arises in the heart, the honour thereof belongs to the

* John vi. 45.   † John v. 40-44.   ‡ John x. 26.
§ John viii. 42.   ‖ John iii. 16, 17.

drawing of the Father.* As regards the true connection between grace and moral freedom, He no more expressly pronounces a judgment in this Gospel than in the Synoptics: enough, He distinguishes, and at the same time unites, the two factors.

7. In this world, thus blinded and divided, Christ appears as the highest revelation of the Father. That He appears is the fruit of the love of God, who will give light and life. The universality of the Divine plan of salvation is so expressly declared by the Lord,† that only a sophistical mode of interpretation employed in the interest of a self-chosen theological system can derive the opposite from His words. In obedience to the will of the Father, the Lord came down from heaven as the living bread, to give life to the world.‡ That this will of the Father is, however, at the same time His own, is manifest from the fact that He was not only sent, but also came forth,§ so that destiny and deed are for Him blended in a higher unity.||

8. Christ is the *light* of the world, especially by His appearing and work on earth. But He is so also by His word. In order to give testimony to religious truth (ἀλήθεια), He arose.¶ On this account He approves of His disciples calling Him Master,** and inculcates, under the form of a new commandment, the principal requirement of His Gospel.†† As in the Synoptics, so also in John, the Lord attaches Himself

---

* John vi. 44.   † John iii. 16, 17 ; xii. 32 ; xvii. 21.
‡ John vi. 33, 38.   § John xvi. 28. || John x. 17, 18 ; xiv. 31.
¶ John xviii. 37.   ** ὁ διδάσκαλος. John xiii. 14.   †† John xiii. 34.

as closely as possible to the Scriptures of the Old Testament, which may in no case be broken.* Yet the truth, even that already declared, now for the first time appeared before the world in its full light. In His person it is concentrated, and reveals itself to the once-closed eye.† And this revelation of the truth is one with the communication of life. He calls Himself the Resurrection‡ and the Life, not because He himself rises, but because He—"the personal power of both, the Raiser and the Quickener" (Meyer)—raises others.§ This life He gives already in the spiritual sense; and will one day also bestow in the natural sense, upon all the dead (John v. 28, 29).

9. This life and this resurrection, however, is not attained to without judgment. Christ is come into the world for judgment (John ix. 39): His appearing and His work bring about a separation between man and man. The inner distinction of their different spiritual tendencies, reveals itself in their relation to Him. He is here already in fact a Judge, although the primary design of His appearing was to be a Deliverer.‖ His judgment consists in this, that the darkness becomes manifest as darkness;¶ and this judgment is the more clearly seen, the more His life

* John x. 35; xiii. 18; xv. 25; compare John v. 39; vi. 45; vii. 38.
† John viii. 12; xii. 35; xiv. 6.   ‡ John xi. 25.
§ Compare John v. 25, 26.
‖ John iii. 17; xii. 47; compare v. 45; viii. 11. For the genuineness of John vii. 53-viii. 11, see a (German) article by E. Graf, in the "Quarterly for German and English Theology." Edited by Dr. M. Heidenheim, Zurich, 1866, iii. 2, pp. 152-179.
¶ John iii. 18.

hastens to its end. Precisely in His death is the Prince of this world sentenced;* and one day, at the end of the ages, the great inner separation will also become outwardly manifest before the eyes of all.† It lies in the nature of the case that the Messianic judgment passes upon all; but the believer is not placed on his trial,‡ inasmuch as he is already in the possession of everlasting life, and is freed from the sentence of death and condemnation (John iii. 18).

10. A work like that of Jesus must necessarily call forth opposition. His work closes in sufferings and death; but even these, instead of counteracting the design of His appearing, must, according to His own declaration, effect the very opposite: His death is destined to overcome the world.§ In the Fourth Gospel, also, the Lord predicts His sufferings and death; at first occasionally, and in figurative language,‖ afterwards explicitly and unequivocally.¶ We are also here witnesses of the natural sorrow** with which He looks forward to His approaching "hour," but also of His voluntary resolve, out of obedience†† and love, ‡‡ to drink the bitter cup. Here, also, the suffering belongs to the definite counsel and will of the Father:§§ here it has the same cause as elsewhere, but also the same glorious aim and the same precious fruit. It is, on His part, wholly unmerited,‖‖ and is imposed upon Him by the wicked-

---

* John xii. 31, 32; xvi. 11.   † John v. 27-29; xii. 48, b.
‡ εἰς κρίσιν οὐκ ἔρχεται. John v. 24.   § John xvi. 33.
‖ John ii. 19; iii. 14; iv. 37.   ¶ John viii. 40; x. 17, 18.
** John xii. 27.   †† John xiv. 31.   ‡‡ John xv. 13.
§§ John x. 18; xix. 11.   ‖‖ John xv. 25.

The Son of God in His Relation to the World. 159

ness of men;* but has, as its aim, to prepare for men the highest blessing. He calls His flesh heavenly bread, which He will give for the life of the world.† As the Good Shepherd, He gives His life for the sheep, to deliver them from otherwise inevitable destruction.‡ His lifting-up upon the Cross has the same aim as the lifting-up of the brazen serpent in the wilderness.§ With this design, the fruit of His sufferings corresponds. This fruit is not simply for the benefit of His first disciples, for whose sanctification He presents Himself voluntarily a sacrifice to God,‖ but also for a wider circle, for His kingdom —the grain of wheat which has died rises again in other stalks;¶ for the world—it is judged, and its Prince cast out;** for Himself—He is glorified through suffering,†† because, as He (in John also) repeatedly and clearly asserts, He will arise again from the dead.‡‡ Thus His dying becomes in the fullest sense not the *end*, but the *crown* of His work.

11. The salvation brought by Him is not, however, conferred upon all without distinction: the Lord, on the contrary, in John, as in the Synoptics, makes participation therein dependent on faith in Him, which is termed a coming to the Son, but at the same time, also, a contemplating of Him with the eye of the spirit.§§ If the expression *faith* ($\pi i \sigma \tau \iota s$) is

* John viii. 37-40; xv. 20.
† John vi. 51, The words $\mathring{\eta} \nu$ $\mathring{\epsilon} \gamma \omega$ $\delta \acute{\omega} \sigma \omega$, we believe, are to be retained. Compare our *Life of Jesus*, ii. p. 453.
‡ John x. 11-13.   § John iii. 14, 15.   ‖ John xvii. 19.
¶ John xii. 24.   ** Compare John viii. 24; xii. 31.   †† John xvii. 1.
‡‡ John x. 17, ii. 19; compare Matt. xxvii. 63.   §§ John vi. 35-40.

not met with in His discourses according to John, yet the demand for believing (πιστεύειν) is constantly made; and in what the nature thereof properly consists is easily deduced from this Gospel. Although here, also, the notion of giving credence need not be excluded—especially where πιστεύειν is construed with ὅτι, or with the infinitive—yet the deepest essence of faith is *trust*, the confiding of the heart, which most closely unites to Him, and receives Him.* He himself is the object of faith;† and this faith is of such value in the sight of God, that properly speaking this alone is demanded by Him above all self-imposed work.‡ And this with good reason. Christ has truly credentials such as none before Him and none after Him have ever had.

12. The grounds on which the Lord demands faith in himself and in His heavenly dignity are of a threefold nature. They are derived partly from the past, partly from the present, and partly again from the future. In the past the Father testified of Him§ both by the writings of the prophets (which render unbelief absolutely inexcusable) and by the mission of John (to whose ministry the Jews themselves went forth). As regards the present, the Lord appeals both to the testimony of His works (in which the Saviour speaks not exclusively, or even principally, of His miracles; but in general of all the revelations of His Divine glory, miracles included) ‖ and to the inward testimony of the heart and conscience (which, in the

* John xiii. 20.   † John iii. 16, and elsewhere.   ‡ John vi. 29.
§ John v. 33-39.   ‖ John v. 36; x. 38; xiv. 11.

The Son of God in His Relation to the World.

word of Jesus, saw their own innermost wants satisfied).* In the future He looks for the vindication of His cause by the evidence for the truth of His words which is afforded by their fulfilment.† Especially His death upon the cross will serve to open the eyes even of His enemies,‡ and the Holy Spirit will wage a victorious warfare for His cause against an unbelieving world.§

13. Since, then, there is sufficient ground for faith in the Lord, unbelief is inexcusable, although not inexplicable. Moral causes are to be adduced for this unbelief—causes which can be overcome only by a higher power.‖ The perverse bent of the mind darkens the understanding, and renders averse to the Gospel. The truth is essentially an object not merely of the understanding, but also of the life. He who will not do the truth, cannot see it.¶ Yet this perverse bent can be so little defended that even an appeal to Moses suffices to show how unreasonable it is.** Although He does not accuse them, yet He could accuse them to the Father. In the Father, therefore, can the cause of the evil by no means be sought, although the praise belongs to Him alone, when in many a one the force of evil principle is truly overcome. For those who have become the possession of the Son have been given to Him by the Father.†† Compare on the whole subject our *Christologie*, ii. p. 89 and following; Reuss, *l. c.*, ii. p. 387 and fol-

---

* John vii. 17.   † John xiv. 29.   ‡ John viii. 28.
§ John xvi. 8-11.   ‖ John vi. 44.   ¶ John iii. 21.
** John v. 45-47.   †† John xvii. 2.

lowing; Schmid, *l. c.*, i. p. 248 and following; on single points C. E. Schmid, *Doctrina de Diabolo in libris Joh. proposita*, Jena, 1800; B. Nachenius, *de notione* τοῖς ἔργοις *et* τῷ ἔργῳ, *quae Jesus sibi vindicat, tribuendâ*, Amstel., 1841; F. L. Rutgers, *de fundamento quo Joh. auctore, fidem sibi habendam niti voluerit Christus*, Lugd. Bat., 1860; H. Jonker, *het Evang. van Joh.*, Amst. 1867, p. 7-52.

POINTS FOR INQUIRY.

Do the sayings of the Lord in the Fourth Gospel justify the assertion that He favoured the theory of a dualism in the moral world?—Is John viii. 44 spoken only of the Devil, or also (Hilgenfeld) of the Devil's father?*—Do the anthropological expressions of the Johannine Christ leave room for the ideas of free-will and human responsibility?—How is John iii. 17 to be reconciled with xii. 48?—Is there sufficient ground for regarding v. 28, 29, and the last words of vi. 40, 54, and xii. 48 as genuine?—Did the Lord speak the words iii. 14, 15 (compare xii. 32, 33), really of His exaltation on the cross?—Are the words of the Master rightly explained by John ii. 21 and vii. 39?

* The latter the view of the Gnostics. Compare Tholuck or Lange *in loc.*

SECTION XXI.

The Son of God in Relation to His Disciples.

THOSE who have been given by the Father to the Son, and in consequence thereof have come through the Son to the Father, have entered into a living communion with this Son (and through Him with each other), the peculiar character of which is recognised only in the way of spiritual experience, and whose beneficent effects make themselves felt throughout the entire domain of the inner and outward life. By the sending of the Holy Spirit after the Lord's departure from the earth, this communion has been modified, but by no means interrupted.

1. On the one hand, it is stated in John that the Father draws to the Son;* on the other hand, that without the Son it is impossible to come to the Father.† These two modes of conception do not

* John vi. 44, 45. † John xiv. 6.

absolutely exclude, but rather complement each other. The Divine drawing (ἑλκύειν), which is also distinguished in the Synoptics from outward calling (καλεῖν), is a psychological impulse;* but not by any means a mechanical compulsion. It does not exclude man's own action; but, rather, on the other hand, presupposes and encourages it.

2. Those who are drawn to the Father, and through Him to the Son, no longer exist for themselves alone, but become most closely united with the Lord and with each other. Only on one single occasion does Jesus speak in John of the kingdom of God;† but the ideal which is realised by this kingdom stands in its full glory before His eye, even on the last evening of His life.‡ As regards the outward forms under which this communion is instituted and maintained, we find even less spoken in this Gospel than in the Synoptics. A birth of water and Spirit is demanded,§ an eating and drinking of his flesh and blood is represented as absolutely necessary;|| but Baptism and the Supper, as external ceremonies, receive no further mention. Even the washing of the disciples' feet¶ is not prescribed as a sacrament, but serves as an example and a symbol. Greater emphasis, however, does the Lord lay upon the essence of the communion which unites himself with His own.

3. It is well known that in the Fourth Gospel we find no parables, properly so called, such as are contained in such great numbers in the first three. On

* John vi. 45. † John iii. 3, 5; compare John xviii. 36, 37.
‡ John xvii. 21-23. § John iii. 5. || John vi. 53. ¶ John xiii. 14.

the other hand, we find here a number of similitudes, so greatly extended that they here and there approach the form of a parable.* As the parables relate to the kingdom of God, so do all these metaphors relate to the communion between himself and His people, and represent in varying form what they would be without Him, what they may find in Him, and what they must become for Him. He is the Bread of Life,† the Light of the world,‡ the good Shepherd,§ the true Vine.‖ As regards these comparisons, it must be observed that they do not so much set forth the value of the doctrine as of the whole person of Jesus, and that as the value He has for all His people; that further, they point not merely to the indispensable necessity for this salvation, but also to its priceless worth, which only by experience can be known and duly prized; and that, finally, they have relation to a mutual fellowship, which, on His side, certainly is not forcibly imposed,¶ and on their side is only preserved by a steadfast persevering in faith and love, without which it is necessarily broken.**

4. To this spiritual communion with the Lord no one attains without the new birth.†† As in the Synoptics He calls for an entire change of mind,‡‡ so here a birth of God is required, without which it is impossible even to see the kingdom of God. The necessity for this new birth has its ground in the fact that the

---

* *E.g.*, John x. 11-16; xv. 1-6.   † John vi. 48.
‡ John viii. 12.   § John x. 11.   ‖ John xv. 1.
¶ John xv. 16.   ** John xv. 6; compare xvii. 12.
†† John iii. 5-8.   ‡‡ Matt. xviii. 3.

fleshly—*i.e.*, natural man—losses all capacity for the reception of the spiritual kingdom of God. Its production is just as mysterious, but also just as easily to be recognised, as the operation of the wind in creation; and it is *possible* because God has given, and yet gives, new life to the world through Christ.

5. The communion with Christ, brought about in such a way, naturally reveals itself in rich and glorious fruits.* He who is Christ's disciple learns to understand the truth, and becomes by it free from sin.† But he becomes at the same time partaker of a life which is in all things different from his former life. It is a life rich in joy;‡ but, at the same time, in spiritual fruits which bring glory to God.§ The noblest of these fruits is the mutual love of believers to each other as brethren; which in this form is the new commandment of Christianity, and the invariable mark of the disciple of the Lord;|| but above all is it necessary in a world which, from its nature, cannot but hate the true disciple ¶ Love stands at the same time in the closest connection with their personal sanctification, which is the object of the Lord's self-surrender unto death;** and reveals itself in the faithful fulfilment of the commandment,†† and in an exact following of the example of ministering love which He himself left them before His departure.‡‡

6. Such a moral height would be unattainable, if

* John xv. 5. † John viii. 32-36. ‡ John xv. 11; xvi. 22.
§ John xv. 8. || John xiii. 34, 35. ¶ John xv. 9-16.
** John xvii. 17-19. †† John xv. 14. ‡‡ John xiii. 13-17.

communion with Christ were interrupted by His death. It was indeed modified on His departure from the earth, but by no means destroyed. On the other hand, He promises the Holy Spirit unto His people before His death,* and repeats this promise in a symbolical manner after His resurrection.† As concerns the nature of the Holy Spirit, the Lord distinguishes Him as well from himself as from the Father.‡ He terms Him the Spirit of Truth, the Spirit of the Father,§ the Paraclete, who remains with and in His people for ever.‖ In this Spirit He comes again invisibly to His people, although as regards the body He leaves them ¶

7. The work of the Holy Ghost has relation partly to the disciples, partly to the world, partly to Christ himself.** The disciples are through His influence reminded of that which has been before spoken, are in the present guided into the knowledge of the truth, and enlightened, as necessity arises, concerning the future of the kingdom of God. The world is, by His mission, assured of the sin of rejecting the Lord, of the justice of His cause, and of the judgment which has been pronounced upon its Prince.†† Christ himself is thereby glorified,‡‡ and revealed in His true dignity. While, however, the mission and work of the Holy Spirit are rendered possible only by our Lord's departure from the earth, this departure is at

---

* John xiv. 16, 17.   † John xx. 22.   ‡ John xiv. 16.
§ John xv. 26.   ‖ John xiv. 16.   ¶ John xiv. 13.
** John xvi. 7-15.   †† John xvi. 8-11.   ‡‡ John xvi. 14. a.
§§ John xiv. 28, xvi. 7.

the same time, in other respects, no loss, but rather an unspeakable gain for His disciples.*

8. This operation of the Holy Ghost replaces indeed, the earthly action of the Lord, but by no means excludes His heavenly action. It has often, but without justice, been asserted, that according to the Fourth Gospel the dominion of Christ consists only in the dominion of the Spirit of truth; so that, properly speaking, any continued personal action and dominion of the exalted One is not to be thought of. On the contrary, the Holy Ghost himself is sent only at the prayer of the Son.† He it is who will do what His people desire of the Father in His name.‡ He sends forth from the Father the Spirit of truth,§ and Himself gathers the sheep which belong to another fold.‖ Such expressions were perversion itself, if He who made use of them were not fully conscious that He would continue to live for His people, and to exert an influence upon them. It must, however, be confessed, that this action, even in John, is rather presupposed than described at large. The same thought also underlies the assurance that He is going hence to prepare a place for them.¶ In the Holy Spirit He comes and remains ever with His own, until, in the consummation of the ages, He shall be revealed in yet higher glory.

Compare Reuss, ii. p. 415; Schmid, vol. ii. p. 293,

---

* John xiv. 28, xvi. 7.   † John xiv. 16.
‡ John xiv. 14.   § John xv. 26.   ‖ John x. 16.
¶ John xiv. 2. (The second clause of this verse is to be read as a question.)

and following; C. Tischendorf, *de Christo pane vitæ*, Lips., 1839; Hugenholz, Diss. *de dictis Jesu*, Joh. xiv-xvi., *ejus reditum spectantibus*, L.B., 1834; Van Teutem, *de laatste nacht des Heeren*, Rott., 1850; E. Worner, *das Verhaltniss des Geistes zum Sohne Gottes, aus dem Joh. Evang. dargestellt*, Stuttg., 1862.

POINTS FOR INQUIRY.

WHAT is the sense of John vi. 44?—Wherefore are there in the Fourth Gospel no parables properly so called?—Does John vi. 41-59 shed any light upon the Lord's Supper?—Is the feet-washing designed by the Lord as a perpetual ordinance?—In what sense does the Lord speak of a new commandment, John xiii. 34?—General survey and criticism of the most important explanations of the Lord's parting promise as to His coming and return.—Connection and diversity of the action of the exalted Christ, and of the Paraclete, according to the words of the Johannine Christ.—Can it be fairly disputed that the various expressions designating a mystical union of the glorified Christ with His people originate with Himself?—What is the meaning of John xvi. 26?

SECTION XXII.

The Son of God in His Future.

THE everlasting life which even here on earth is a fruit of personal enduring communion with Christ outlasts the death of His people, and passes over after their death into infinite blessedness. According to the Christ of John, as well as of the Synoptics, we must look for a resurrection of the dead, a universal judgment, and an irrevocable decision on the last day.

1. According to the prevailing conception of the Fourth Gospel, the believer has, even in this world, everlasting life in Christ.* It consists in the true knowledge of God and of Christ,† and in the satisfaction for all wants of the soul therefrom proceeding.‡ It is true there are not wanting statements from which it is clear that the enjoyment of this everlasting life is by no means confined to the earth. In many instances it is unmistakably clear that the Lord

* John v. 24.   † John xvii. 3.   ‡ John vi. 35.

has reference also to a world beyond;"* but in general in this Gospel He understands by everlasting life the sum of all that blessedness which the believer receives immediately upon his entering into communion with Christ, and which is diametrically opposed to being for ever lost.†

2. This life is already in its essence something indestructible. He who possesses it lives already an imperishable and happy life, and will live this life in yet greater fulness after death. Instead of being annihilated, it is developed beyond the grave to unmixed blessedness. In the Christ of John, as in the Christ of the Synoptics, there is found no trace of a sleep of the soul until the morning of the resurrection. On the contrary, when Martha looks for the re-animation of her brother only at the last day, the Lord assures her that the believer who dies has not on that account ceased to live.‡ And if we inquire as to the nature of the happiness of His people beyond the grave, there are not wanting in this respect very suggestive hints. The higher life is preserved and assured to us by the sacrifice of the natural life.§ Whosoever serves Him shall be honoured of His Father, shall be where Christ himself is, and in communion with all the redeemed shall behold His glory.‖ As a friend, He himself goes before to prepare His people a place, and comes again in the hour of death.

3. The continuation of life through which death is

* Such as John iv. 14; vi. 27; xii. 25.   † John x. 28.
‡ John xi. 25, 26.   § John xii. 25.   ‖ John xii. 26; xvii. 24.

not seen unto eternity (viii. 51) is nevertheless not in itself the completion of blessedness. In the Fourth Gospel also the Lord speaks of a resurrection and a judgment at the last day*—of a resurrection of all men, of a judgment which is delivered to Him of the Father, and in which His own word will be the standard. From the brevity and sporadic character of these hints it cannot be denied that it is not easy to bring them into perfect harmony with the before-mentioned teachings. Yet this fact does not justify us (with Scholten) in rejecting them as the interpolation of a later hand; or, destroying the clear force of the words, to explain them of a purely spiritual resurrection, or of an individual judgment; and the less so, since the Lord repeatedly promises the having of everlasting life and the arising from the dead at the last day in one breath;† so that, in his opinion, the one does not exclude the other, but rather the latter is the crown of the former. The question how a resurrection can yet be spoken of in the case of those who are already partakers of eternal life here, is not without its solution—if we only distinguish between a spiritual quickening and a resurrection of the body which has died, which, according to the constant teaching of the Lord, will take place only at his final return.

4. Although He certainly (in John also) throughout describes His coming as a spiritual one, we yet hear Him on several occasions‡ speak of this coming in

* τῇ ἐσχάτῃ ἡμέρᾳ, John v. 27-29; vi. 39, 40, 44; vi. 54; xii. 48, b.
† John vi. 40, 54.   ‡ John xxi. 22.

The Son of God in His Future.

such a manner that we cannot possibly think of anything else but His last appearing, and that in the sense in which this return is ever spoken of in the Synoptics—a proof indeed that even in the domain of Eschatology the much-spoken-of opposition between the utterances of the Synoptical and the Johannine Christ is not absolute, although important. The imagery of the first three is sought for in vain in the Fourth Gospel, but not so the main thought which dominates these gospels.

5. The Johannine Christ, also, teaches no restoration of all things in the sense which has since been given to these words. Though He promises that, lifted up upon the cross, He will draw all men to himself,* we must not from these words suppose that any irresistible constraint is intended, through which all must necessarily at length be saved. The Prince of the World is judged †—*i.e.*, just as little *annihilated* as *saved*, but cast out; so that He is no longer in a condition to disturb the harmony of the now perfected kingdom of God. The unbeliever dies in his sins,‡ without any future prospect of life being opened up to him. Under *one* Shepherd all indeed become *one* flock;§ yet only the all of those sheep who voluntarily hear His loving voice. The resurrection unto salvation stands in irreconcilable opposition to that unto perdition;‖ and though in the Fourth Gospel no *Hades* and no *Gehenna* is spoken of, yet we can hardly believe that, according to the view of speaker

* John xii. 32. † John xii. 31. ‡ John viii. 24.
§ John x. 16. ‖ John v. 28, 29.

or writer, the ungodly who have been raised unto perdition are to be sought anywhere else than there. Compare Reuss, ii. p. 453, and following; Schmid, i. 321, and following; Cramer, *Bijdragen op het gebied van Godgel. en Wijsbeg.* i. p. 284; H. Jonker, *het Evang. van Joh.*, p. 47, and following.

POINTS FOR INQUIRY.

THE connection of everlasting life and knowledge; of losing life and preserving it; of temporal death and spiritual life. —The conception of Θάνατος in the Fourth Gospel.—Is the idea well founded that the κρίσις here spoken of takes place exclusively on this side the grave?—Unity and diversity of the two ideas, everlasting life and resurrection at the last day.—Does the Johannine Christ hold forth the prospect of ultimate annihilation, or of an unending chastisement of the obdurate sinner?

THIRD DIVISION.

HIGHER UNITY.

SECTION XXIII.

Diversity and Harmony.

THE difference between the utterances of the Synoptical and the Johannine Christ is certainly not of such a kind that the impartial investigator can regard only one or the other series as genuine or trustworthy. On the contrary, upon any attentive comparison, the higher harmony meets the eye at almost every point; and the difference, however considerable, is not only perfectly explicable, but is to be regarded as in more than one respect exceptionally important.

1. The separate treatment (Sec. xvii. 1) of the doctrines of the Johannine Christ has been justified by the result. Thus much was at once seen, that the

Lord in the Fourth Gospel spoke quite otherwise than in the first three. From this, however, it by no means follows that we find in John another Christ than in his predecessors. This would be the case only if we heard Him on the one hand deny what He had asserted, or assert, on the other hand, what He had denied. We were, on the contrary, even more struck with the fact that here there is no distinction as between *yea* and *nay*, but only as between more and less; and it is absolutely impossible to contradict the words of the Synoptical Christ by an appeal to the Christ of John, provided we only bring both into the true light of history. The difference is brought into its just proportions by a word of Godet.* "As far as the religious side of the contrast is concerned, it is remarkable that the conscience of the Church has never been perplexed by it, and that it is exclusively the learned who pronounce it insoluble. This fact proves, in any case, that for the pious and believing heart the Jesus of the Synoptics has never been, and will never be anything else than that of John. The difference does not therefore reach the depths of the religious and moral life." The justice of this remark is felt if we regard even the form, but yet more if we bring the contents of the Lord's words in John into comparison with the contents of His words in the Synoptical Gospels. In both respects the difference is only relatively great, and is perfectly explicable.

2. **As** far as the form is concerned, the striking harmony which prevails between the language of the

* *See* his "*Examen des princip. Quest.* cet." p. 48.

Diversity and Harmony.

disciple himself, and that of Jesus in John (compare Sec. xvii. 3) is to be explained partly from the great affinity of spirit between the Master and the disciple, which has formed his style of writing after that of the Master's speech; partly from the apostolic freedom with which, under a higher guidance, he records the Lord's discourses. The absence of the parables in the Fourth Gospel will appear less strange when we consider that we have here, for the most part, the Lord not in the midst of the Galilean multitude, but confronting the Jews of Jerusalem; whilst, moreover, the metaphors (παροιμίαι) here employed are so greatly developed that they here and there approach the form of the parables. Besides which, both metaphors and parables are chosen out of the domain of nature and of daily life, and the assertion that the Christ of John derives nothing from nature is at least entirely unproved. In like manner the vigorous pregnant expressions, the apparent paradoxes which frequently characterize his teachings here are by no means wanting in the Synoptics. A misunderstanding of his words, which here often gives occasion for a fuller explanation, is also met with in the first three Gospels.* That there is less variety of discourses of the Lord in John is a consequence of the strict plan on which this Gospel is formed, and which must of itself lead the author to make a particular selection from the rich treasures at hand.† In part at least are these discourses not less called forth by the occasion, and

* *E.g.* Matt. xvi 6, 7; xix. 10, 11; compare xxii. 45.
† Compare John xx. 31; xxi. 25.

manifold in their character, than those of the earlier Gospels; and that the Jewish, or rather Israelite, character of the exalted Speaker is by no means laid aside in the Fourth Gospel is clear even from the letter,* and yet more from the spirit and tendency of the discourses therein preserved.

3. As far as the substance is concerned, it is by no means proved that the idea of God from which Jesus proceeds in the Fourth Gospel is essentially different from that which He expresses in the other Gospels. Here as there He presents God to His disciples clearly as His and their Father,† and designates as the children of God only those who in a moral aspect bear His image and character.‡ Here as there He presents this God at the same time as animated with fatherly compassion towards sinners, § and men as unable to effect their own deliverance, but yet capable of receiving salvation through the intervention of a higher power. In both cases He promises and prepares this deliverance by means of a kingdom of God, which is indeed in its tendency universal, but which comes first to Israel; and the foundations of which have been carefully laid in Israel, especially through the Old Testament economy. In both cases, also, is the relation of this kingdom to the kingdom of darkness, and the nature of the kingdom of darkness itself, described as the same; ‖ and the Lord remains ever

* John iv. 22; v. 45, 46; vii. 37, 38.   † John xx. 17.
‡ Matt. v. 9; compare John viii. 42.
§ John iii. 16; compare Matt. xviii. 10-14.
‖ Luke x. 18; compare John xii. 31.

consistent with Himself when He announces *Himself* as the way by which to become a member of His kingdom.*

4. If we compare that which Christ testifies in the Synoptics concerning His person and work with that which He testifies in John, we can come to no other conclusion. To the Christ of the Synoptics belongs a superhuman character and dignity (Sec. x. 5), whilst the Christ of John is in the true sense of the word man (Sec. xvii. 3), and reveals himself as man. According to both sources He displays, as such, a higher knowledge, but no boundless omniscience;† unsullied purity, which, however, is subject to the human condition of exposure to temptation;‡ in a word, Divine majesty, but in the lowly form of a servant.§ Arising as a Teacher (Matt. xxiii. 8; compare John xiii. 14), He proclaims at Jerusalem and in Galilee *one* Gospel, and appeals to the same credentials of His authority; both in the Synoptics and in John we hear how He attributes to his miracles an essential power of proof, although not the very highest proof, for His Divine mission and dignity, and condemns as entirely inexcusable the unbelief which rejects Him.‖ Not His own honour, but that of the Father,¶ and the salvation of all that are lost,** is

* Compare, for example, Matt. v. 6, vii. 21, xi. 28, xviii. 3, with John vi. 35, vii. 37, xiii. 14-17.
† Compare Mark xi. 13; with John xi. 34.
‡ Matt. xvi. 23; compare John vi. 15; xii. 27.
§ Luke xxii. 27; compare John xiii. 14.
‖ Matt. xi. 20-24; compare John viii. 24.
¶ Mark v. 19; compare John vii. 18.
** Luke xix. 10; compare John vi. 37.

the highest object of his effort. For this He lives and labours, and will, moreover, according to God's will and counsel,* suffer and die. His suffering and death is, on the one hand, an event in the order of providence to which, not without deeply feeling it, He obediently submits ;† on the other hand, an act which He accomplishes with the greatest freedom.‡ As respects the causes, the aim, and the fruits of this suffering and dying, the Johannine Christ expresses himself in essentially the same manner as the Christ of the Synoptics (Sec. xiii. 7 ; compare Sec. xix. 6). The little also which He speaks in the Fourth Gospel concerning His resurrection cannot without great violence be explained otherwise than of a bodily resuscitation from the dead ; and in the Gospel, not less than in the Synoptics, His continued personal relation to His people, even after His departure from the earth, is most certainly taught (Sec. x. 5 ; compare Sec. xxi. 8).

5. The greatest difference is found no doubt in the domain of eschatology. But whilst this is manifest, we shall not seek in vain for a deep and important harmony. It is nowhere denied that the believer outlives death, and is happy after death ;§ according to both sources, however, a resurrection of the body at the last day is presupposed and promised. even to those who here on earth were partakers of the higher life. (Sec. xv. 5 ; compare Sec. xxi. 3). Upon the

* Matt. xxvi. 54 ; compare John x. 17, 18.
† Matt. xxvi. 38 ; compare John xii. 27, 28.
‡ John xiv. 31 ; compare Matt. xxvi. 46.
§ Luke xvi. 23 ; xx. 38 ; compare John xi. 25.

mountain in Galilee,* and at the festival at Jerusalem,†
the Lord proclaims himself the Judge of the future,
exalted above all creatures, yet conscious at the same
time of His entire dependence upon the Father.‡
According to both sources, He promises the same
future salvation,§ which is to be attained by each of
His people in the way of self-denial and suffering.∥
In neither does He hold forth to the impenitent sinner
any prospect of ultimate annihilation, or of the diminution or removal of future chastisement. His Parousia
(coming) which is *there* generally but not always more
figuratively, *here* more spiritually presented, brings in
and reveals the glorious end of all things.

5. No doubt there are single thoughts of importance
in the teaching of the Lord which are communicated
on the one hand only in John, on the other hand
exclusively in the Synoptics. How can it be otherwise, when none of the Evangelists sought for systematic unity, much less for completeness, in this
respect? What John gives in addition seems only as
the complement, and is the crown of that which his
forerunners had recorded; and where he is silent it
must never be forgotten that he needed not to repeat
what he could presuppose was sufficiently known
from the work of his predecessors. Many a peculiarity in the teaching of the Lord according to John
is quite sufficiently explained by its historic connection. If here, for instance, the command of love is

* Matt. vii. 21-23; compare Matt. xxv. 31 *cet.*   † John v. 24-29.
‡ Matt xxiv. 36; compare John xiv. 28.
§ Luke xii. 37; compare John xii. 26.
∥ Matt. xvi. 25; compare John xii. 25.

called a new commandment,* while it is elsewhere designated as old and well known,† the reason is that the Lord is here speaking not of the general love of one's neighbour, but of that Christian love of the brethren which His people henceforth are called to exercise in following Him. If it is only in John that Jesus speaks of praying in His name,‡ this is because it is spoken on the last evening, in those farewell discourses which are preserved only by John. If, on the other hand, the idea of forgiveness of sins retires almost entirely into the background—compare, however, John xx. 23—it is because the historic connection in which the Lord, according to the Synoptics, speaks thereof, is wanting in John. At the same time, the love of God towards guilty men is here also proclaimed with no less emphasis. The Lord without doubt speaks in John more fully than elsewhere of the promise and operation of the Holy Spirit, but here, as in the Synoptics, He promises the Spirit to His people both before and also after His death,§ and the help He leads His people to expect partakes in both cases of the same character.‖ Thus there is shown afresh the truth of the observation, "The profound discourses which St. John relates are only the development of the energetic and concise words which the three first Evangelists collected by preference" (De Pressensé), or with another writer, in point of conviction a converted Tübingen Critic, "The presentation

* John xiii. 34. † Matt. xxii. 39. ‡ John xvi. 23.
§ John xx. 22 ; compare Luke xxiv. 49.
‖ John xiv-xvi. ; compare Matt. x. 19, 20.

of the teaching of Jesus, as made by the three first Gospels, demands its complement in the discourses of John." (A. Ritschl).

7. While the real difference between the teaching of the Christ of the Synoptics and the Christ of John is neither absolute nor inexplicable, it is on more than one account of importance. It is a no less unconstrained than indisputable proof of that *unsearchable riches of Christ*,* which no Evangelist is able to exhaust. It serves, moreover, to confirm the trustworthiness of narrators who, while they show themselves not unacquainted with the work of others, proceed each one from his own stand-point, with so much independence and accuracy. It explains to us, finally, how out of the teaching of Jesus—with all its depths, so simple— so rich a diversity of Apostolic doctrines could spring. Precisely because the teaching of the Lord was so many-sided, was it able to serve as the basis for more than one form of Apostolic proclamation, in which now one, now another side of this teaching was brought into prominence, without the Apostle becoming untrue to the spirit or intention of his Master. The soil is here fruitful enough to bear diverse plants, which attain various heights, but evidently belong to the same order, and bear like fruits.

Compare E. A. Borger *de constanti et aequabili J. C. indole*, &c., H. C. 1816. Our *Life of Jesus*, i. p. 147. *Christologie*, ii. 113-121. The *Gospel of John* (Engl. transl.) E. de Pressensé, *Jesus Christ: His Times, Life, and Work* (pp. 291-306 of Eng. trans.) **F. de**

* Ephes. iii. 8.

Rougemont, *Christ et ses temoins*, Paris, 1856, i. p. 137, and following. Godet, *Commentaire*, ii. pp. 750-770. W. Beyschlag, *Christologie des* N. T., p. 54, and following. Where it is truly remarked: "All the main themes of the Johannine discourses are found in the Synoptics, only in scattered traces, half lost sight of; but just as certainly as Christ must have discoursed of them with infinitely greater fulness than would appear from the Synoptics, just so certainly does a comparison of the Synoptics with John confirm again even in this particular the authenticity of John."

POINTS FOR INQUIRY.

IN what respect is the doctrine of the Synoptical Christ explained and confirmed by the word of the Johannine Christ? —Wherein consists the difference of the παραβολή in the Synoptics and the παροιμία in John?—Is the appellation *Son of man* employed by Jesus in the one and the other in the same sense?—Whence arises it that the Lord, in the Fourth Gospel, speaks of His Messianic dignity, His death, and His resurrection, so much earlier than in the others?—On what points is the Lord silent in John, while in the Synoptics he speaks with more or less of explicitness?—And what is to be inferred from this silence?—Review of the different modes of regarding and explaining (Lange, Godet, &c.) the utterances of Jesus, recorded only in John.—Proof of the harmony between the utterances of the Lord as preserved in John and those in the Synoptics, in the history of the suffering, death, and resurrection of Jesus?—Apologetical significance of the results obtained.—The careful comparison of the didactic contents of the Synoptics and the Johannine Gospel is the abiding task of the Biblical Theologian of our days, and a field on which many a weed has yet to be rooted up, but **also many a precious flower is still to be gathered.**

SECTION XXIV.

𝔑esult.

IN its harmonious diversity, the doctrine of the Lord, communicated by the Evangelist, is on the one hand the explanation, development, and fulfilment of the Word of God, spoken by Moses and the Prophets; on the other hand, at the same time, the basis and starting-point of a series of Apostolic testimonies in regard to the way of redemption, which on their side, in turn variously modified, contain, interpret, and confirm His teaching.

1. At the end of this our Second Part, we naturally look back upon those foundations first laid in the Old Testament. The impression which the study of the Lord's teaching, then, makes upon us, whether we listen to John or the Synoptics, cannot be better expressed than in a reverent *Amen* to the declaration of the Sermon on the Mount, "I am not come to

destroy the Law and the Prophets, but to fulfil."* If the opposition between the Old Testament and the New is not to be passed over, the connection between the words of the Lord and those of Moses and the Prophets is rendered by way of comparison the more striking. We receive here an explanation of many a mysterious word of the Old Testament; an explanation, the high importance of which cannot be ignored, when we regard the Lord in the light in which, according to *all* the Evangelists, He so often represents himself; on the other hand, the doctrine of earlier days is, in its most important points of faith and morals, so explained and fulfilled, that to many questions only raised there, the most satisfactory answer is here given; and again, we perceive in the words of Jesus a fulfilment of earlier prophecies and expectations, which cannot possibly be explained from a merely natural and accidental course of things. If, consequently, the words of the *Word* are in a certain respect such as were before unknown, they are, on the other hand, the echo of the mighty voice of prophecy, and the Old Testament confirms again its right to the honourable title of "a great prophecy—a type of Him who should come, and is come." (De Wette.)

2. Just because the doctrine of the Lord is a living unity, it is anything but a dead uniformity. *A priori*, therefore, we might expect that the word of the Apostles would be something else than a

---

* Matt. v. 17.

mechanical repetition, and, *à posteriori*, it will be seen that here nothing less than a new, though by no means strange, world of thought opens before our eyes. "In the discourses of Jesus, we have the pregnant germ and kernel, the root, the simple but firm foundation; in the Apostolic teaching, as the other New Testament writings give it, we have the off-shoots and branches, the plant grown forth from the germ; we have the completed edifice, which rests upon that simple but firm foundation. However full of life and energy this Apostolic doctrine appears, equally original, equally pregnant, equally presenting the Christian impress in the first form, do the discourses of the Lord in the Gospels appear: and both were equally adapted, the Apostolic teaching to the relations of the Apostles in their further development, as the discourses of the Lord were in accordance with the relations of His personal life." (Schmid). The investigation now following will be a continued evidence for the truth of this observation.

Compare our *Christologie*, i. p. 33, *seq.*, ii. p. 130, *seq.* Lutterbeck, *l. c.* ii. p. 161, *seq.* Schmid, *l. c.* ii. p. 7. Baur, *l. c.* p. 122-126. A recent work of great merit— B. Weiss, *Lehrbuch der biblischen Theologie des Neuen Testaments*, Berlin, 1868—may also be profitably consulted on this and the following divisions.

POINTS FOR INQUIRY.

To what extent are the utterances of Jesus himself, in regard to His relation to the Old Testament economy, confirmed by the results of our investigation?—Jesus as expositor of the words of Moses and the Prophets.—Christ's interpretation of Scripture, and later Hermeneutics.—What is that which is properly new in the Gospel of the kingdom of the Synoptics, and the testimony concerning himself of the Johannine Christ?—What in the domain of doctrine?—What in the domain of morals and of ritual?—Does the doctrine of Jesus stand in one and the same relation to that of all the Apostles and of their fellow-labourers?—**Transition to the treatment of** the Theology of the **Apostles.**

THIRD PART.

THE THEOLOGY OF THE APOSTLES.

SECTION XXV.
General Survey.

THE investigation of the Theology of the Apostles extends to the sum of the doctrines—so far as we can speak of a sum of doctrines—of all those men whose testimony concerning the Lord Jesus Christ is given in the New Testament, and which testimony, even on historical grounds, is of unspeakable value for us. In the investigation of this testimony, also, we must no more overlook the manifest diversity than the higher unity in the testimony of the several witnesses; and in making this examination we must proceed so as gradually to rise from the simplest to the more complicated and involved system of doctrines.

General Survey. 191

1. In the strict sense of the word, the title of Apostle can be given only to the twelve, who were called by the Lord himself to the apostolate,* and whose number was filled up, after the death of Judas, by Matthias.† Nevertheless, in addition to these, Paul also lays claim to this title of honour,‡ which is moreover given to the fellow-labourers and friends of the first witnesses of the Lord,§ yea, once even to Jesus himself.‖ We follow this example the more readily, since the greater part of those who were Apostles in the exact sense of the word have left no writings behind them. We shall here, consequently, examine the doctrines of all the writers of the New Testament, but of these only. Those spiritually allied, whose writings have not been received into the canon of the New Testament, remain consequently without the circle of our investigation. (Sec. ii. 3.)

2. The distinction between the Theology of Jesus Christ and that of the Apostles is the fruit of a sounder view as to the inspiration of the sacred writers. From the stand-point of the mechanical theory of inspiration it was entirely a matter of indifference whether a text of Scripture was to be found in the Old Testament or the New, proceeded from the Lord himself or from one of His witnesses: enough, it was in the Bible. A mode of dealing with Scripture more in accordance with historic principles prepared the way for a juster distinction, which,

* Luke vi. 13. † Acts i. 26. ‡ Gal. i. 1
§ Acts xiv. 14; Gal. i. 19. ‖ Heb. iii. 1.

without doubt, is according to the mind of the Lord and His Apostles.

3. The question as to why the Apostolic testimony possesses binding authority for the faith and life of the Christian, belongs not to the domain of historic, but of systematic Theology. Yet, even from the standpoint of historic theology, it is easy to see that the word of such witnesses as stood nearest of all to Christ, cannot be too carefully listened to.* We may safely admit that not all the Apostles were naturally men of high and extraordinary gifts; but even the priority of their testimony, the fruit of that first impression which the manifestation of Christ makes upon a susceptible mind, assures to them a position entirely unique; and justice is not rendered to the importance of their writings if these are regarded merely as feeble attempts (Reuss) to express Christian truth as well as possible, attempts which forthwith were in part successfully replaced and supplemented by others. Nearest the fountain-head the water is unquestionably purest, and where it is a question of witnesses to historico-religious facts, a plain man who has received the first impression aright has the precedence over a man of greater culture who later philosophises in a distinguished manner, but—*after the lapse of centuries.* At the same time, the Apostolic testimony concerning Christ cannot be placed unreservedly in one line with the testimony of Christ concerning himself. There is found here a distinction similar to

* Compare John xix. 35 ; Acts i. 21 · 2 Peter i. 16.

that between the Messianic period as a whole and that of the Apostles. Their word must be tested by that of the Master, not the reverse. But if their doctrine is to that extent subordinate to His, it nevertheless stands high above that of later writers. What a distance between the Christian literature even of the second century and that of the first!

4. The fountain-head, from which the knowledge of Apostolic Theology is derived is the New Testament. "What we learn in addition from other sources, concerning the teaching of this or the other Apostle, is in any case to be accepted only so far as it agrees with the teaching of the New Testament." (Messner).

Concerning the relation in which our investigation stands to the isagogics of the New Testament we have already expressed ourselves (Sec. i. 4). The Biblical theologian of the New Testament, who proceeds from the stand-point of the supernatural, has to regard scruples as to the genuineness of his sources only when they display a better origin than that of a one-sided, naturalistic criticism. He must not, however, exclude the light which, through the examination of the *contents* of the New Testament writings, may also be shed upon their *genuineness*.

5. To the question, how far the theology of the Apostles derived from these sources can be regarded as a whole, no answer can, at this stage of our investigation, be given. It is well known that the doctrine of the Apostles is presented to us in a multitude of doctrinal types (τύποι διδαχῆς), but nowhere in a system of doctrines closely reasoned out.

When, therefore, we speak of the doctrinal system of an Apostle, we mean only "the sum of his isolated doctrinal utterances reduced to an orderly and systematic whole." Such a doctrinal system is the more easily formed, the greater the number of the ideas which we gain from a rich store of Apostolic *dicta*. No one, for instance, will think of placing on a level in this respect the writings of James or Jude with those of Paul. The unity of the Apostolic doctrine is certainly anything but a mere uniformity; and it is to be reckoned among the merits of the modern supernaturalism, that it has, far more than the earlier, an eye and a heart for the rich variety of ideas which is found in the different writers of the New Testament. Nevertheless, this variety gives no right to the assertion that, "rightly regarded, very little unity in their testimony concerning the faith is to be found among the Apostles" (Pierson), as though we were here contemplating different limbs, but no body—loose stones, which, however, were too dissimilar in size and form to be erected into one building. Certainly, there is nothing easier than to oppose to each other a number of Apostolic utterances, and then to speak of the conflicting views of the different New Testament writers. But such an anatomical criticism, which knows, indeed, how to separate, but has not learnt how to combine, and which, from its close attention to each particular tree, is not able to take in the whole forest at one view, has already shown itself as weak as it is one-sided; and the "*divide et impera*" is more aptly inscribed upon the banner of the assailants of Christianity than upon the school of believing theology. What was to be expected *à priori* is also exegetically and historically justified : there exists among the Apostolic writers a diversity of gifts, but unity of spirit ; they are unlike in regard to their point of departure and the method and depth of their teaching, but agree in their convictions in regard to the faith, in their principles and expectations ; their colour is varied, but not so the original light ; their tones change, but thereby the higher harmony is rather increased than disturbed. The Jewish-Christian cast of thought of the one writer is by no means irreconcilably opposed to the more Grecian colouring of thought in another ; and a continued investigation always leads to the discovery of a harmony even in those cases where it was before doubted, perhaps entirely overlooked.

6. The main divisions of our subject have been before indicated (Sec. iii. 2), and must be justified by the progress of our investigations. As far as the execution of it is concerned, our design is neither to condemn nor to defend, but simply to afford an objectively accurate representation of the doctrine of the Apostolic writers. This, however, must be undertaken in the spirit of the writer, and with regard to the peculiarity, the main thought, and the definite method of each one. Instead, therefore, of grouping together under one head (*e.g.*, of Theology, Anthropology, Christology, Eschatology) what is taught by the different Apostles, the classification and analysis of the ideas of one Apostle—Paul, for instance—must be

made in a very different manner from the classification and analysis necessary in the case of another—as Peter or John. It is impossible to understand a witness for the truth so long as we do not take into account his stand-point and his characteristic mode of viewing his subject. At the same time, it is of importance to consider the genetic and psychological development of the thoughts of the writer, and so, also—where it is possible, and so far as is necessary—to take into consideration the chronological order of his writings. Here, as elsewhere, any sharp line of separation between the dogmatic and the ethical side of the Apostles' teaching would be both useless and hurtful. Only when the doctrinal system of each Apostle has been separately regarded in its facts and as a whole, can good fruits be looked for from the comparison of the doctrinal system of the one with that of the other.

7. As regards the means of help available for this part of our investigation, and the spirit in which it must be carried on, we direct attention to what we have before said (Sec. ii. 3, and iii. 3). Only it is necessary again to remind the student that he who contemplates the doctrines of the Apostles from a stand-point which is in irreconcilable antagonism with their own, can neither understand nor appreciate their testimony. The Apostolic writings, like the Gospels, can be understood only in the light of that Spirit by whom their writers were inspired.

Compare on the Theology of the Apostles, besides the writings mentioned (Sec. ii. 3), G. C. R. Matthaei,

Der Religionsglaube der Apost. Jesu, u. s. w., 2 vols., Gott. 1826. E. de Pressensé, *Early Years of Christianity*, pp. 207-259. F. Bonifas, *Essai sur l'Unité de l'Enseignement Apostolique*. Paris, 1866. Ph. Schaff, *History of the Early Church*. (Eng. trans.)

POINTS FOR INQUIRY.

ORIGIN, sense, and various uses of the name of Apostle.—What is the significance of Luke x. 16 as compared with John xx. 21?—What is to be learnt from post-Apostolic literature in regard to the doctrine of the Apostles?—Which Apostolic system of doctrine appears, after a preliminary examination, the deepest, most perfect, and richest?—What is necessary to penetrate as deeply as possible into an Apostolic system of doctrine?—Characteristics of the Apostolic teaching, as compared with the oldest Patristic literature.

FIRST DIVISION.

THE PETRINE THEOLOGY.

SECTION XXVI.

Summary.

THE prior treatment of the Petrine theology is justified as well by the especial place which this Apostle takes in the history of the first century of the Christian Church, as by the peculiar character of his doctrine itself. If this theology is to be drawn from the purest sources, the First Epistle of Peter and the Acts of the Apostles occupy the first place; but also single Pauline Epistles (*e.g.*, that to the Galatians) contain in this respect important hints. The Second Epistle of Peter is in this investigation no more to be quietly placed on one side than to be raised without examination to an equality of rank with the First; but it must be separately examined and compared. The whole doctrine of this Apostle contained in the New Testament affords us, at the same time, the spectacle of a harmonious development, and the traces of a strongly expressed but sanctified individuality.

1. There is nothing arbitrary in the fact of begining our investigation with the theology of Peter. If we are to ascend from the simplest to the more complicated and highly-developed system of doctrines (Sec. xxiv.), we must in no case begin with Paul or John. Just as little can we bring ourselves (with Schmid) to accord the first place to James, since his claim to the name of an Apostle in the narrower sense of the word is more than doubtful; and his Epistle bears an almost exclusively practical character. Besides this, Peter affected much more powerfully than James the spirit of the whole Apostolic age. It was Peter who exerted an influence upon the earliest form of the Gospel, which is entirely ignored in the romantic presentation of the history of the Apostles in favour just now (Renan). Even Paul has afterwards only built upon the foundation laid by Cephas in the Jewish and Gentile world. (This is not in contradiction with Rom. xv. 19, 20; Paul's labours being the natural outgrowth of the principles laid down by Peter, Acts xv. 7-11; and of his example, Acts x. 34-43). Although Rome has exalted this Apostle in a one-sided manner, it would be an act of ultra-Protestant unfairness to overlook the special impor-

tance of his person and word. In union with Matthew, Mark, James, and Jude, he affords us the purest source for learning what was the faith of the earliest Churches of Palestine.

2. The fountain from which the Apostolic writers derive their testimony concerning the way of salvation is with all essentially the same; but this testimony has been in the case of each one of them more or less modified. All are enlightened by the Holy Spirit, who leads them into the sanctuary of truth; but not all attain to the same height of spiritual life. Sent forth by this Spirit, Peter speaks distinctly as an eye-witness of the deeds and sufferings of the Lord.* At the same time, he appeals more than many others to the Scriptures of the Old Testament, which are manifestly better understood by him after the day of Pentecost than ever before. He also appeals to special revelation granted to himself.† Above all, his own matured Christian experience gives to his testimony its peculiar character and its indisputable value.

3. Upon a superficial examination it might appear as though among the sources whence our knowledge of the Petrine doctrine is drawn, the Acts of the Apostles must occupy the first place. But, while the trustworthiness of this book is to be acknowledged, it is self-evident that for our purpose a writing of the Apostle himself is of much greater importance than some of his discourses which have been communicated by another, years after their delivery. For this reason we give the first place among the sources

* Acts v. 31; 1 Pet. v. 1.   † Acts x. 28; compare 2 Pet. i. 14.

through which we become acquainted with his theology to the First Epistle of Peter; and the more willingly, since its genuineness is raised above all reasonable doubts, and it moreover manifests a thoroughly subjective character. Next to this, however, we rank the Acts of the Apostles, and place so much the greater confidence in this source, inasmuch as we ever afresh observe that the Peter with whom we become here acquainted corresponds in so many respects with that of the First Epistle.* The Apostle Paul also is able to render us important service in our seeking to come to a true knowledge concerning the natural bent and disposition of Peter's mind. Not to speak of the correspondence between some of the Pauline and some of the Petrine modes of conception (which is pushed to an extreme by some of the Tubingen school), we may think of 1 Cor. i. 12, ix. 5, xv. 5; of the account given in Gal. ii. 7-9; of the statement that Peter was the Apostle of the Circumcision, one of the pillars of the Church, &c.

As far as the Second Epistle is concerned, the modest assertion that "no one who is experienced in things of this sort can be found to defend the genuineness of this Epistle" (Loman) serves only as an example of the peculiar manner in which a certain school grants to its own disciples alone the well-known "right of speech." Different voices have been raised in our time in defence of its genuineness, which was early assailed. Yet the advocates of its genuine-

* Compare Acts ii. 14-38, iii. 12-26, iv. 9-12, v. 29-32, x. 34-43, xi. 4-17, xii. 11, xv. 7-11.

ness will willingly admit that the scruples raised in regard to this Epistle are by no means entirely unfounded. As matters now stand, it is neither to be quietly set on one side, nor to be placed without reserve on the same level with the First. If the one course betrays a prejudice, the other is not scientific: to exclude it would be precipitate, but to distinguish is a duty. Only the science of isagogics can discuss in their full extent the objections raised against this Epistle: the Theology of the New Testament has fulfilled its task when it has developed the doctrine, and compared it in every respect with that of the First Epistle.

4. The Petrine Theology, as known from these different sources, offers the charming spectacle of a harmonious development. For all the Apostles of the Lord, and especially for our Apostle, life ceased not to be a continual growing. During a period of about thirty years we hear how the consciousness of Peter in regard to the faith expresses itself ever more fully, more powerfully, and more clearly. Nowhere do we find self-contradiction demanding the recal of former utterances, but everywhere a progress which reminds of the words of Solomon: "The path of the just is as the shining light, that shineth more and more unto the perfect day." The Christology, for instance, from Acts ii. 22, to 2 Pet. iii. 18 *b*—the genuinensss of the latter presupposed—exhibits a glorious climax. The great facts of salvation, presented with such force even in his earliest discourses, **are, as** occasion calls for it, presented in his First

Epistle in all their dogmatic power. From all this the literal fulfilment of the promise of the Lord in John xvi. 13 is manifest; and the comparison one with another of the testimonies of the Apostle at different periods of his life is, at the same time, an undesigned confirmation of the trustworthiness of his statements.

5. Not less are there seen in the doctrines of this Apostle the traces of a strongly-expressed but sanctified individuality. Even in the Gospel narrative he comes, as is well known, strikingly into the foreground, and displays a spiritual physiognomy which is not easily interchanged with that of any other. Peter is the impulsive disciple, the man of feeling and action, not given to abstract thinking, but living and moving in the sphere of the concrete and of that which is immediately present. We should not expect of such a man that he would write much, would make his statement in detail, or would develop one and the same idea on all its sides. He will be more at home in a circle of historical than of speculative ideas, will attach himself without difficulty to the course of thought and form of expression employed by another, and will be in some respects inferior to more distinguished labourers. And all this we actually do find to a certain extent in the discourses and Epistles of Peter. Even after his conversion he is one of those unlearned and plain men,[*] by whom the form of the moral world was changed. His testimony is precisely what we might expect from the Simon Peter we have known before. This clearly-marked individuality is pene-

[*] Acts iv. 13.

trated with the flame of a zeal and a love which alone could qualify him to testify of Christ in such manner as he actually did.

6. Somewhat more closely do we become acquainted with this individuality in the important address with which Peter—before the Pentecost, but already sealed by the Holy Spirit*— introduced the election of Matthias.† It becomes at once manifest how conscious he is of his Apostolic mission to be a witness of the Lord Jesus, and especially of His resurrection.‡ He appeals, moreover, repeatedly during this short address to the prophetic scriptures,§ showing thereby that he occupies a purely Israelitish stand-point. Finally, he is the first to lift up his eyes and make provision for the future, as though by his first Apostolic act he would lay claim to the honourable distinction of "the Apostle of Hope." As the leading thought of a symphony becomes apparent even in its overture, so do we learn even from these traits to know the Apostle aforehand, as he will show himself afresh in his discourses and writings. Simon Peter occupies for us the successive positions of Apostle of Jesus Christ, Apostle of Circumcision, and Apostle of Hope.

On the personality of Peter and his theology in general, compare an article of J. P. Lange in Herzog; the commentaries of Huther, Wiesinger, Besser, Fronmüller (Lange's Series), upon the Petrine epistles; especially B. Weiss: *der Petrin. Lehrbegriff*, Berl. 1855. On the genuineness of the Second Epistle our

* John xx. 22. † Acts i. 15-22. ‡ Acts i. 22. § Acts i. 16, i. 20.

Christol. des N. V. p. 162-176. On the credibility of the Acts of the Apostles in regard to Peter, besides our prize essay (Soc. of the Hague, 1846) C. F. Tripp: *Paulus nach der Apostelgesch.* Leiden, 1866. Lechler, *l. c.* p. 7, and following. Meyer: Commentary on the Acts, Introduction, Sec. ii.

POINTS FOR CONSIDERATION.

The personality and character of Peter, as they are known to us from his own words and writings.—The importance of his labours in the doctrinal development of the Apostolic age.—Nature and value of later accounts of his doctrine (the Clementines).—The true conception of growth in its application to the doctrinal system of an Apostle—To what extent can the personality of Peter be regarded as the source of his doctrines?—Is the proposal of Peter, Acts i. 16-22, to be condemned, to be justified, or to be commended?

SECTION XXVII.

Peter an Apostle of Jesus Christ.

As an Apostle of Jesus Christ, Peter testifies with increasing clearness, in word and deed, to the whole unique dignity and greatness of the Lord. The great facts of His earthly and heavenly life are brought by Peter emphatically into the foreground; such, also, as in the discourses and writings of other Apostles are not at all, or scarcely, indicated. With the historic presentation of these facts is united in his teaching, in an increasing degree, the apprehension of their dogmatic import and the appreciation of their practical worth.

1. In dealing with the Petrine system of doctrines, we properly begin with that which Peter has in common with all the other Apostles, thence to rise to that which is found in him of a nature peculiar to himself. As all the others, so he also is a witness

(μάρτυς) of Christ, although he is the only one who calls himself by this name;* and one may say that the text of the testimony which he delivers as such, is to be found in the words of this Apostle on his first appearance before the Council in Jerusalem.† The infinitely glorious and exalted form of the Saviour is not, however, contemplated on the same side by all. Of Peter it may be said that he lays special stress upon its historic character. Without plunging into reflections concerning the nature of the Lord, he places his person at once in the light of history, and gives Him—so to speak—to live on in the preaching of His Apostle.

2. Even on the day of Pentecost, he begins to speak of Jesus as the Nazarene, who had arisen among his contemporaries, a man whom God had approved by powers and well-known miracles.‡ He begins, consequently, by placing Him upon a level with the most illustrious servants of God, immediately after to raise Him above all, as that man whom God had made both Lord and Christ.§ The great proof for this assertion is found in His resurrection, and the outpouring of the Holy Ghost, and even His death of the Cross—which is by no means passed over in silence, but is charged home upon the Jews as an act of iniquity. Just because he is the Messiah, the historic fact of the descent of the Lord from David, has, for Peter, an especial significance.‖ Since He was promised by the Father, He is called the Holy One of

* 1 Peter v. 1.   † Acts iv. 12.   ‡ Acts ii. 22.
§ Acts ii. 36.   ‖ Acts ii. 33.

God,* the Prophet,† God's holy Servant, Jesus ($παῖς$)‡ —a name, not indeed equivalent to the more usual term Son ($υἱός$) of God "which appellation is not found in Peter" but which is far above the title of bond-servant ($δοῦλος$) a term the Apostles usually employ in speaking of themselves, and is derived from the prophetic representation of the perfect servant of Jehovah (עֶבֶד יָהּ). Besides this theocratic dignity of the Lord, Peter exalts His moral greatness. Christ is for him the Holy One and the Just,§ whose death condemns the whole nation. This impression was made by Christ's whole manifestation upon the man who had once (Luke v. 8) sunk down at the the Saviour's feet with the confession of his own impurity. In the sufferings of the Lord, more particularly does he point with admiration to His perfect sinlessness,‖ especially as this manifested itself in self-control and never-failing meekness. Thence it is he exalts these sufferings not merely (in common with all the Apostles) as expiatory, but also expressly as affording us a type and example.¶ But nothing can be further from the Apostle's mind than the thought that the Lord was only the best and greatest of men. In the historic manifestation of Christ, on the contrary, he gives us to behold traces of a super-human greatness. Even in the Pentecostal address it was said, with manifest reference to Christ's own words, that He had "received of the Father" the promise of the Holy Ghost ;** and whilst His relation

* Acts ii. 27.   † Acts iii. 22.   ‡ Acts iii. 13 ; iii. 26 ; iv. 27.
§ Acts iii. 13, 14.   ‖ 1 Peter i. 18, 19 ; ii. 22 ; ii. 23.
¶ 1 Peter ii. 21.   ** Acts ii. 33.

to the Father is not for the moment more closely defined, yet with the first proclamation of the Gospel among the Gentiles, the address of the Apostle is emphatically prefaced with the statement that God was, in a very especial manner, with Him.* This higher Christologic element comes yet more clearly into the foreground in his First Epistle. The Trinitarian distinction made at the very beginning † would be as unsuitable as the joyful proclamation of God as the Father of our Lord Jesus Christ, had the Lord been, according to the view of the Apostle, nothing more than a human being surrounded with Messianic glory. But even the mentioning of the Spirit of Christ ‡ as having been in the prophets, would at least sound strange, had Peter only meant by it that the spirit which animated the prophets was the same as that with which Christ was afterwards filled. The expression leads us rather to suppose a previous being and activity; and this supposition is yet strengthened when we hear that the Lamb of God was "foreknown indeed ($\pi\rho o \epsilon \gamma \nu \omega \sigma \mu \acute{\epsilon} \nu o s$) before the foundation of the world, but *was manifested* in these last times,"§ which would scarcely have a meaning had He not before this had an existence. If we add to this that several Old Testament utterances, having reference to God, are transferred, without limitation, to Christ,‖ and that, according to the simplest explanation of 1 Peter iv. 11 *b*, Jesus Christ is the subject of a reverential doxology: then, the testimonies of

* Acts x. 38. † 1 Peter i. 2, 3.
‡ 1 Peter i. 11. § 1 Peter i. 20.
‖ 1 Peter ii. 3; compare Psalm xxxiv. 8; 1 Peter iii. 15; Isaiah viii. 13.

Peter in regard to the supernatural character of the Lord, though comparatively few, are by no means ambiguous or unimportant.

3. It must nevertheless be acknowledged that the metaphysical side of the question with him by no means occupies so prominent a place as the historical; and if we inquire about the facts on which the Apostle lays a special emphasis, foremost of all is the resurrection of the Lord. In all the Petrine discourses preserved by Luke, this is defended with enthusiasm, and what he demands every Apostle should be,* he himself is in the fullest sense of the word—a witness of the resurrection. For him the Lord, especially the risen Lord, is the Prince (Author) of Life;† yea, the thought that Christ is not risen‡ is for him something self-contradictory. He holds firmly by the truth of the resurrection in the presence of the Jewish council;§ and, so far from being troubled by the objection that the Risen One has not manifested Himself to all the world, he rather gives prominence to this fact, and observes that he and his fellow-witnesses have eaten and drunk with Him risen. In the beginning of his First Epistle‖ he speaks of the blessing of regeneration in immediate connection with Christ, a fact easily explicable when we remember what the joyful message of the resurrection was for Peter himself.¶ As he himself was thereby born again to a new hope, so also, by this very resurrection, hope itself became for the first time a living, energising hope. The

* Acts i. 22; ii. 32.   † Acts iii. 15.   ‡ Acts ii 24.
§ Acts iv. 10.   ‖ 1 Peter i. 3.   ¶ Luke xxiv. 34

Peter an Apostle of Jesus Christ. 211

resurrection and glorification of Christ stands in immediate connection with faith and hope in God ; * and even baptism obtained its delivering power only through this resurrection.† Since, consequently, only a risen Christ is for Peter the true Christ, we cannot be surprised that on one occasion he characterises him, in his vigorous oriental and figurative manner, as the " living stone."‡

4. The Apostle, however, fixes the attention of his hearers and readers not upon this principal fact alone. He does not pass over in silence the fact that God has raised up His perfect servant,§ but just as little—what is found in no other Apostolic utterance—that God has anointed Him with the Holy Ghost and with power.‖ He is probably thinking of that which took place at the baptism of the Messiah.¶ And least of all does he neglect in recounting the miracles of the Lord,** to mention also the healing of those that were possessed, while he magnifies the whole public life of the Lord as *one* great act of blessing.†† He is manifestly unable to be silent about that which he has seen and heard.‡‡ Especially when he is speaking of the suffering and death of Jesus, he immediately shows himself an eye-witness. Whilst (in the Acts of the Apostles) standing in the presence of enemies, he regards this as the cruel act of Jewish transgression, yet not without

---

* 1 Peter i. 21. † 1 Peter iii. 21. ‡ 1 Peter ii. 4.
§ Acts iii. 26. ‖ Acts x. 38. ¶ Compare Isaiah xlii. 1 ; lxi. 1.
** Acts ii. 22 ; x. 38. †† Acts x. 38. ‡‡ Acts iv. 20.

seeking some extenuation of guilt for its authors.*
He dwells upon it in his epistle, in which he is speaking to Christians, as the revelation of the greatness of Christ, and as the source of the most glorious benefits. Of the Cross he often speaks as the tree (τὸ ξύλον)† perhaps in allusion to Deut. xxi. 23. But what took place upon the Cross, took place—and this was for Peter himself assuredly the first point of light in the darkness—in accordance with the determinate counsel and foreknowledge of God.‡ With this testimony concerning the sufferings of Christ,§ there come also spontaneously into the foreground single details in the history of His suffering ;‖ and he shows clearly by the whole way and manner in which he relates them, that he contemplates these sufferings in the light of prophetic Scripture, especially of Isaiah liii. In this manner, the offence of the Cross has now ceased for him also. Christ the Righteous One (compare Isaiah liii. 11) has, in opposition to those sacrifices which must often be offered, suffered for sins once for all,¶ and did this not merely to afford an illustrious example, but thereby to take away the load and burden of sin.** He suffers consequently for (ὑπέρ) the unjust; and although the expression in itself does not suffice to indicate a substitution, it is clear †† that Peter is thinking of a suffering through which others are delivered from the

* Acts iii. 17 ; compare Luke xxiii. 34.
† Acts v. 30 ; x. 39; 1 Peter ii. 24.   ‡ Acts ii. 23.
§ 1 Peter v. 1.   ‖ Acts iii. 13, 14; 1 Peter ii. 22, 23.
¶ 1 Peter iii. 18.   ** 1 Peter ii. 21-24.
†† 1 Peter 3, 18 ; ii. 24.

sufferings which are their due; in other words, of a bearing of chastisement in the place of others.* In consequence of this suffering, Christians were healed, and at the price of this blood redeemed from their former vain mode of life, with the definite aim that they, being dead to sin, should live to righteousness; first delivered from the guilt and chastisement, they were now also set free from the dominion of sin.†

5. Since Christ has once suffered for *sin*, He stands henceforth out of all relation to *sins*:‡ he who suffers in the flesh is made free from sin and the world. No wonder that He who as to the flesh was put to death, was precisely thereby made alive as to the spirit.§ Death breaks the bonds which had held captive the higher life, and opens up to Him an unbroken field for an activity rich in blessing. Of this work of the departed spirit of the Lord, the Apostle Peter gives repeated testimony.‖ Our design does not admit of our adducing at large all the different views which have been brought forward in all centuries, of these enigmatical words of the Apostle, far less to discuss them. Enough that we reject as entirely arbitrary, as well the opinion that a work of the spirit of the Lord at the time of Noah is here to be thought of, as

* Compare Lament. v. 7.

† 1 Peter ii. 24. 1 Peter iv. 1 does not belong to this place, since the words "*for us*" are not found in the best MSS. Neither does 1 Peter i. 2 belong directly to this class of texts, if it is true—what we assume with Weiss and others—that the blood of Christ, with which believers are sprinkled, is here distinctly conceived of as "the blood of the covenant."

‡ 1 Peter iv. 1.   § 1 Peter iii. 18.
‖ 1 Peter iii. 19-21; iv. 6; compare Acts ii. 31.

the view of Baur, that the spirits here spoken of were fallen angels (2 Peter ii. 4). Evidently, the Apostle is speaking of a work of the spirit of the Lord himself, which intervenes between His being made alive according to the Spirit and His exaltation to heaven,* and through which the Gospel of reconciliation was proclaimed to the dead, even the unhappy dead—of whom *one* generation is mentioned by name. Whether this activity was confined to this one generation, what form it assumed, what result it had—to all these questions the Apostle gives no answer. He has, manifestly, to do only with the assurance that the Christ who had died for sins did not remain inactive after death, thereby to bring into so much the greater light the far-extending consequences of the salvation brought by Him. He does not even speak of this mysterious event as something hidden, which was communicated to him by (an especial) revelation; but in passing, as a thing which is equally well known to his readers as the Lord's dying and returning to life. We might even call it a constituent part of Peter's Gospel, and one which peculiarly belongs to that Gospel.

6. The suffering and death of Christ, which are ended with this work of his departed Spirit, prepare the way for a glory which, not less than the previous sufferings, is an object of intense interest, even for the angels.† As with the Lord himself (Luke xxiv. 26), so with Peter, also, are Christ's sufferings and glory most intimately connected. This glory is manifested

* 1 Peter iii. 19, 22.   † 1 Peter i. 12.

even in the resurrection, of which Peter expressly says that it took place on the third day,* and which, on this account (as an event taking place on earth), is clearly distinguished from the glorification of the Lord in heaven.† The Apostle was, according to his own words, no less a witness of this exaltation, accomplished by the right hand of God, ‡ than of the resurrection which preceded it; § we must, therefore, following his guidance, regard it as a visible manifestation. From that which he tells us of its glory and its consequences, ‖ it is clear that he is by no means speaking exclusively of a spiritual rule in the sense in which that term is often used. The glorified Christ continues also his personal activity for the advancement of the highest interests of His people. He is and remains the shepherd and guardian of their souls; ¶ although invisible, object of their continued love and joy,** and through Him alone can their spiritual sacrifices be acceptable to God.††

7. Even though we should proceed no further, it would yet be clear enough that, if the Christology of Peter is not the richest, it yet leaves no single side of the person and work of the Lord out of sight, and thereby manifests just that character which (taking into account the brevity of his First Epistle) was to be expected from an individuality like his. His whole teaching confirms his right to the honourable title of Witness and Apostle of Jesus Christ, but at the

---

* Acts x. 40. † 1 Peter iii. 21, 22. ‡ Acts ii. 33.
§ Acts v. 31, 32. ‖ 1 Peter iii. 22. ¶ 1 Peter ii. 25.
** 1 Peter i. 8. †† 1 Peter ii. 5.

same time to that of a disciple of John the Baptist
(John i. 35-42). This last observation prepares the
way for observing a new characteristic of this Apostle.

Compare, besides the writers mentioned in the
preceding section, on the appellation *Servant of the
Lord*, C. I. Nitzsch, in the Stud. u. Krit. 1828, ii.
p. 331, and following. On 1 Peter iii. 19-21 ; iv. 6,
see our *Christol.* ii. p. 196-202 : the Commentaries of
Meyer and Alford *in loco*. An important history of
the interpretation of this passage is found in Weiss,
Der Petrin. Lehrbegriff, p. 216-227.

POINTS FOR INQUIRY.

WHAT is the sense of Acts iv. 12 ?—Whence comes it that
in the first discourses of Peter, yet more stress is laid upon
the resurrection than upon the death of the Lord ?—The
Petrine teaching concerning the appearing of Christ in
the spirit-world compared with that in the Gospel of Nico-
demus.—Probable source and abiding value of this teaching.
—What peculiar significance is attached to the resurrection
of the Lord in 1 Peter i. 21 ; iii. 21 ?—Does Peter, as well
as the other Apostles, give any hints as to the nature of the
relation between the glorified Lord and his people ?

SECTION XXVIII.

Peter the Apostle of the Circumcision.

ALTHOUGH Peter, as the Apostle of Jesus Christ, proclaims salvation in Him as absolutely necessary for all, and as attainable for all, yet the substance and form of his teaching justifies the name of the "Apostle of the Circumcision." This name, however, is not to be taken in a one-sided separatistic sense.

1. The fact that salvation in Christ is indispensable alike for all is powerfully expressed by Peter before the Council at Jerusalem.* The *name* of Christ, mentioned with warmth by him, especially in his first discourses,† is for him in the fullest sense the banner of redemption. Without reason it has been supposed that a different spirit is to be found in the mild words addressed (Acts x. 34, 35) to Cornelius. He there by no means asserts that God-fearing men are without distinction acceptable to God (δεκτός) in

* Acts iv. 12.
† Acts ii. 38, iii. 6, 16, iv. 10, 12 ; compare Luke xxiv. 47.

such a sense as that they should be saved without Christ, but only that they should be received into the kingdom of God, thus to be saved. Were it otherwise, of what use were preaching and baptism to the whole Gentile house? "*Non indifferentismus religionum, sed indifferentia nationum, hic asseritur*" (Bengel).

2. This perfect indispensableness has its ground in the universality of sin. In itself the doctrine of sin is with Peter but little developed. As to its origin he does not directly express himself; while Paul ascends to the source, he points out only the turbid stream. The sin of the Jewish nation culminates before his eye in the rejection of the Messiah;* that of the Gentiles is the fruit of the ignorance which blinded them in their pre-Christian state.† Whilst fleshly lusts are in themselves sinful,‡ their manifestation in all kinds of perverseness is especially in antagonism with God's will, and brings back the confessors of the Gospel to a former heathen stand-point.§ Even the Christian is continually exposed to the danger of sinning,‖ and is not therefore saved without a great struggle.¶ After all, there is for Jews and Gentiles only one way of salvation—the grace of the Lord Jesus Christ, even without the oppressive yoke of the works of the law.**

3. That which is so necessary for all is also equally attainable for all. Even in the Pentecostal address distinct reference is made to this universal destination of salvation in Christ. To the greatest sinners among

---

* Acts ii. 36. † 1 Peter i. 14. ‡ 1 Peter iv. 2. § 1 Peter iv. 3, 4.
‖ 1 Peter v. 8. ¶ 1 Peter iv. 18. ** Acts xv. 10, 11.

the Jews grace is proclaimed, and no obscure allusion is made to the calling of the Gentiles also.* If Peter at first thinks that the Gentiles must be brought as it were over the bridge of Judaism into the kingdom of God, we see this limiting condition fall away after the revelation of Acts x. He even lays evident stress upon the fact that God has broken down the wall of separation† in giving the Holy Ghost both to Jews and Gentiles, and purifying the hearts of both through faith. There is consequently no ground for accusing Peter of a narrow-hearted separatism which has been supposed to lead him to see in the Jews, if not exclusively, yet especially, the heirs of the kingdom of God. Even the memorable words in which he teaches that God had *first* sent His servant Jesus to the Jews,‡ furnish in themselves a proof to the contrary.

4. The conditions of partaking of salvation in Christ are, according to Peter, exceedingly simple. In his addresses to the unbelieving Jews, we hear him—entirely in the spirit of the Baptist and of the Messiah—repeatedly call them to repentance and conversion.§ In this repentance ($\mu\epsilon\tau\acute{a}\nu o\iota a$) is included that faith which in his address to Cornelius he urges as pre-eminently essential,|| and which is manifested by the centurion's voluntary submission to baptism—an act of obedience with which is associated the reception of the forgiveness of sins and the gift of the Holy Ghost, without, however, any supernatural efficacy being supposed to dwell in the baptismal water itself.

---

* Acts ii. 39. † Acts xv. 8, 9. ‡ Acts iii. 26; compare John iv. 22.
§ Acts ii. 38, iii. 19. || Acts x. 47.

Only to *that* baptism is value ascribed which is accompanied with the promise of preserving a good conscience before God.* Such a baptism saves, even as the water of the flood saved the family of Noah in the ark, and he who receives it begins here on earth to be a partaker of the salvation ($\sigma\omega\tau\eta\rho\iota a$) which is in Christ. Whatever any was before, the one has no distinction on that account above the other, for Christ is Lord of all,† and the Holy Ghost has raised all to the same freedom and dignity.‡

5. However purely Christian all this may be, even the form in which the Apostle expresses these ideas, and yet more the nature of these ideas themselves, is such that we recognise in Peter, before all others, the Apostle of the Circumcision. Both in the Acts and the Epistles he stands before us as a man who is entirely penetrated with the Spirit of the Old Testament, and most willingly clothes his thoughts in its language. No writing of the New Testament contains more citations from the Old, more allusions thereto, than the First Epistle of Peter. In the Pentecostal discourse, also, we hear how he appeals in regard to the Resurrection and Exaltation of the Lord to the xvi. and cx. Psalms. At once (Acts iii.) the promise of the great "Prophet" serves as his text, and again (Acts iv.) the Psalm of the "corner-stone." All the prophets, from Samuel onwards,§ he appeals to as witnesses. Christianity is for him the fulfilment of prophecy. Even to the prophets it was revealed that the things which they proclaimed should

* 1 Peter iii. 21. † Acts x. 36. ‡ Acts xv. 8, 9. § Acts iii. 24.

Peter the Apostle of the Circumcision. 221

not be granted to themselves, but to Christians ;* and the Apostle who makes this assertion has sat at their feet. In their words, even when he does not expressly mention them,† he sets forth and defends his opinion. The main requirement of the law‡ and the promise of prophecy§ are expressly adduced ; and the principal persons in the history of the Old Testament, *e.g.*, a Noah with his family, a Sarah in her relation to Abraham, yea, the holy women of old time in general, are presented as patterns for believers.|| Those who walk after this example are distinguished with titles of honour like those conferred upon the Old Testament Israel. They are called *Elect*,¶ *a royal priesthood*,** and form together the *house of God*.†† The name Church or Congregation (ἐκκλησία) is not used by this Apostle ; but instead of this is found the expression *people of God*,‡‡ *flock of the Lord*,§§ which is so often in the Prophets and Psalms used of Israel, and which has for Peter without doubt a peculiar value.|||| The Old Testament idea of Election¶¶ everywhere underlies his discourses and his writings. Yea, our Apostle takes his stand so firmly upon the basis of a teleologic view of the world, that he even acknowledges the fulfilment of the counsel of God

---

* 1 Peter i. 12.

† 1 Peter i. 24, 25, compared with Isaiah xl. 6-8 ; ii. 3, compared with Psalm xxxiv. 8 ; iii. 10-12, compared with Psalm xxxiv. 12-16 ; iv. 18, compared with Prov. xi. 31 ; v. 7, compared with Psalm lv. 22.
‡ 1 Peter i. 16. § 1 Peter ii. 6. || 1 Peter iii. 5, 6, 20. ¶ 1 Peter i. 2.
** 1 Peter ii. 9.   †† 1 Peter iv. 17.   ‡‡ 1 Peter ii. 9-10.
§§ 1 Peter v. 2, 3. |||| Compare John xxi. 15-17.
¶¶ Compare Deut. vii. 6.

when the disobedient stumble at the word of Grace (1 Peter ii. 8).

6. In the idea of God, also, from which Peter proceeds, the Old Testament tone prevails. Without doubt it is a distinctive privilege of Christians to be able to call on God as Father (1 Peter i. 17)—it is as though the "Our Father" were before the mind of Peter when he wrote these words—but this Father gives sentence at the same time as Judge, without respect of persons. He is the faithful Creator (1 Peter iv. 19), and with this attribute of His faithfulness—so celebrated by Israel's prophets—come forth His power, holiness, omniscience, and righteousness. Christ also, the Son of God, is here contemplated less from the metaphysical than from the theological stand-point. Peter is the only Apostle by whom he is called a *Lamb* (ἀμνός),* an expression which is also derived from Isaiah. The Holy Ghost also is unquestionably mentioned by Peter,† and brought into the closest connection with the Godhead;‡ but with him, as in the Old Testament, the doctrine of the Spirit is but little developed.

7. No other character is borne by the prevailing description of the Christian life according to Peter. That which is of the greatest importance with him is the fear of God, accompanied by works of righteousness.§ It is true that believers are called children,‖ even little children.¶ Israel also in the old time

---

* 1 Peter i. 19 ; compare Isaiah liii. 7.
† Acts v. 32 ; 1 Peter i. 12, iv. 14. ‡ Acts v. 3, 4.
§ 1 Peter ii. 17 ; compare Acts x. 35. ‖ 1 Peter i. 14.
¶ 1 Peter ii. 2.

eceived like names of tenderness—but they nevertheless remain the bond-servants of God (δοῦλοι),* who are called to walk with fear.† Faith and obedience are with Peter correlative ideas;‡ and not so much filial love as filial reverence is the ground tone of the spiritual life here described. If, also, the yoke of the law has been broken,§ the precept of the law yet remains the standard for the conduct and action of the disciple of the Lord.‖ In that they together serve God, they fulfil the task which in ancient time was especially set before one of the tribes of Israel. We may say that the doctrine of the universal priesthood of believers¶ is especially Petrine. It is not so emphatically expressed in any other of the epistles—only in the Apocalypse, i. 5, 6, v. 8, 9. But this idea also is, in principle, as much an Old Testament idea as the description of Christians as strangers and pilgrims.** Such peculiarities are so much the more noteworthy if it is true, as seems borne out by certain texts,†† that the first readers of the Apostle's letter were mainly indeed, but by no means exclusively, Jews. Such, also, as formerly sat in the darkness of heathenism are here addressed as having part in the blessing of Israel, but at the same time, also, as being called to the realisation of the ideal of all the Old Testament economy of salvation.

8. That which has been remarked concerning the

* 1 Peter ii. 16.   † 1 Peter i. 17.   ‡ 1 Peter i. 2, ii. 7.
§ Acts xv. 10.   ‖ 1 Peter iii. 8-15.   ¶ 1 Peter ii. 4 9.
** 1 Peter ii. 1; compare Psalm cxix. 19 *a*, and other places.
†† Compare 1 Peter i. 14, ii. 10, iv. 3, 4.

Old Testament colouring of the Petrine theology determines its character, but does not at all detract from its importance. Two things are true: the New Testament is at once the fulfilment of the Old Testament and its opposite. Paul lays the chief stress upon the latter, Peter upon the former side of the question. Precisely on account of this peculiarity he was so much the better adapted to be the bearer of the Gospel to Israel; and as this Israel itself was in the fullest sense a people of hope, so also their first Apostle became at the same time the Apostle of Hope.

Compare Weiss, *Petrin. Lehrbegriff*, pp. 98-197, and the literature there cited; van Teutem, *Blik op den eersten Brief van Petrus*, Leid. 1861, p. 31, and following; Koch, *de Petri Theologiâ, per diversos vitæ, quam egit, periodos, sensim explicatâ*, L.B., 1854; Fronmüller, *Commentary*, Introduction, § 4.

POINTS FOR INQUIRY.

WHAT is the sense of Acts ii. 40 *b*?—In what relation does Peter place himself and his companions in faith to the Old Testament economy of salvation (Acts xv. 7-11)?—How is Gal. ii. 11-13 to be reconciled therewith?—What does Peter teach concerning baptism?—What concerning the call of the Gentiles?—What place does the doctrine of predestination occupy in the theology of Peter?—In what points is there an agreement in the use the Lord makes of the Old Testament, and in what points a difference?

SECTION XXIX.

Peter the Apostle of Hope.

As well the discourses as the First Epistle of Peter teach us to recognise this Apostle especially as the Apostle of Hope, in this sense, that the return of the Lord equally dominates his whole presentation of Christian truth, as his whole conception of Christian life. While this characteristic of the Apostle is to be fully explained by an acquaintance with his person, it at the same time affords us the key by which to understand the progress of his ideas, and the standard by which to determine the value of his doctrinal system.

1. The appellation, "Apostle of Hope," by no means indicates a feature of character which belongs exclusively to Peter, but only a peculiarity which comes forth more strongly in his doctrinal system than in that of others. In the mouth of no Apostle is wanting the name and praise of Christian hope ($\dot{\epsilon}\lambda\pi\iota\varsigma$); but the Petrine theology bears more than

others an elpistic character. Christian hope forms not merely the conclusion, but makes the centre of his whole doctrinal scheme. The Gospel is in his eyes, on the one hand, the fairest fulfilment, on the other, the richest promise. Ever does he love to speak of this hope, and constantly does he return to it by preference. Whether we direct our attention to his discourses or to his first Epistle, ever is it the expectation of the future which breathes life and warmth into his whole presentation of truth.

2. In the very beginning of his Pentecostal address, Peter points forward—availing himself of the prophecy of Joel—not merely to that which is granted in the present, but also to that which is to be expected in the future ;* and although he addresses his words exclusively to the house of Israel, he yet cannot omit to cast a glance forth upon all "that are afar off."† In the discourse which follows he urges repentance unto conversion,‡ "that the time of refreshing may come," through the appearing of Christ, who now, for a time, has taken possession of the heavens, but who is ready in Israel to set up His kingdom, and to bring about a restoration of all things. The address to Cornelius hastens also, so to speak, to the mention of Christ as the divinely-appointed Judge of the Quick and the Dead ;§ and even in the brief address in the Apostolic Council at Jerusalem there is an undertone of expectation of a blessedness as yet, at least, partially future (Acts xv. 11).

* Acts ii. 16-21. † Acts ii. 39.
‡ Acts iii. 19-21. § Acts x. 42.

3. Yet more strongly does this peculiarity come out in the First Epistle of Peter. He begins with a doxology,* by which we are involuntarily reminded of that in the Epistle of Paul to the Ephesians. But whilst Paul in general makes mention of the spiritual blessings in Christ, Peter, above all, gives thanks for regeneration to a living hope through the resurrection of the Lord. A definite reason for the mentioning of this particular blessing can scarcely be given; but it is precisely that which is nearest to his heart. The object of hope, this heavenly inheritance, is described in a series of expressions which designate closely-allied and yet separate ideas. "It is incorruptible" (intransitory), because it belongs to the realm of everlasting things; "undefiled," for it is subject to no desecration through sin; "unfading," not only enduring, but also ever fair. This eternal, holy, glorious inheritance is fully assured to believers (ver. 4); it is reserved for them, and they are preserved unto the salvation which is already on the point of being revealed (ver. 5). The present suffering (ver. 6) endures only for a short time,† and increases the joy (ver. 7) at hand. Their joy of faith is already glorious (ver. 8), and is present there where its object is, and whence they look for the end of their faith, the salvation of their souls (ver. 9). Christian life is, for this reason, a perfect hoping for grace.‡ That not only their faith, but also their hope, may be directed towards God,§ Christ was raised and glorified. The

---

* 1 Peter i. 3.
‡ 1 Peter i. 13.
† Compare John xvi. 16.
§ 1 Peter i. 21.

character of the God-fearing women of the Old Testament is designated by a single trait: they hoped in God.* In like manner, also, must Christians especially be able to give an account of their hope.† Assuredly, the time which we shall live in the flesh is only short: Christ is ready to come to judgment.‡ Judgment is already beginning on the Church,§ and that, also, which shall come upon the world shall not long be expected in vain. As far as the Apostle himself is concerned, there is for him nothing more desirable, next to that of a witness of the sufferings of Christ, than the name of partaker of the future glory.∥ Pointing forward to the recompense of the future serves him as the most powerful exhortation (ver. 4), and the Christian vocation to everlasting glory after a brief suffering is the theme of his doxology (ver. 10). Without doubt, all this is entirely in the spirit of the Lord,¶ but is also the expression and fruit of a personally felt necessity for irradiating the darkness of the present with the light of the future. The expectation of this glory is, as it were, the axis around which the Apostle's doctrine turns. Nowhere is there found a hint that he yet looks for a prolonged struggle of the members: their head is ready to come. The condition of Christians after death, the resurrection of the just, the endless chastisement of the wicked, is here entirely, or almost entirely, passed over. Far beyond all this extends the glance of the

---

* 1 Peter iii. 5. † 1 Peter iii. 15. ‡ 1 Peter iv. 3-7.
§ 1 Peter iv. 17. ∥ 1 Peter v. 1. ¶ Compare Luke xxiv. 46.

Apostle to the glorious end, the personal parousia of the Lord.

4. As a proof that we have rightly characterised the teaching of this Apostle, there follows here a scheme of the First Epistle from the before-mentioned point of view. First he celebrates in an exalted strain the glory of hope (i. 3-12), in that he shows its sure basis (ver. 3-5), its joy (ver. 6-9), and its exalted character (ver. 10-12). Immediately after, he makes a powerful effort to call forth and strengthen the life of hope. The general exhortation to his readers to place their hope fully upon grace (ver. 13) may be taken as the pregnant text, which is at once the result of all that precedes, and the theme of all following exhortations and consolations. These are partly (A) of a more general kind (i. 14—ii. 10), and call all believers, without distinction, to personal sanctification (i. 14-21), mutual love (i. 22—ii. 3), and the common glorifying of God and the Saviour (ii. 4-10); partly, also (B), they have a more definite relationship (ii. 11—v. 5), and apply either to Christians in the world and social life (ii. 11—iv. 6), as subjects, servants, married persons, or members of the whole suffering and militant Church; or concern the mutual relationship of Christians to each other (iv. 7—v. 5), in that they are called for each other to live (iv. 7-11) with each other to suffer (iv. 12-16), and to each other to be subject (v. 1-5). In conclusion (C), all is once more summed up in the general exhortation to look upward with humility (v. 6, 7), to look within with diligence (v. 8), to look around with sympathy (v. 9),

and to look to the future with hope (v. 10, 11). But among all these exhortations there is scarcely one which is not directly or indirectly connected with that first and general one (i. 13): " Place your hope entirely upon the grace which is brought unto you in the revelation of Jesus Christ."

5. The elpistic character of the Petrine theology is at the same time as easily explicable as it is indisputable. It takes its root in the individuality of the Apostle, whose First Epistle might be called "a portrait in letters." Even as an Apostle of Jesus Christ (Sec. xxvii.), Peter is an Apostle of Hope: his hope is founded upon the Master's own word.* Also as Apostle of the Circumcision he must be so (Sec. xxviii.) : the utterances of the prophets were only in part accomplished by the (first) appearing of Christ in humiliation: " *Pièrre est un homme, formé à l'école de l'A. T., mais qui a compris les choses nouvelles dans toute leur richesse et dans toute leur grandeur.*" (Bonifas). But he is, above all, Apostle of Hope because he is Simon Peter—no Thomas or John—the man of warm and sanguine temperament, for whom the former longing and endeavours after a glorious future have been moderated indeed, but not by any means taken away. " *Gratia non tollit, sed sanat naturam.*" The more the new man here and there still feels the influence of the old (Gal. ii. 11), so much the greater must be the longing within him for perfect redemption.

6. The value of the Petrine doctrines is by no

* Matt. xix. 28-30.

means diminished by the observation that the hope of the Apostle has not been fulfilled in the form in which it was cherished and confessed. The day of the Lord's parousia, not more nearly defined by the Lord himself, remained, and remains, a point of individual expectation, upon which only time can shed the true light. If Peter shared in this respect the expectation of the whole Apostolic age, the event itself which he looked for remains none the less the object of expectation for all future ages, and the hope commended by him is still an inexhaustible fountain of consoling and sanctifying influence. The manner in which in his writings he justifies this hope is so interesting that the question can hardly fail to arise whether he has not, at a later time, further expressed himself on this subject. This question naturally leads us to the investigation of the Second Epistle which bears his name.

Compare Weiss, *l. c.*, p. 25, and following. Mayerhoff, *Histor. Krit. Einl. in die Petrin. Schr.* Hamburg, 1835, p. 102, and following. (*Expository Lectures* on the First and Second Epistles of Peter, by Dr. John Brown, of Edinburgh). On 1 Peter i. 3-12, the *Dissertatio* of Dr. J. Ruitenschild, Leid. 1825.

POINTS FOR INQUIRY.

WHENCE the general expectation of the Apostolic age—expressed also by Peter—in regard to the speedy parousia of the Lord?—In what connection does his eschatology stand with that of the Synoptical Christ?—What does he understand (Acts iii. 21) by the ἀποκατάστασις πάντων, and what does he expect therefrom?—What are, according to him, the heralds of the parousia?—What does he teach concerning the reward and the punishment of the future?

SECTION XXX.

The Second Epistle of Peter.

ALTHOUGH very serious objections to the Apostolic origin of the Second Epistle ascribed to Peter have been raised, yet the doctrines therein contained bear—with all their peculiarity—an unmistakably Petrine stamp. This Epistle itself shows so many traces of the individuality of Peter as the Apostle of Jesus Christ, as the Apostle of the Circumcision, and as the Apostle of Hope, that, so far as the internal evidence is concerned, there is much more to be adduced in favour of its genuineness than against it.

1. Doubts as to the genuineness of the Second Epistle of Peter arose in the very earliest times. Irenæus, Tertullian, Cyprian, and others, know only one Epistle of Peter; Origen and Eusebius question the authenticity of the Second; and in the oldest Syriac translation (Peshito) it is not found. Even Erasmus and Calvin express themselves doubtfully or unfavourably in regard to it, and in our own time the

majority of critics decide against its genuineness. Yet it has found defenders, even in our age, in Hug, Flatt, Kern, Heidenreich, Windischmann, Dietlein, Thiersch, Guericke, Fronmüller, Steinfass, and others; and Weiss and Brückner evidently incline to its recognition; so that the science of New Testament isagogics cannot yet regard this case as closed. The theology of the New Testament can only draw attention to its teaching with the purpose of discovering how far this bears a Petrine character, or how far it does not.

2. Without doubt there is here and there a difference between the dogmatical and ethical contents of the Second Epistle and those of the First. Much greater stress is laid upon the knowledge ($ἐπίγνωσις$) of the Gospel; many an idea expressed in the First Epistle is here entirely or almost entirely passed over; and throughout there prevails a correspondence between our Epistle and that of Jude greater than is found between any other two writings of the New Testament. Nevertheless, these and other peculiarities can be explained, partly from the altered requirements of the readers, partly from the special aim of the writer, partly, also, from the individuality of Peter himself. In no case do they detract from the thoroughly Petrine colouring of this Epistle, which is even acknowledged (however explained) by those who contest its genuineness. Often there is a confirmation, and that in a surprising manner, of the words of Lutterbeck: "The Second Epistle of Peter shows apparently the opposite, in reality the same thing, as the First Epistle."

3. The writer of this Second Epistle also speaks in fact as an Apostle of Jesus Christ. As in the First, the historical Christ is the centre of his whole conception of the truth; the pre-existence of the Lord is not, however, expressly mentioned. He is the Saviour,* and the principal blessing which believers owe to Him consists in being cleansed from their former sins.† He has redeemed them,‡ and ceases not after his departure from the earth to stand in the closest relation to them.§ A shadowing forth of the glory which He now enjoys (and which He shall manifest at his parousia, i. 16), the author has seen on the Mount of Transfiguration ‖—a special event in the life of the Lord, of which mention is made in no other Epistle of the New Testament; just as another not less mysterious event is mentioned only in the First Epistle of Peter (1 Peter iii. 19-21). No wonder that Christ stands before the eye of the author in the radiance of a truly Divine dignity. What has been pre-supposed or indicated in the First Epistle is here distinctly affirmed. Besides the name of Saviour, the Lord receives the name of *God*;¶ and the doxology rendered to Him at the end of this Epistle** sets the seal to this appellation. In short, we see how the train of thought beginning in the Acts and the First Epistle is here completed.

4. A no less real correspondence do we find when

* 2 Peter iii. 2. † 2 Peter i. 9; compare 1 Peter i. 2.
‡ 2 Peter ii. 1; compare 1 Peter i. 18.
§ 2 Peter i. 14.; compare 1 Peter ii. 25. ‖ 2 Peter i. 16-18.
¶ 2 Peter i. 1. ** 2 Peter iii. 18.

we take in hand the Second Epistle and think of Peter as the Apostle of the Circumcision, as we learnt to know him in the First Epistle. The Old Testament colouring observed there is found afresh here, both as to the form and the contents of the ideas. The *righteousness* of God occupies the most prominent place;* and presently after he refers to the election (ἐκλογή) of believers as their peculiar privilege.† The same high estimate of the prophetic word, with the same view of its Divine origin, meets us here,‡ as we found in the First Epistle. Once also, as in the First Epistle, the Old Testament is expressly cited;§ but considerably greater is the number of those places in which there is an allusion thereto, or in which its style is unconsciously adopted. Here, also, mention is made of the age of Noah and of Abraham;|| this time, however, on account of this special aim of the Epistle, not in reference to the obedient Sarah, but to the God-fearing Lot.¶ Here, also, repeatedly, the most appropriate use is made of that which might be presupposed as known from the Scriptures of the Old Testament.** To this category belongs also the mentioning of the Last Day as the Day of God,†† which is entirely in the spirit of ancient prophecy. The New Testament is consequently here

---

* 2 Peter i. 1. † 2 Peter i. 10.
‡ 2 Peter i. 19-21; compare 1 Peter i. 10-12. § 2 Peter ii. 22.
|| 2 Peter ii. 5, 6. ¶ 2 Peter ii. 7-9.

** 2 Peter ii. 13-16, compare Num. xxii. 16-34; ii. 22, compare Prov. xxvi. 11; iii. 5, compare Gen. i. 2; iii. 7, compare Gen. ix. 11; iii. 8, compare Psalm xc. 4; iii. 13, compare Isaiah lxv. 17.

†† 2 Peter iii. 10.

also, from beginning to end, the completion and crown of the Old—never its opposite.

5. Also the Apostle of Hope is revealed in this Epistle to an attentively listening ear. From the beginning the author directs the attention of his readers to the Divine promises,* and urges them especially by appealing to the future—to the work of continued sanctification (i. 11). Also, the "putting off the tabernacle"† recalls to our mind the "pilgrimage" of the First Epistle.‡ What most engages our attention here, however, is that place in which he expresses himself so fully as to the destruction of the present order of the world,§ and the stupendous consequences thereof, where we find almost an Apocalypse in miniature. The difference in regard to eschatology which is found between the doctrinal system of the Second and that of the First Epistle is only relative, and is easily explicable. If some time had passed between the composition of the two Epistles, the Apostle might and must perceive that the return of the Lord, so ardently desired, might remain longer unaccomplished than he had at first expected. He could the less be insensible of this delay since occasion was taken from it by scoffers who ridiculed this hope, against whose attempts to seduce he here arms believers; whilst in the First Epistle he consoles under sufferings by pointing forward to the coming glory. Here, however, as there, is his look directed with longing to the future; and the exhortation to

* 2 Peter i. 4.   † 2 Peter i. 14.   ‡ 1 Peter ii. 11.
§ 2 Peter iii. 3-15.

hasten * unto the coming of the day of the Lord bears an equally Petrine † stamp with the urgent exhortation to holiness with which the life of hope, in this Epistle also, is brought into immediate connection. And finally, as to the main contents of the expectation here enunciated, it must be remarked that they attach themselves entirely to the prophecies of the Old Testament seers and the utterances of the Lord himself. If any conception in this Epistle is according to the view of a later age untenable, this does not by any means prove that Peter therefore could not entertain and give expression to it.

6. It is true there are more or less important differences opposed to the correspondence we have adduced; but difference of thoughts or of form in two different writings prove nothing against the identity of the author, least of all when this author manifests an individuality like that of Simon Peter. Enough, in no single point do these two Epistles contradict each other, and assuredly only the *appearance* of contradiction would be avoided with the most anxious care by one who, in counterfeiting his Epistle, abused the name of Peter. There is at least no greater difference between the First and the Second of the Epistles called after Peter, than between many of the writings of John or Paul, as to the genuineness of which no unprejudiced person has a doubt.

* σπεύδοντες, 2 Peter iii. 12.

† Thrice the genuinely Petrine word σπουδάζειν occurs in our Epistle, and only seven times in all the Epistles of Paul. Would an anonymous imitator of Peter's style have bethought himself of reproducing such slight psychological traits?

7. Other objections, arising from the internal evidence which concern the difference of style in the First and Second Epistles, the relation of the latter to the Gospel narrative, to the Epistles of Paul, to the General Epistles of Jude, or to the Gnosticism which was rising at the time, or which have to do with the mysterious character of some of the utterances in this Epistle, lie without the province of our investigation. If we confine ourselves strictly to its doctrinal contents, we must, as the result of our investigation, express the judgment that the Second Epistle contains absolutely nothing that prevents our supposing Simon Peter to be its author; and, on the other hand, not a little that justifies our belief in its Petrine origin. We find ourselves consequently ever shut up to the inexorable alternative: Either Peter himself wrote the Epistle, or an unknown person, for the advancement of his particular ends, evidently wished to pass for our Apostle, and, with this intent, imitated his style and his ideas as exactly as possible. Whether such a literary fiction is so lightly to be accepted as is believed on many sides, and whether this solution harmonises with the moral character of the writer, as we learn from this Epistle, is a question with the answering of which we have not here to do. Had the Second Epistle of Peter appeared anonymously, perhaps the inner criticism would have attached a high degree of probability to the supposition that this writing originated in no other than the Apostle Peter.

Compare, on the doctrinal system of the Second

Epistle of Peter in connection with its genuineness, Messner, *l. c.* p. 54-70; our *Christol. d. N. V.*, p. 162-176; Fronmuller *l. c.* p. 68, and following; Steinfass, *Der Zweite Br. d. heil. Petrus*, Rostock, 1863; B. Weiss, *Zur Petrin. Frage*, Stud. u. Krit. 1865 and 1866.

POINTS FOR INQUIRY.

WHO have combated the genuineness of the Second Epistle of Peter, mainly on the ground of its doctrinal contents?—What peculiarity is manifested in the doctrinal and moral contents of our Epistle, as compared with the First?—To what extent are these peculiarities to be explained from the special aim of this Epistle, and the individuality of the writer?—The relation of this Epistle to that of Jude, and those of Paul?—The eschatology of this Epistle, as compared with the expectations of the Gentile nations and the prophecies of Old Testament Scripture.—Peter's Second Epistle the crown of his whole Apostolic testimony, **and his testament for the Church and the World.**

SECTION XXXI.

Kindred Types of Doctrine.

THE Petrine conception of the Gospel stands by no means alone amongst the writings of the New Testament. Without violence to the individuality of each writer, it harmonises in a remarkable manner with that which is either presupposed or expressed in the Gospels according to Matthew and Mark, and especially in the General Epistles of James and Jude.

1. We have learnt to recognise the Petrine idea of Christian truth in its many-sidedness. To this type of Christianity, without doubt, those Jewish Christians attached themselves, who found in Peter their leader and representative; and, since he occupied so important a place in the history of the Apostolic age, it may be assumed, *à priori*, that there would be by no means wanting men of kindred spirit with him among the sacred writers of the New Testament. This conjecture becomes a certainty when we cast a glance at the different parts of the New Testament in which

the spirit of our Apostle distinctly reveals itself, or in which ideas are expressed which more or less resemble his.

2. This is, first of all, the case with the Gospel according to *Mark*, on whose contents and composition Peter, according to tradition, exerted an influence, the nature and extent of which cannot here be further determined. The more philosophic stand-point of John's Gospel is equally wanting here as in the discourses and epistles of our Apostle. The Second Gospel begins immediately with the baptism of John, to end with the resurrection and exaltation of Jesus, and moves thus precisely within that circle which had been marked out by Peter himself,[*] for the witness of the Lord. Jesus appears there as Peter was wont to describe Him, and with such traits of character as were, for Peter's personal remembrance of Him, of the greatest value. The dramatic force of the representation, the varying tone, the rapid transition in the narrative, involuntarily reveals to our mind that witness of the Lord whom we have just learnt to know in his words and writings.

3. Somewhat similar may also be observed in regard to *Matthew*. Whatever we may think as to the intricate questions which this Gospel presents to us, thus much is certainly indubitable, that it bears a purely Palistinean type of character, and that the author is, to that extent, rather allied to Peter than to Paul or John. The manifest tendency of the First Gospel to present Jesus in the light of prophetic

---

[*] Compare Acts i. 21, 22.

Kindred Types of Doctrine. 243

Scripture as the promised Messiah, is entirely in the spirit of our Apostle. As Peter, in his proclamation of Christ,* attaches especial value to the miracles of the Lord, so here, also, a number of His miracles are grouped together (chapters viii. and ix.); and as Peter, so also Matthew, proclaims the Lord as Israel's Messiah, while excluding the Gentiles just as little as does Peter. Nowhere, finally, are the eschatological discourses of the Lord, which are of such priceless value for the Apostle, related so fully and in such order as in the First Gospel.

4. Yet less is it to be denied that *Jude*, the brother of James, so far as he is known to us from his epistle, stands on the same platform with Peter. Whatever conclusion we may come to as to his person, and the resemblance of this Epistle to the Second Epistle of Peter, the conception of Christian truth peculiar to Peter is also unmistakably present here. As a witness of Jesus Christ, Jude also, although in few words, places the Lord in the foreground. For Him Christians are preserved;† He is the only Ruler and Lord ‡ for whose compassion unto everlasting life they wait,§ and through whom God is glorified in the Church.|| Thus, Jude builds—as with all the Apostles, so pre-eminently with Peter—upon one and the same foundation; although, like Peter, he rather presupposes and hints, than actually declares, the Divine nature and dignity of the Redeemer. The

---

* Acts x. 38.   † Jude 1.
‡ Jude 4.   § Jude 21.
|| Jude 25.   Upon all these places, consult Alford or Tischendorf.

Old Testament colouring also belongs to his teaching, in common with that of Peter. Even as Peter, he avails himself largely of sacred history, as that of Sodom,* of Moses, of Balaam, and of Enoch.† He seems also, in regard to this last, to have drawn upon an apocryphal writing, which he accepts as authoritative. The hope of the future is also brought into great prominence in this short epistle, even though —having regard to untruth and unrighteousness—it is especially contemplated on its terrible side. Even as Peter (1 Peter i. 5), so Jude also lays especial stress upon the preservation of believers unto everlasting life.‡

5. Especially, however, must we here mention the Epistle of *James*, which occupies, indeed, no pre-eminent position, but, nevertheless, an important one, in the first development of Christian doctrine. The doctrine of this witness of the Lord contains also— besides that which it has in common with Peter's— much that is peculiar to itself, especially as regards the exhibition of the person and work of the Lord. The actual name of Jesus Christ is here only twice mentioned,§ although in many other places it may at least be questioned whether it is not alluded to.‖ On the great historic facts in the life of Christ he pre-serves an entire silence. The high-priestly work of the Lord also falls into the background, even His royal glory is spoken of only in passing ¶ ; but louder

---

* Jude 7. † Jude 9, 11, 14. ‡ Jude 1, 21, 24.
§ James i. 1 ; ii. 1.   ‖ James ii. 7 ; v. 6 ; v. 7, 8 ; v. 14.
¶ James ii 1.

Kindred Types of Doctrine. 245

than elsewhere we here catch the faithful echo of His prophetic word. Many an exhortation of the Epistle of James is, as it were, an echo of the Sermon on the Mount,* and proves how deeply the author was penetrated with the spirit of his glorified Brother. In the conception of God, it is principally the moral attributes of God upon which stress is laid ; even His unchangeableness is not only a characteristic, but a virtue.† Not less peculiar is the conception he forms in relation to sin on the one hand, and grace on the other. James lays great stress upon the fact that man was created originally after God's image ;‡ but none the less does he expressly affirm that sin is absolutely universal,§ and, above all, that it is man's own fault.‖ That he does not ignore the demoniacal origin of moral evil is clear ;¶ but the arising of sin within the man at a particular moment he describes especially on its psychological side,** as also in the word sin (ἁμαρτία) he thinks rather of the sinful act than of the sinful principle (with him ἐπιθυμία). On that account, he rather combats actual sins, *e.g.*, those of the tongue,†† or of the rich against the poor,‡‡ than (as, for instance, Paul, Romans vii.) probes to its depths the discord and conflict within the sinful heart. But as this sin, in the widest sense of the word,§§ brings forth death, grace is revealed—it is true in its forgiving,‖‖ but—especially in its sancti-

* *E.g.* James iii. 11, 12 ; iv. 4 ; v. 12.
† James i. 13-17.   ‡ James iii. 9 ; compare Gen. ix. 6.
§ James iii. 2.   ‖ James i. 13-18.   ¶ James ii. 19 ; iii. 15 ; iv. 7.
** James i. 14, 15.   †† James iii. 1-12
‡‡ James v. 1-6.   §§ James i. 15 ; v. 20.   ‖‖ James v. 15.

fying and new-creating* power. Grace is received through faith, but only through such a faith as is proved genuine by works.† The peculiar sense in which the words *justification, faith,* and *works* are used by James as compared with Paul, serves as a clear proof that his object is not to wage war against the ideas themselves, which are found in the writings of this Apostle, but to place a bridle upon the onesided Paulinism which showed itself in his vicinity. One must certainly share Luther's antipathy for this "epistle of straw," before asserting with him that "the Holy Ghost allowed Sanct James to stumble a little." James, no less than Paul, recognises a faith which is nothing less than a firm confidence of the heart ;‡ but it is here not so much an opposition of sin and grace as of knowing and doing (compare John xiii. 17) which dominates his whole mode of thinking. He does, it is true, also contemplate Christianity from its devotional, but especially from its ethical side. We hear how, in this short epistle, he exhorts repeatedly to prayer, even to intercessory prayer,§ an exercise of the Christian life, to which is assured, according to James, not merely a psychological influence, but also a direct answer. ‖ He brings, as a rule, the commandments of the Second Table into greater prominence than those of the First ; and one might say that the text and ground-tone of all his exhortations is contained in a single sentence ;¶ just as

* James i. 18.　　　† James ii. 14-26.　　　‡ James i. 6-8
§ James i. 5 ; iv. 2, 3 ; v. 13-18.
‖ James i. 5-8 ; v. 14, 15.　　　¶ James i. 19.

1 Peter i. 13 is the basis of all the following exhortations of that Epistle of Peter. Moral beauty is that at which James, above all, aims,* and Christianity is the great means of bringing man to this perfection, and thus raising him to the highest rank.† In self-denial and love to one's neighbour consists that act of true religion which is here, above all others, commended.‡ The Gospel itself is, according to his view, a perfect law of liberty, whose precepts are all inseparably connected, and governed by the great principle of love.§ The whole Epistle of James bears, consequently, rather a practical than a dogmatic character, and contains (partly in highly poetic language) a moral teaching which attaches itself partly to the utterances of the Lord, partly to the precepts of the Book of Proverbs, and partly, also— what is nowhere else met with in the writings of the New Testament—to those of the son of Sirach. It is the task of Isagogics to find the key to this and other peculiarities of this beautiful Epistle, in the individuality of the writer, in the circumstances of his readers, and in the peculiar aim of his writing. The Biblical theology of the New Testament can only show that here, within a small compass, is laid up a rare wealth of original, deeply Christian thoughts, which show indeed the unquestionable independence of the writer, but also his spiritual kinship with Peter.

6. In a Christological aspect, it is less rich than that of Peter, even than that of Jude; but the funda-

* τελείος, i. 4, 25; iii. 2. † James i. 18.
‡ James i. 27.   § James ii. 8-13.

mental conception of Christ's person belongs to the same circle of thoughts, and the Christian life, as it is here and there described, shows an unmistakable relationship. The express mention of regeneration through the Word,* the powerful exhortation to moral perfection,† to Christian joy, even under the severest trials, yea, on account of them,‡ and not less the exhortation to compassion and love, made in connection with the future judgment,§ is common alike in both. We may say that the twofold tendency of the two Epistles of Peter, *consolation* and *exhortation*, is, in the Epistle of James, blended in one. The Old Testament character, also, of the Epistles of Peter will not be sought in vain in the Epistle of James. Entirely in the spirit of the ancient prophets is the mention of the jealousy ‖ of God: also the appellation Jehovah Sabaoth,¶ which is found only here in the New Testament, is in this respect noteworthy. "James conceives of the old under new forms" (Neander). Only in one respect is there an essential difference: Peter conceives of the Gospel as, above all, the fulfilment of prophecy; James, on the other hand, as the fulfilment of the law. Finally, as regards the elpistic character of both epistles, the more calm and practical James, though he has not the longing desire of the ardent Peter, yet has this in common with him, that he also constantly

* James i. 18; compare 1 Peter i. 3, 22.
† James iii. 1; compare 1 Peter i. 15
‡ James i. 2-4; compare 1 Peter i. 6-9; iv. 14.
§ James ii. 13; v. 20; compare 1 Peter iv. 8.
‖ James iv. 5. ¶ James v. 4.

directs the eye from the present to the future, and avails himself of the approaching parousia, urgently and powerfully to exhort to a Christian spirit.* *His* eye also is fixed upon the Crown of Life,† which is promised to the faithful warrior, but he has also regard to the retribution with which the oppressor of the poor brother is threatened.‡ We must divorce expressions like these last entirely from their connection, and regard them with very prejudiced eyes, to find here no higher conception than that of a tolerably flat specimen of Ebionitism (Réuss).

Compare, in addition to Schmid, Reuss, and Messner, on this subject, especially P. H. Friesema, *Jacobus, ein waardig tegenhanger van Paulus en Joh.* Utr. 1842. Lange, *Commentary*, Introd. to Epp. of James and Jude. De Pressensé, *Early Years of Christianity*, pp. 207-219. Bonifas, *l. c.* pp. 27, and following. R. Stier, *Der Brief Judä, des B. d. H.* Berl. 1850.

POINTS FOR INQUIRY.

ORIGIN and extent of the Petrine element in the Second Gospel.—Peter and Matthew.—The relation between the Epistle of Jude and the Second Epistle of Peter in regard to dogmatic contents.—How is the use of an apocryphal writing in the Epistle of Jude to be explained, and what judgment are we to form as to its citation?—Connection between the Epistle of James and the Synoptical Gospels.—

* James v. 7-9. † James i. 12 ; compare 1 Peter v. 4.
‡ James v. 1-6.

Influence of Solomon, and Jesus the son of Sirach, upon the contents and form of this Epistle.—The peculiarity of its representation of faith and works.—What is the sense of James i. 27 ?—The doctrine of the oath in James in connection with the Sermon on the Mount.—Does James ever write polemically ?—Are there to be found in his Epistle traces also of Ebionitish ideas ?—How are the opposite judgments concerning this Epistle in earlier and later times to be explained ?

SECTION XXXII.

Result and Transition.

THE contents and form of the Petrine system of doctrines correspond entirely to that which was to be expected of our Apostle as we already knew him, and bear the unmistakable stamp of a rich originality. Although it is not to be denied that between the ideas which are to be found in the Apostle's First Epistle and many Epistles of Paul there is a certain affinity, yet the Petrine theology is by no means a feeble copy of the Pauline, but preserves alongside the other its independent character; always, however, in such sense that, in the riches and depth of its doctrinal development, it stands not above, but below the Pauline.

1. When, at the end of this section, we sum up for ourselves the total impression we have received, we find that in many respects confirmed which we have earlier (Sec. xxv.) said, concerning the agreement of

the Petrine system of doctrine with what we have learnt from other sources as to the individuality of this Apostle. This agreement, rightly understood and used, affords no despicable contribution to the defence of the historic character of the discourses, and the genuineness of the Epistles ascribed to Peter. But, at the same time, a glance at the kindred systems of doctrine has convinced us of the great influence which the Gospel of Peter exerted within his immediate circle, and consequently, also, so far as it can be inferred therefrom, of the power of his personality. *His* Gospel also forms an organic whole, by no means an aggregate of incoherent thoughts.

2. It is true we find in many an Epistle of Paul, especially in those to the Romans and Ephesians, utterances by which we are even involuntarily reminded of the First Epistle of Peter.* The investigation as to the causes of this remarkable phenomenon belongs to the sphere of isagogics. But this phenomenon itself, on which so much has been said, by no means justifies the Tübingen school in the assertion that the First Epistle of Peter should have been called only an apology for Paulinism, and that it was palmed off by some unknown adherents of Paul upon the Petrine Christians. Neither does it in any way affect the originality of the Petrine conception of the Gospel, even in the highly improbable case that the said agreement must be explained by the use made, on the part of Peter, of the Pauline epistles. In Peter we find

* Compare, *e.g.*, 1 Pet. i. 3, *seqq.*, with Eph. i. **3**; 1 Peter i. **6-9** with Rom. v. 3-5; 1 Peter ii. 6, 7, with Rom. ix. 33.

Result and Transition.

not the echo of another, but an independent, clear, and powerful voice of his own.

3. By this, however, we do not intend to say that the Petrine system of doctrines comes up to, or even towers above, the Pauline in riches, depth, and power. The contrary will soon be manifest from a contemplation of this latter. Fundamental thoughts of the Gospel of Paul, as, for example, the doctrine of justification through faith, are not found in this form in Peter. Truths and duties, of which both remind us, are treated by Paul more deeply and in a more many-sided way than by Peter, whose literary remains are also much smaller than those of his fellow Apostle. For one Petrine idea which is not touched by Paul, there stand probably ten Pauline ones which are passed over in silence by Peter. But much which is more fully explained by Paul has been already hinted at by Peter; and so far we may truly say, "Pièrre appartient à la même école que Jacques, mais il a depassé le point de vue de l'école de la Loi, *et nous a fait déjà pressentir le point de vue de Paul*" (Bonifas.) The best proof for the justice of this remark will be the treatment, in the following division, of the Pauline theology itself.

Comp. Weiss, *l. c.* pp. 375 and following. Messner, *l. c.* p. 55. Baur, *l. c.* pp. 227-297.

POINTS FOR INQUIRY.

In what respect do single utterances of James and Peter correspond in subject-matter and form with those of Paul?

—Can we fairly maintain that the Epistles of James and Peter show a determined attempt at reconciliation between Paulinism and Judaism?—To what extent does the Petrine theology, regarded as a whole, rise above the Ebionitism of the Apostolic age?

SECOND DIVISION.

THE PAULINE THEOLOGY.

SECTION XXXIII.

General Survey.

THE Pauline doctrinal system embraces the rich contents of all that which the Apostle Paul himself has called *his* Gospel, so far as this is known to us from the Scriptures of the New Testament, and especially from his own letters. The introductory survey will delineate roughly the leading thoughts, character, source, value, and history of the Pauline theology, in order at the close to give an answer to the question how its treatment is to be conducted.

1. A much richer field than is to be found in the Petrine theology opens itself to us in the Pauline. As the former makes us acquainted with the Gospel which

was proclaimed to the Jewish Christians, so this more especially makes known to us the glad tidings of salvation which Paul proclaimed in the Gentile world. With all that the doctrine of the Apostle of the Gentiles has in common with that of a Peter or a John, there is manifested, at the same time, so much that is peculiar to himself that Paul was fully justified in speaking as he does of *his** Gospel.

2. The Gospel of Paul is made known to us, not indeed exclusively, but yet principally from the Scriptures of the New Testament. Besides the Second Epistle of Peter,† the Book of Acts‡ makes us especially acquainted with the main contents of this Gospel. But, above all, it is the thirteen Epistles which have come down to us under his name, which—some more, others less—afford us important materials for the prosecution of this investigation.

The question, on what ground we ascribe all these Epistles to Paul, belongs to the province of criticism and isagogics. In this place the assurance must be accepted that, in our estimation, the genuineness of the whole thirteen is certainly to be acknowledged, although we admit that this genuineness in the case of some can be more satisfactorily defended than in the case of others. Of the authenticity of the greater part, a powerful defence has been quite recently put forth ; of others, the authenticity has, on scientific grounds, never been disputed. We retain, in this

* Rom. ii. 16, and elsewhere. † 2 Peter iii. 15, 16.
‡ Acts xiii. 16-41; xiv. 15-17; xvi. 31 ; xvii. 3 ; xvii. 16-31 ; xx. 18-35; xxii. 3-21; xxiii. 6; xxiv. 14-25 ; xxvi. 6-23 ; xxviii. 15-28.

respect, absolutely the stand-point which, until within the last few years, was accepted by almost all theologians, whether of a more conservative or more advanced school, both within our own country and beyond it; and we continue to hold it, not because the new is unknown to us, but because therein something of an uncritical and arbitrary nature constantly usurps the place of thorough and impartial science. While, for this reason, we do not entirely except from our examination any one of the Pauline epistles, they must naturally—at least in regard to the most important points—be consulted in that order in which there is good ground for believing they were written. During an interval of about twelve years, which passed between the composition of the earliest and the latest epistle, the spiritual development of a Paul was certainly not stationary. They are probably to be arranged in the following manner:—1. The two Epistles to the Thessalonians; 2. The Epistle to the Galatians; 3. The two Epistles to the Corinthians; 4. The Epistle to the Romans; 5. Those to the Ephesians, Colossians, Philemon, and Philippians; 6. The Pastoral Epistles.

It cannot by any means be shown that another Gospel is to be read in those epistles whose genuineness has been denied, or held suspected, by critics of the Old or New Tubingen school, than in the four which the first-named have magnanimously left to us. It is on this account not necessary on every point to consult these four before listening to the testimony of either of the others.

On disputed points, however, of special importance, we cannot, at the present time, entirely neglect this distinction. Besides this, also, an especial value in regard to specific subjects is to be attached to particular epistles above others : *e g.*, for soteriology, the Epistles to the Romans and Galatians; for ecclesiology, that to the Ephesians ; for eschatology, those to the Corinthians, &c.

3. In order to become at home in the Pauline theology, it is of importance to discover the ground-thought which, to a certain extent, shapes the dogmatic teaching of this Apostle. It is the doctrine of justification through faith which, more than anything else, according to Paul, makes the Gospel to be God's power unto salvation.* Not only in the Epistles to the Romans and Galatians, but also in that to the Philippians,† this truth is expressed, evidently as a favourite one with the Apostle, and expressed in a form which links it at once with the declaration of the Old Testament‡ and with the teaching of the Lord Himself,§ a form also especially familiar and attractive for Jewish Christians. The utter impossibility of justification on the ground of the works of law, and the perfection of the justification by grace in Christ, this is the ground-thought which Paul, ever afresh, expresses in manifold forms, and applies to every variety of necessities and conditions.

4. By this ground-thought of the Pauline theology, the peculiar character of the form and subject-matter

* Rom. i. 16, 17. † Phil. iii. 4-10.
‡ Gen. xv. 6. § Luke xviii. 14.

is at the same time determined. The character of the subject-matter is in general Soteriological; salvation in Christ is here, as far as possible, on all sides presented for contemplation, whilst the great antithesis of sin and grace is ever anew placed in the foreground. Yet more decidedly may we say that this doctrine bears an Anthropological character. Paul does not, like Peter, take his point of departure in the prophetic Scriptures, or, like John, in the person of the Saviour, but in *Man*, with his deepest wants, as they are awakened indeed by the law, but can be satisfied only by the Gospel. And this satisfaction, according to the genuine universalism of the Apostle, is designed and attainable, not merely for some, but for all. The fact that Christianity is the religion for the world, although ignored by none of his fellow-witnesses, is yet testified by none so powerfully as by himself.*
The form also in which all this is expressed by him is in the highest degree striking and appropriate; for in point of form the whole Pauline theology is decidedly antithetical. Law and Gospel, works and faith, flesh and spirit, death and life, condemnation and justification, form a succession of powerful antitheses which do not fail to produce their impression. The key to this peculiar character of his whole doctrinal system, both as to subject-matter and to form, is to be found in the experience of the Apostle's own life.

5. The source of the Pauline theology was partly, but not entirely, the same as that of his fellow-

* Compare Acts xiii. 38, 39; Rom. iii. 21-24.

witnesses. From 2 Cor. v. 16* it would seem that he had not personally known Christ; certainly he had not (like the Twelve) held converse with Him and received instruction from Him. He himself says that he received not his Gospel of man, or by man, and points to a special revelation of Jesus Christ as the source of his teaching.† The revelation granted to him at and after his conversion was later continued from time to time in regard to particular points.‡ Christian tradition also was, as to its substance, known to him.§ The revelation of God in nature, history, and the conscience, had been attentively observed by him;|| and even his education by Gamaliel¶ had not been by any means without influence on his after mode of thinking. Accurately acquainted with the Old Testament, and the peculiar mode of interpreting Scripture prevalent in his day,** and even with Greek literature,†† he could perceive the truth more clearly than many others, and express it with greater force. All this, however, would not have made Paul to be Paul, had not the gift of the Holy Ghost been bestowed upon him in rich measure,‡‡ through which the mystery of the Gospel was revealed to him in immediate connection with his own inner need and his own life experience. Consequently, we may say that the sanctified personality of Paul—or, traced back to its

---

* κατὰ σάρκα, after a fleshly standard. † Gal. i. 1-17.
‡ 1 Cor. vii. 25; Eph. iii. 3; 1 Thess. iv. 15.
§ 1 Cor. xi. 23, παρέλαβον. || Romans i. ii.
¶ Acts xxii. 3.   ** Compare Gal. iv. 24.
†† *E. g.*, Acts xvii. 28; Tit. i. 12; 1 Cor. xv. 33.
‡‡ 1 Cor. ii. 13; vii. 40; xii. 7.

General Survey.   251

first beginning, his conversion—was the source of his whole doctrine. The theology of Paul was, in the deepest and richest sense of the word, the theology of experience [experimental].

6. The value of the Pauline theology has been sometimes ignored, sometimes over-estimated, the latter, in the case of the Tübingen school, which has discovered in Paul the father of Christian universalism; the former by the common Rationalism, where it has placed the zealot of Tarsus far beneath, yea, in opposition to the Rabbi of Nazareth, a position to which modern theology is in danger of sinking, whenever in attempting to make Paul the apologist of its so-called liberal sentiment, negation is seen to be futile and hopeless. Avoiding both extremes, it is certain that the Pauline theology is of the highest value, partly in itself, in that it contains a many-sided, profound, faithful, and powerful presentation of the Gospel; partly in comparison with others, which it either surpasses (Peter and James), or for which in turn it prepares the way (John); partly, finally, on account of the great influence which the testimony of Paul has exerted in the course of the ages, and still continues to exert. Though he was not the founder of Christianity,[*] he has yet been privileged to be the founder of the Gentile Church, and the spiritual father of millions.[†] Augustine and Luther sat at his feet; his spirit is again awakened in Protestantism, and even the little which the criticism of the present day allows to be genuinely Pauline, suffices to

[*] 1 Cor. i. 13   [†] 1 Cor. iv. 15.

convince of folly the naturalistic unbelief which decks itself with the name of Christianity.

7. It is on this account gratifying that the history of the scientific treatment of the Pauline theology, although dating only from the beginning of this century, is by no means insignificant. Without saying anything in this place of the earlier and less successful attempts, we draw attention to the meritorious work of L. Usteri, *Paulin. Lehrbegr.*, sixth edition, 1851. Himself a pupil of Schleiermacher—of whom, by the talent displayed in this work, he shows himself a worthy successor—he has penetrated more deeply than his predecessor into the spirit of the Apostle. Deserving also of attention is the examination of the Pauline theology in the second part of Neander's *History of the Planting and Training of the Christian Church* [English translation], and that of F. C. Baur in his *Paulus*, Stuttgart, 1845, pp. 505-670. The writings of A. F. Dahne (1835) and E. C. J. Lutzelberger (1839), on the Doctrinal System of Paul, will not bear comparison with the three fore-named. At the same time, besides what is contained in the writings so frequently adduced of Schmid, Messner, and Reuss, more or less of attention has been devoted to the matter and manner of Paul's teaching, in the treatment of the history of the Apostolic age by Lechler, Schaff, De Pressensé, Ritzschl (second edition) and others. Among the Dutch theologians, Dr. I. Da Costa's *Paulus* (2 parts, Leiden, 1846, 1847) is especially worthy of mention. The theologians, also, of the Groningen school, in their first issues of

Waarheid in Liefde (1837 and following), with different writers of the Leyden and Utrecht schools, afforded their contributions to the understanding of single parts of the Pauline system.

8. After a glance at so many examples—partly warning, partly encouraging—the question as to the best manner of dealing with the Pauline doctrinal system cannot be difficult to answer. The ground-thought of the Apostle's teaching before observed, determines at the same time the course of our investigation, which naturally attaches itself to his own utterance, Rom. iii. 21, 22. We must especially have regard to the Apostle's distinction of the time *before Christ* and *after Christ*, and must necessarily occupy ourselves for a much longer period with the latter than with the former. We hear, consequently, first what he testifies of humanity and the individual man, *out of* Christ, and then what he testifies of both *in* and *through* Christ. When, after taking into account, as far as possible or necessary, the chronological succession of his Epistles, we have examined his doctrine in relation to the one and to the other, and have brought it into a compact whole, we shall —as at the end of the previous division of our subject —stay to examine the kindred cycles of doctrine.

Compare, on Paul and the Pauline theology in general, besides the oft-named works of Schmid, Reuss, Messner, Baur, and others, the consultation of whom, even without constant reiteration, is tacitly recommended for all the following Sections, especially the article *Paulus*, by Lange, in Herzog, as also the

General Introduction to his Commentary on the Epistle to the Romans. Also A. Monod, *St. Paul, cinq Discours* (English translation); Conybeare and Howson, *Life and Letters of St. Paul;* Haldane, *Commentary on the Epistle to the Romans;* Symar, *die Theol. des H. Paulus dargestellt*, Freib. im Br. 1864 (R.C.); Hausrath, *Paulus der Apostel Jesu;* Trip, *Paulus nach der Apostelgsch.*, Leid. 1866. On the genuineness of the Thirteen Epistles, Scholten, *Inl. N. T.*, Leid. 1856. On *the Gospel of Paul*, a Latin *Dissertatio* of J. van Loenen, Gron., 1863.

POINTS FOR INQUIRY.

WHAT is the meaning of Paul by *his* Gospel, Rom. ii. 16; xvi. 25; 2 Tim. ii. 8?—What knowledge of Paulinism, beyond that derived from the New Testament, can we draw from the early Christian literature? Is the Paul of the Acts and of the Epistles the same?—What is the sense of 2 Cor. v. 16?—What of Gal. i. 16?—What of 1 Cor. xi. 23? To what extent was Paul an empiric? - In what relation does Paul place himself to his fellow-Apostles?—How is the great influence of the Pauline theology to be explained? General survey and criticism of some other divisions and modes of treatment of the subject.

FIRST SUBDIVISION.

HUMANITY AND THE INDIVIDUAL MAN, BEFORE AND OUT OF CHRIST.

SECTION XXXIV.

The Gentile and Jewish World.

According to the teaching of Paul, the whole Gentile world lies sunk in a condition of godlessness and immorality which can neither be extenuated nor excused, and which must, therefore, endure and experience God's righteous judgment. Although the Jewish world was originally irradiated by purer light, it stands in a moral respect so little above the other, that it also deserves the same judgment. Since both, consequently, are under sin, the whole world is exposed to condemnation before God, and is by no means in a condition to justify itself before Him.

1. Although the misery of the individual man and of humanity before and out of Christ is either presupposed or actually expressed by all the Apostles, yet no one has given so full a description of this condition as the Apostle Paul. His extensive knowledge of the world and of men, combined with the personal experience of his life, qualified him for this work; and his object—to prove that the reception of the Gospel was absolutely indispensable—could scarcely be better attained. The *locus classicus* on this point is Romans i. 18 and iii. 20, with which must especially be compared Acts xiv. 15-17; xvii. 24-29.

2. Heathenism is, in the view of the Apostle, by no means merely a lower stage of the religious life, but in its origin and growth the consequence of a melancholy defection from God; for the heathen had the capacity for recognising God, and even to a certain extent have actually recognised Him.* He revealed himself not only through the works of nature, but also in the original light of conscience.† In consequence of this, they possessed some natural acquaintance with God, and were conscious of that which God demands.‡ Notwithstanding all his degradation, man was, in the words of one of their own poets, of Divine descent, and felt, as such, an obscure but powerful impulse to seek Him in whom the true foundation of his being lay§ The Apostle does justice to the æsthetical worth of heathenism,

---

* Romans i. 18-21.   † Romans ii. 14, 15; compare Acts xiv. 17.
‡ Romans i. 32.   § Acts xvii. 27, 28.

as well as its religious aspirations;* but beneath this transparent robe he sees a corruption whose depth, with firm hand, he probes and lays bare.

3. Heathenism, which prides itself upon its wisdom, is the fruit of a darkened understanding; and this blinding of the understanding has its source in a heart estranged from God.† The declension of the heart first became manifest in a self-justifying neglect. It rendered not to God the praise and glory which was His due, and through unrighteousness forcibly restrained the operation of the truth.‡ When, in this way, the first trace was lost, men began to contend about the truth which the darkened eye could no longer clearly see, and attained to the climax of a folly which in turn was made manifest in the most terrible transgression. In the estimation of Paul, the highly-lauded heathenism is nothing but a deification of nature,§ an abuse of the creature for the purposes of idolatry, *i.e.*, a theoretical and practical denial of God—godlessness in the garb of religion.

4. Sin necessarily brings with it its own punishment: man who has lost God, loses also himself. Immorality is a natural consequence of ungodliness; but a consequence which has its reason in God's holy will, and is, therefore, a revelation of His righteous judgment.‖ Impure desire, which even manifests itself in an unnatural form, first becomes associated

---

* Acts xvii. 22, 23. † Rom. i. 21 ; Eph. iv. 18.
‡ Rom i. 18, κατέχοντες τὴν ἀλήθειαν. § Rom. i. 21-25.
‖ Rom. i. 18.

with idolatry; and sinful passion unites with harshness and hatred towards all that which opposes the gratification of unbridled sensuality and selfishness.* Thus is sin chastised by sin; and this chastisement is the more appropriate, not only because the evil is wrought in spite of a better knowledge, but also—a fine pyschological trait, although a terrible one—because at the same time there is united with this an unconcealed pleasure in those who do the same. †

5. Upon a superficial observation, it might appear as though Judaism stood, in a religious and moral aspect, far above heathenism. It had, in reality, inestimable privileges and advantages. God had allowed the Gentiles to walk in their own ways, in that He conferred upon them no extraordinary revelation, while, on the other hand, this was granted to Israel.‡ But so much the less might the Jew exalt himself above the Gentile, since he, notwithstanding, became guilty of the same sins.§ It is true, *his* perverseness shows itself in another form: according to Paul, not so much voluptuousness as pride is the ruling sin of the Jews—self-conceit and harshness,|| united with an obdurate impenitence in presence of the judgments of God.¶ But so far from this modified form of sin deserving a lesser chastisement, the Jewish transgressor has, on the other hand, to expect especial tribulation and anguish, because he has sinned—not only as the heathen—against a natural

* Rom. i 25-31. † Rom. i. 32.
‡ Acts xiv. 17; Rom. iii. 2. § Rom. ii. 1.
|| Rom. ii. 17, and following. ¶ Rom. ii. 4, 5.

law, but against a positive command.* Outward circumcision avails nothing: conscientious Gentiles deserve the preference over unconscientious Jews.† Thus these last have not the slightest advantage in a moral respect, although they are privileged in a theocratic sense, and—Paul expresses it with the same inflexible severity as John the Baptist and Jesus himself—the pharisaic pride must be silenced. After he has powerfully repelled the possible objection that upon such a supposition the whole value of circumcision vanishes,‡ he appeals for the justice of this his judgment§ to their own law,‖ *i.e.*, to words of the whole Old Testament, especially regarded in its moral aspect. The description there given of the wickedness of the people of God, applies not less to the Jews than to the Gentiles; and since these two represent the totality of the sinful world, it is easy to infer the judgment of Scripture upon the melancholy condition of the same.

6. It is, then, manifest that all are "under sin."¶ *i.e.*, not merely sinners, but governed by the power of sin. The absolute universality of sin is for Paul a fact proved successively by Scripture, by experience, and by the consciousness; and had he foreseen the objection that his representation of the then Jewish and Gentile world, even supposing it to be a purely accurate one, proves nothing in regard to other individuals living at a later period, he would assuredly have answered that human nature remains

* Rom. ii. 9-12. † Rom. ii. 25-29. ‡ Rom. iii. 1-8.
§ Rom. iii. 9-19. ‖ Rom. iii. 19. ¶ Rom. iii. 9.

the same in all ages. He directs the eye to the mass, as it divides itself in this way into two only apparently dissimilar halves, but thereby expresses also his judgment upon the individuals themselves.* Result: "All the world is guilty before God," *i.e.*, subject to the curse with which the law visits transgression.†

7. Therefore, also, it follows that no flesh can be justified by works of law. In this inevitable conclusion ‡ is pronounced the righteous judgment of God upon the whole Jewish and Gentile world. How heavily this judgment presses upon it, we shall hereafter see. For the present, we are concerned, above all, with the question, What is the cause of such a lamentable condition?

Compare, for the explaining and confirming of Paul's judgment on the Gentile and Jewish world, in addition to the well-known writings of Tholuck, Sepp, De Pressensé, and others, our *Leven v. J.* 2nd edition, i. p. 265, and following. On Paul's Natural Theology, Hebart, *Die Natürl. Theol. des Ap. P.*, Nürnberg, 1860.

POINTS FOR INQUIRY.

Does Paul's judgment upon heathendom, Acts xvii. 16, and following, perfectly agree with his judgment in Rom. i. 18, and following?—Value of his judgment upon Judaism.—What is the sense of Rom. ii. 14, 15?—What argumentative value has the analysis, Rom. iii. 9-20?

---

* Compare Rom. iii. 23; v. 12; xi. 32.
† Rom. iii. 19; Gal. iii. 13.   ‡ Rom. iii. 20.

SECTION XXXV.

The Cause of this Condition.

THE cause of this condition lies in the moral corruption of man, which, arising from the disobedience of our first parents, infects his whole nature, manifests itself in various degrees and forms, and—being by the law not only bridled, but also nourished—necessarily leads to death as the wages of sin.

1. The question, Whence moral evil? was not only the life question of Gnosticism in the second century, but also a main question of the Christian gnosis of the first century. Paul also furnishes an answer to it, and it is only without reason that there has been seen in this answer nothing more than an impure remainder of his former Jewish theology. Hardly would the Apostle have adopted into his Christian doctrinal system something from the Old Testament, without having—enlightened by the Spirit of truth—regarded it as the true solution of the question in point. With full confidence, we will now direct our

attention as well to his historical as to his psychological explanation of the origin of sin.

2. Sin (ἁμαρτία) is not for Paul, as with James and Peter, a sinful act, but a culpable principle, a power which, at a given time in the history of the world, began to rule. Sin "by one man entered into the world."* What is suggested by this word (εἰσῆλθε) is confirmed by other texts. Yet more fully than any of his predecessors does Paul declare himself as to the origin of a kingdom of darkness, of personal evil spirits, divided into different classes,† who, as it seems, have fallen through pride,‡ and who, constantly active in the idolatrous heathen world,§ show themselves most hostile to the kingdom of Christ and His servants.‖ That he regards Satan as the author of the Fall, is not, indeed, directly stated, but is in the highest degree probable.¶ (Compare also Book of Wisdom ii. 23, 24.) He does not, however, enlarge upon this point, because he has not to do with the metaphysical, but with the historical origin of evil. He contemplates the world of men (κόσμος) as a unity, and says that into it sin entered by one man, *Adam*, not Eve, as has been inferred from 1 Tim. ii. 14. He implies thereby not only that Adam was the first sinner, whose example all others at once followed, but—as becomes evident from the opposition instituted between Adam and Christ—that between this first act of transgression and the sin which afterwards reigned, there existed a definite connection. In what

* Rom. v. 12. † Ephes. vi. 12. ‡ 1 Tim. iii. 6. § 1 Cor. x. 20.
‖ 2 Cor. ii. 10, 11. ¶ 2 Cor. xi. 3, 14; compare John viii. 44.

this connection consisted is indicated by that which immediately follows: "Death by sin, and so death passed upon all men, for that (ἐφ' ᾧ) all have sinned;" and that not only *in Adam*, but also in *themselves*, as is manifest from the fact that death is universal, even among those who have not, like Adam, broken a positive command (v. 13, 14). Yet more clearly does the Apostle point out the true connection when he says (v. 19) that, "through one man's transgression many were made (constituted) sinners." If, in addition to this, we follow out the hint he gives us in his assertion, that the Jews as well as the Gentiles were by nature (φύσει, *indole sua*)* children of wrath, and in his more general statement, that death came through a man (δι' ἀνθρώπου),† we have a perfect right to maintain, that, according to Paul, human nature has become corrupt in consequence of its descent *from*, and its connection *with*, the first transgressor; and that death is by no means the consequence of the original organisation of our nature, but a chastisement, the wages of sin.‡

Paul evidently implies, therefore, that the first man was originally neither sinful nor mortal. This is not in any way opposed by the fact that he elsewhere speaks of the first man as earthy,§ for earthy (χοϊκός) is not the same as evil. It is, moreover, scarcely to be supposed that Paul regarded matter (ὕλη) as the origin of sin, which would necessarily lead to the execrable conception of God as the cause of sin.‖ He speaks,

* Ephes. ii. 3.   † 1 Cor. xv. 21.   ‡ Rom. vi. 23.
§ 1 Cor. xv. 45-47.   ‖ Rom. iii. 8.

on the contrary, of the image of God in man,* and designates knowledge and holiness as lineaments thereof. While the first man, as such, was, indeed, a material being, there was involved in this the *possibility*, not the necessity, of dying. That the possibility became a reality, is the especial consequence of sin. Sin and death are with Paul correlative ideas.

3. Since, then, sin has infected human nature, it lies in the nature of the case that it has defiled the whole man. In order rightly to apprehend the Apostle's conception of the physical origination and compass of sin in man, we must learn to understand his anthropology. Paul is a trichotomist—that is, he distinguishes body, soul, and spirit. This is shown with especial clearness in his prayer for the Thessalonians.† Even to the man who is yet unregenerate, the Apostle ascribes a soul (ψυχή) and a spirit (πνεῦμα); this spirit, however, must be entirely renewed.‡ To the spirit there is opposed, in the natural man, as a ruling power, the σάρξ, *i.e.*, the flesh—by no means equivalent to *body*, σῶμα—the proper seat of sin.§ By the word flesh, we are not to understand the dominion of the senses—in this case, contrary to the assertion of Paul (1 Tim. iv. 8), bodily discipline (asceticism) would be the best way to perfection, and it would be absolutely inexplicable how precisely the most spiritual of all sins, pride and want of affection, could be

---

* Ephes. iv. 23, 24 ; Colos. iii. 9, 10.   † 1 Thes. v. 23.
‡ Ephes. iv. 23.   § Rom. vii. 17, 18.

reckoned among the works of the flesh*—but (in the ethical sense of the word) the unsanctified human nature, as it opposes itself in a hostile manner to God, and all that is of God.† As the sinful man stands, through his spirit, in relationship with God, so does he, through his flesh, stand in relationship with the visible world, which offers to the desire of the flesh (ἐπιθυμία) a thousand attractive but forbidden objects. Life according to the flesh is consequently of necessity not a life of love, but of selfishness,‡ the poisonous root, out of which grow of themselves, as it were, two opposite branches, the sins of pride and of sensuality.

Sin, now, as a principle (sinfulness) manifests itself in the act of disobedience—in the doing of all that which is not becoming. This Paul indicates by different words—παράπτωμα, παράβασις, παρακοή, ἀπείθεια, ἀδικία. Out of the heart, the central point of the personality, proceeds this evil power, darkening the understanding, and misusing, like a tyrant, the different members of the body as so many weapons (ὅπλα) wherewith to wage its shameful warfare against God and that which is good.§ If man yields to it, he becomes, in his whole inner and outer life, entirely under the dominion of the flesh—sold under sin. Hence the expressions, "to be in the flesh," "to live after the flesh," "to mind the things of the flesh," as

---

* Gal. v. 20 ; Colos. ii. 18-23.

† Σάρξ is not = σῶμα, but = σῶμα + ψυχή, in opposition to πνεῦμα. On this account, also, the same thing is in the main implied by σαρκικός and ψυχικός ἄνθρωπος.

‡ 2 Cor. v. 15.   § Rom. vi. 13.

indicating this melancholy condition. Without doubt, Paul concedes to the sinful man the power of free self-determination, inasmuch as in the exercise of free-will, yea, even with full self-satisfaction, he sins against God;* for how could man otherwise be held guilty and worthy of chastisement?† Yea, even the heathen has in his conscience a lawgiver and an inflexible judge;‡ and in this very conscience does the Gospel seek and find in every man its secret point of contact.§ But in the sinner, understanding and conscience are both defiled;|| and where his heart has become insensible, he has given himself up entirely to the service of unrighteousness.¶ In speaking of such a condition, there can be no longer any room for question as to the moral freedom of the sinner; sin is, in Paul's eyes, no weakness, but a fatal power, which, in spite of all protests of the reason and conscience, bears away the victory over the natural man. It may rise so high as not merely to blind, but harden the man, and even to cause him to find a natural pleasure in moral evil as such.**

4. After what has been said, we cannot be surprised that the Apostle declares the mind of the flesh to be enmity against God and His law.†† So much the more natural, however, is the question, in what relation, according to his view, the law stands to sin. When Paul mentions the law (ὁ νόμος), he ordinarily means the Mosaic law, in its whole compass of moral and

* Rom. i. 28.   † Rom. ii. 1.   ‡ Rom. ii. 15.
§ 2 Cor. iv. 2; v. 11 b. || Tit. i. 15.   ¶ Eph. iv. 19.
** Rom. i. 32; Eph. iv. 19.   †† Rom. viii. 7.

The Causes of this Condition. 277

ceremonial commands, as the rule of life ordained by God. The law is by no means something sinful in itself, much less the cause of evil. It is true, indeed, as a general fact, that no sin is possible without law, but then, law is possible without sin. The law is, in its contents and aim, holy, just, and good.* It was given "because of the transgressions,"† *i.e.*, in order to restrain them it was added to the promise; it was like a stern disciplinarian, who brings unruly boys under control by holding over them the rod.‡ To this extent it exerts, after its own manner, a healthful reaction against the power of sin, and teaches man to recognise it as sin, *i.e.*, as the cause of guilt and punishment.§ But in spite of this, its excellent aim, the operation even of the best law can, for the sinful man, be only fraught with destruction. Without the law sin is dead, ‖ and only through the commandment does it revive. The law awakens in the sinner the slumbering desire after that which is evil, and calls forth on his part reaction against its own imperative requirements. Thus it becomes the power of sin¶— a power which not only reveals sin, but also constantly increases it; yea, even was with this last aim appointed by God himself, inasmuch as He willed that, through the increase of evil, the necessity for redemption should be **more** deeply felt, and the revelation of His grace so much the more highly prized.** The law, however, produces only wrath;††

* Rom. vii. 12; Gal. iii. 12. † Gal. iii. 19.
‡ Gal iii 24, 25. § Rom iii. 20; vii. 7. ‖ Rom. vii. 8.
¶ 1 Cor. xv. 56. ** Rom. v. 20. †† Rom. iv. 15.

the transgression of it calls necessarily for the manifestation of its displeasure, and thereby brings the transgressor into a condition of slavish fear, which excludes all love, and renders the estrangement only greater.* On this account, also, no law is able to give life to the sinner,† that is to say, to give him the true life of the spirit, which would enable him to fulfil God's will out of love to God. By works of law, therefore, *i.e.*, works which the sinful man performs from the stand-point of law, can no flesh be justified before God.‡ To him who fulfils the law, life is promised; he who transgresses it has thereby forfeited his life; to win God's favour again by the fulfilling of the law is so impossible that all who proceed on this principle must, on the contrary, expect the curse.§

The Mosaic law had, in a word, only a temporary and provisional worth; this is clear, if we contemplate it from a Christian stand-point. There was a time when all mankind were yet living objectively,‖ and Paul subjectively,¶ without the law. A time arrives for the Christian, in which he no longer stands under the dominion of the law as a commanding and condemning power.** So long, however, as this time has not yet come, sin and misery are only increased by the law. It can hold forth the ideal before the sinner's eye, but can never render the attainment thereof possible.

5. Thus sin brings death, just because it is wrought in opposition to the command of the law. Necessarily

* Rom. viii. 15.   † Gal. iii. 21.   ‡ Rom. iii. 20.
§ Gal. iii. 10.   ‖ Rom. v. 13.   ¶ Rom. vii. 9.   ** Rom. vi. 15

it is now imputed,* as well on this side as on the other side the grave. The sinner comes short of the glory (δόξα) of God, *i.e.*, of the honour which he would have had with God, had he not sinned and become exposed to the righteous judgment which concentrates itself in death.† The Pauline idea of death is not easy to define in its whole fulness. We are just as little entitled to restrict it to the idea of physical death alone, as we are entirely to exclude this idea. In every case the idea of spiritual death is included ;‡ and we cannot overlook the fact that death is, in the full sense, the wages of sin, inasmuch as it ends in everlasting perdition (ἀπώλεια). That Paul had also this latter in his mind, is clear from the antithesis of death and the gracious gift of everlasting life.§ In the idea of death there is united, consequently, that of the greatest temporal and everlasting wretchedness; and in the language of the Apostle, now this, now the other side of his subject comes into greater or lesser prominence. Spiritual death leads to temporal, and this passes over into eternal death.‖

Compare, on the principal points herein treated of, especially Ernesti, *vom Ursprung der Sunde nach Paul. Lehrgehalt*, 2 vols., Gott. 1863-64. Tijssen, *Diss. Theol. Pauli Anthropologiam exhibens*, Gron. 1847. On the law, Hamerster, *Diss. Theol. de lege e Pauli Ap. sententiâ*, Gron. 1838. A. Ritzschl, *die*

---

* Rom. v. 13.   † Rom. vi. 21 ; compare Gen. ii. 17.
‡ Ephes. ii. 1, 5 ; Colos. ii. 13 ; Ephes. v. 14.
§ Rom. vi. 23.   ‖ 2 Cor. vii. 10.

Entstehung der Alt-Kathol. Kirche, 2nd ed., 1857, pp. 63-76.

POINTS FOR INQUIRY.

By what peculiarity is the demonology of Paul distinguished?—What significance for his demonology has the history of the Fall?—The trichotomy of man in the writings of Paul.—Paul's doctrine of the conscience.—What is the sense of Gal. ii. 19?—What of 1 Tim. i. 8-10, as compared with the view taken of the law in the Epistles to the Romans and Galatians?—Is, in Paul's teaching, even natural death regarded as a definite chastisement of sin?

SECTION XXXVI.

Its Consequences.

SUBJECT to the power of sin and death, man finds himself in a condition of melancholy discord, the traces of which are apparent even in nature, and the consciousness of which, when it has once been awakened, cannot but render him unspeakably wretched. In the distinct feeling of this wretchedness is, nevertheless, at the same time, given the point at which inner receptiveness for the blessings of salvation begins.

1. However sad the condition into which sin has brought man (Sec. xxxv.), it would be less unendurable if the *man* were entirely sunk in the *sinner*. This, however, according to the teaching of our Apostle, is certainly not the case; the original nature of man has been corrupted, indeed, by sin, but by no means annihilated. In consequence thereof, there naturally arises within the sinful heart a feeling of disharmony, which renders impossible the enjoyment of peace.

2. The Pauline representation of discord in the sinful heart must be distinguished from that which he says of the conflict in the heart of the believer.* Even with believers, flesh and spirit do not cease to war against each other; but in the man who is yet out of Christ, while the spirit (τὸ πνεῦμα) is present, it is as a part of his nature which is slavishly bound; he is by nature fleshly, and sold under sin.† When he begins, like Paul himself before his conversion, to come through the law to self-knowledge and a knowledge of his proper destiny, the law in his mind begins to struggle with the law in his members. There is seen now the discord between the sinful nature and the awakened conscience; but the fruitless conflict ever ends in a painful defeat, and the combatant remains an enigma to himself, unless his weakness is transformed into strength through another power than that of the law.‡

* Gal. v. 17. † Rom. vii. 14.

‡ We have here to do with one of the most difficult, but, at the same time, one of the most important, passages in the Pauline Epistles— Rom. vii. 7-24. The exposition—determined by dogmatic prepossession—which was current for centuries, would perhaps have afforded less room for difference of views, had not two questions been unceasingly confounded:—"Of whom is the Apostle here speaking?" and "To whom is his admirable description still more or less applicable?" That to the latter question the answer was given—" To every believer," will surprise no one who is no stranger to the domain of spiritual life. But from this it by no means follows that Paul is actually describing the life of the believer. Against this supposition is (1) the connection and aim of his reasoning; (2) the fact that he describes a conflict not of the πνεῦμα but of the νοῦς (the inward man) as against the flesh; and (3) his description in ver. 14 is not consistent with the idea of Christian freedom as presented in viii. 2; vi. 17; and Gal. v. 24. He is manifestly describing his former state in the light of his present condition, and the

3. Not in the microcosm of the human heart alone, but also in the macrocosm of the world, is reflected, for the eye of the Apostle, the same element of discord. The whole creation—that is, the whole animate and inanimate nature—is unwillingly and in consequence of sin, subjected, through the will of God, to vanity, and awaits with longing expectation a redemption and glorifying which it shall receive only when the sighing of those who have the first-fruits of the Spirit is heard, and the glory of the children of God shall have been made complete and manifest. Nature suffers with humanity, since its destiny is most intimately bound up with that of humanity: both look for the same thing — redemption.

4. Sinful man cannot be redeemed by the laying aside of the body of death, for death itself is a chastisement which leads to greater misery (Sec. xxxv. 5). Paul speaks of a flaming fire, in which vengeance is taken of those who know not God, and reject the Gospel—of the suffering of punishment even everlasting destruction, in banishment from the presence of the Lord and from the glory of His power.*

---

present in which he speaks is partly to be explained by the vividness of his description, partly by the fact that the after-pains of this melancholy condition were still perceptible, inasmuch as perfect redemption was not yet enjoyed. In Rom. vii. it is just as little the mere natural man who is described as the Christian in his normal state; but the sinner under the law, who is beginning to awaken and strive after better things, the object of the *gratia præparans et præveniens*. Paul's words will recall the words of many an earnest-minded heathen: *e. g.*, the "*Video meliora, proboque*," &c.

* 2 Thes. i. 9.

Elsewhere, also, it is seen that he represents this judgment under like figures as do his contemporaries. Nowhere is there found any hint that he looks for any diminution or removal of this chastisement. He proclaims, indeed, diverse heavy judgments, which are determined in degree by the greater or lesser amount of light by which the transgressor was surrounded; but even the heathen do not escape unpunished, when they sin against the light of conscience.* On the part of man, also, nothing is to be reaped from sowing to the flesh except corruption ($\phi\theta o\rho\acute{a}$).† Before rejecting this teaching of the Apostle concerning a last judgment as an unimportant remnant of his former rabbinical learning, we shall do well to ask whether the Apostle in this in any way proceeds beyond that which is warranted by the word of the Lord himself and the prophetic language of the Old Testament.

5. Man, who is conscious of such a division within himself, and looks forward to such a judgment, must necessarily feel himself unspeakably miserable. Nevertheless, that which is his deepest source of suffering becomes, on the other side, his happiness: the sinner—precisely at the time when he feels himself irretrievably lost, and *inasmuch as* he does so feel himself—can be saved. The clear consciousness of his own misery ‡ is at the same time the inner point of contact for the work of redemption. Herein is the fallen man distinguished from the fallen angel, whom Paul never otherwise represents than as taking

* Rom. ii. 9-12. † Gal. vi. 8. ‡ Rom. vii. 23-25.

pleasure in corrupting, and as given up to everlasting perdition. If, however, the salvation of the sinner, which is in this way psychologically possible, is to become an actual fact, it must proceed from God himself.

On Rom. vii. 7-24, see the Commentaries of Tholuck and Lange. On Rom. viii. 19-23, our *Christol. des N. V.*, pp. 300-311. The whole Pauline conception of the depth of this wretchedness has, perhaps, after Augustine and Luther, been better understood by no one than by Blaise Pascal. See the Dissertation on this subject by Dr. Wijnmalen, Utr. 1865.

POINTS FOR INQUIRY.

WHAT opinion are we to form as to the person who is introduced as speaking in Rom. vii. 7-24?—Summary and criticism of the most important expositions of Rom viii. 19-23.—Harmony and criticism of the whole doctrine of man's misery as contained in Paul and in Augustine.—**Its eternal truth and its permanent value.**

SECOND SUBDIVISION.

HUMANITY AND THE INDIVIDUAL MAN THROUGH AND IN CHRIST.

SECTION XXXVII.

The Plan of Salvation.

THE righteousness of God, which, on account of sin, is wanting both to Jew and Gentile, is promised to and conferred upon the sinner in a very different way than that of his own merit. The Gospel of the New Testament proclaims the mystery of a Divine plan of salvation, which, formed before the foundation of the world, was shadowed forth throughout the whole preparatory economy of the Old Testament, and revealed in the fulness of time; which embraces the Jewish and Gentile world, heaven and earth, and in gradual development shows forth, with a lustre before unknown, the majesty and glory of God.

The Plan of Salvation. 287

1. What could proceed from God alone has actually been conferred by God. For Paul it is an equally certain fact that God in Christ has done that which to the law was impossible,* as that He is the cause of all that is spiritually good (1 Cor. i. 30). Therefore, also, God, in the whole fulness of His being, is called the Saviour,† whose love to sinners—a love, however, which had been entirely forfeited by them—bears the character of grace, and bestows upon them that which reason, left to itself, is not able even to comprehend.‡

2. The Gospel of this grace is consequently, according to the view of our Apostle, something absolutely new—not the continuation of the old order, but its direct opposite. It is for him the joyful message of the sinner's justification before God through faith in Christ, and, as such, a revealed secret (μυστήριον). For the word *mystery* has, in the usage of our Apostle, a sense entirely different from that in which it was later used. It signifies a matter which was before unknown, but has now come to light, and on this account ceases to be hidden, although, even after it has been made known to men, it retains its dark and mysterious side.§ "Understanding in the mystery" is obtained only through revelation ‖—a peculiar supernatural act of God, which is indicated by Paul in different words—ἀποκάλυψις, φανέρωσις, &c.—in which, however, it cannot be shown

---

* Rom. viii. 3, 4.

† 1 Tim. i. 1; ii. 3; σωτήρ, a truly Pauline characteristic in the Pastoral Epistles.

‡ 1 Cor. ii. 9. § Rom. xi. 33. ‖ Ephes. iii. 3, 4.

that he sharply distinguishes the one from the other for the indication of a different idea of revelation. What, on the other hand, is yet concealed in the future, remains, on this very account, so long as it is yet future, a mystery which, naturally, we can believe only on the word of him who declares it.* Although Paul enumerates several such mysteries, all of which fall within the domain of Christian knowledge,† yet pre-eminently the Gospel is for him the *one* great mystery of Christ,‡ which reveals a character by no means speculative, but, on the contrary, one especially practical.§

3. That which is new did not on this account come in without preparation having been made for it. In principle, the New Testament is contained in the Old, and is witnessed by the law which is replaced by it, and by the prophets, of whom it is a glorious fulfilment.‖ No Apostle has manifested a deeper insight into the whole course of the world's history than Paul. His philosophic eye sees in the whole pre-Christian period one long age of preparation which was brought to completion only in the coming of Christ.¶ He is the end of the law,** the goal to which its whole economy tended; and while, before his appearing, God allowed the Gentiles, in a certain sense, to walk in their own ways,†† even the most privileged nation under the old covenant resembled

---

* 1 Cor. xv. 51.
‡ Ephes. vi. 19 ; Col. iv. 3.
‖ Rom. iii. 21, 22.
** Rom. x. 4.

† 1 Cor. xiii. 2 ; xiv. 2.
§ 1 Tim. iii. 16.
¶ Gal. iv. 4.
†† Acts xiv. 16.

The Plan of Salvation.

a youth who had not yet come to full age.* On this account, he could regard an abandoning of Christianity only as a relapse into an earlier stage which had been already left behind,† and must look upon the continued unbelief of the Jews‡ as a fruit of the most melancholy blindness. The Gospel, which is of a spiritual nature, cannot possibly be understood by the psychical man as such, for it must be spiritually judged of.§ And no wonder, since it makes acquainted with God's purpose of saving sinners—in former ages hidden from men—a purpose which has been formed and carried into execution in accordance with His own plan.

4. The salvation proclaimed in the Gospel is nothing else than the carrying out in time of that which God had determined within himself from all eternity. Even in his earliest writings, Paul shows that he regards those who believe in Christ as elect of God,‖ in whom the ideal of ancient Israel is most beautifully realised.¶ Especially in the Epistles to the Romans and Ephesians** does this idea come prominently into the foreground. The Apostle speaks of a Divine plan of salvation whose centre is Christ, and whose end is the bright revelation of God's glorious perfection.†† This plan was no more originated in consequence of sin‡‡ than it can be

---

* Gal. iv. 1, and following. † Gal. iv. 9.
‡ 2 Cor. iii. 14; iv. 4. § 1 Cor. ii. 14.
‖ 1 Thes. i. 4; 2 Thes. ii. 13. ¶ Gal. vi. 16.
** Rom. ix.-xi.; Ephes. i. 4, and following. †† Rom. xi. 36.
‡‡ See the author's *Bild Christi nach der Schrift*, pp. 61-64, Hamburg, 1864. Compare also Goodwin on Ephes. i. 9, 10.

permanently frustrated by the power of sin. It is eternal as God, and is founded not on any excellence of man himself, but in God's adorable and unchangeable good pleasure—not *because* believers are holy, but *in order that* they may become so, has God chosen them;* and this their faith is not the cause, but only the sign of their election unto salvation. Without doubt, Paul knows a Divine calling and election to a participation in the blessings of (outward) Christianity; yet he nowhere makes an essential difference between this and the calling and election to everlasting salvation. He could not, indeed, make this distinction, since those to whom he explains this mystery were, as a rule, true believers. Without doubt, he speaks of the choice of the Gentiles in their totality † as opposed to the national rejection of the Jews; but nowhere is there to be found a proof that he entertains any other view than that of personal election to salvation with regard to the individuals of whom this totality is composed (ἡ ἐκλογή). The contrary is manifest from the way in which he consoles believers, and urges them to the work of sanctification, by reminding them of their personal predestination. "All this is singularly clear, and certainly it will not be with exegetical arguments that the system which the Augustines, the Calvins, the Gomars have built up upon these premises can henceforth be combated" (Reuss).

5. The Divine plan of salvation is in itself one and indivisible, but is for the individual only gradually

* Ephes. i. 4. † Rom. ix –xi.

realised. God has known His own from eternity in love (πρόγνωσις), and on this account has foreordained them (προώρισεν) to be conformed to the image of His Son. Only on dogmatic grounds can one desire to draw a sharp line of distinction between these two terms: in an impartial examination of the Pauline system of thought, they flow, as it were, the one into the other. "Willingly will we let pass this distinction, which in fact only conceals without revealing anything" (Schleiermacher). Both belong to the sphere of eternity; in time, on the other hand, falls the vocation (κλῆσις) with which the personal safe-conduct of the believer to the blessedness designed for him begins. The Apostle, in speaking of this vocation, conceives of it not merely as an outward call, but as one which is, at the same time, inwardly understood and comprehended. Wherever there is a calling in the Pauline sense of the word, *there*, at the same time, is the germ of faith and of conversion; and herein lies the logical ground for the called being spoken of as those who are here justified and hereafter glorified. That they are, however, the one and the other, they owe exclusively to the absolute good pleasure of God (εὐδοκία τοῦ θελήματος), which is inseparably one with his moral perfection, and consequently partakes in no degree whatever of an arbitrary character (Eph. i. 5-10).

6. Such a doctrine would appear harsh, considered apart from all connection with the sovereign omnipotence of God on the one hand, and the absolute reprobation due to sin on the other hand. Yet it is precisely to this connection that the Apostle draws

attention, when (Romans ix—xi.) he discusses from the apologetic stand-point the exclusion of the Jews from the blessings of the kingdom of God, as opposed to the reception of the Gentiles. Whilst he gives expression to his heart-felt sorrow for the fate of his nation, he shows (A) that Israel's rejection (ix. 6-13) does not conflict with the unchangeableness of God, since the promises of salvation in the Old Testament are ever made to the true, *i.e.*, the believing Israel; and just as little (B) with the righteousness of God (ix. 14-29), since God is indebted to no one, and, as Lord, has the sovereign disposal of every creature. Still less (C) with His holiness, since this rejection is only the just punishment of Israel's unbelief (ix. 30—x. 21). Least of all (D) with His truth, compassion, and grace, since Israel's fall becomes salvation to the Gentiles; and, moreover, Israel itself is capable of being restored again (Rom. xi.) He does not, indeed, in this manner, remove all objections; but, nevertheless, by a constant reference on the one hand to the pregnant texts and examples of the Old Testament, and on the other hand to the exalted majesty of God, he reduces to silence obdurate gainsaying. His object is manifestly to establish the doctrine of God's free grace, not so much against all working and striving on our part, as against all self-righteousness and all human merit.

7. Belief in God's unalterable decree is for Paul no object of abstract reasoning. "Paul is not here a philosopher, who is deducing scientifically the formulas of metaphysics; he is an advocate who is pleading the cause of God" (Bonifas). Far from

The Plan of Salvation.

commending an *à priori* searching into this revealed mystery, he rather teaches believers, standing, as it were, at the end of their journey, to look back upon that which God has destined for them in Christ; that by meditating thereon, both the fruitfulness and the joy of their faith may be increased. While acknowledging that, even by the manifestation and punishment of obdurate unbelief, God's eternal counsel is fulfilled, he regards this unbelief itself as a fault, for which men are personally responsible. As it is impossible to mistake the plain sense of Romans ix., so also is it unjustifiable arbitrarily to separate this chapter from the tenth and eleventh. The true synthesis of the apparently irreconcilable antinomy between the Divine predestination and human freedom is not afforded us even by Paul. It suffices him to lay upon the second member no less stress than upon the first—not merely to bewail the unbelief of Israel as a sad fact, but as a great sin—and to await from the future the further solution of a problem which is for unbelief a stone of stumbling, but is already for faith an occasion for deepest adoration.

8. This it must be in the widest sense of the word, since God's plan of salvation extends not to this world alone, but to the whole creation. The great thought of God to unite all things under one head has reference not only to men, but also to angels—not only to earth, but also to heaven.* If we meditate somewhat deeply upon this Divine purpose, it manifests to us God's adorable wisdom,† but, above all, the inex-

* Ephes. i. 10; Colos. i. 20.   † Ephes. iii. 9-12.

haustible riches of His grace, and along with these His infinite foreknowledge,* in a light in which they could not otherwise be seen, and which calls forth from the Apostle a strain of exultation,† of which even an Erasmus, full of admiration, exclaimed: "*Quid unquam Cicero dixit grandiloquentius?*" No wonder—the eloquence of Cicero had never such material to dispose of; and not talent, but the heart, guided the pen of Paul.

Compare the following Academical Dissertations: —M. van Staveren, *de Evang. Naturâ*, Gron. 1839. H. van Gesseler, *de præpar. Jud. et Gentil. ad Relig. Chr. accip.*, Gron. 1839. J. Boeles, *de Mysteriis in Rel. Chr.*, Gron. 1843. F. G. B. van Bell, *de Patefact. Christ. indole*, Lugd. Batav. 1849. And, above all, the dissertation of Dr. J. A. Lamping, *(Diss.) Pauli de prædest. Doctrinam exponens*, Traj. 1860. Also the writing of G. W. Krummacher, *Das Dogma von der Gnadenwahl* (Exposition of Rom. ix.-xi.), Duisburg, 1856. Compare also the Commentaries of Ellicott on Galatians and Ephesians; and Goodwin's Exposition of various passages of the Epistle to the Ephesians. 2 vols. (reprinted), Edin. 1861.

POINTS FOR INQUIRY.

WHAT is with Paul the proper essence of the Gospel?— What does he teach by Colos. ii. 16, 17?—The Gospel a revealed mystery.—The way of life under the old covenant, Rom. iv.—The psychological ground for Paul's doctrine of

* Rom. xi. 33-36. † Rom. viii. 31-39.

predestination.—Its relation to the Pauline universalism.—Connection and difference of the Pauline doctrine with that of Augustine and Calvin.—Does Paul teach reprobation as unconditionally as he proclaims predestination to everlasting life?—To what extent has the Apostle succeeded in removing the objection that God is made the author of sin?—Does Paul's doctrine of predestination contain no necessary premises to that of the restoration of all things?—Argument of Rom. viii. 28-30.—Sense, beauty, and power of Rom. viii. 31-39.—The doxology, Rom. xi. 33-36.

SECTION XXXVIII.

The Christ.

THE Divine plan of salvation has for its centre Christ, the Son of God, the Saviour of sinners, who appeared on earth in human flesh, that, as the second Adam, He might be the spiritual head of the new humanity. Relatively little does Paul communicate concerning the Lord's earthly history; but every conception of His person in which He is regarded either as man only in appearance, or as a *mere* man, is expressly condemned by the doctrine of the Apostle.

1. It belongs to the excellencies of the Pauline theology, that he ever considers the plan of salvation in connection with Him in whom it has been realised. Christ is for him the centre, not merely of the Gospel, but of the whole history of the world. Although in his teaching he throughout takes his departure from *man* (Sec. xxxiii., 4), he yet rises unceasingly to Him

The Christ. 297

in whom the ideal of humanity is realised ; and while he manifestly lays greater stress upon his testimony concerning the work of the Lord than upon that concerning His person, he has yet expressed himself regarding the latter in a manner which leaves no room for doubt as to what he really thinks on this subject.

2. The Tubingen school has asserted that the Christology of the latest letters preserved under the name of Paul bears the stamp of another character than that of those four whose genuineness it acknowledges. In itself, this would occasion no difficulty; certainly not if we believe that the Holy Ghost was leading the Apostle, in giving this testimony also, from light to light, from strength to strength. If those Epistles in which we find his loftiest Christological thoughts, *e.g.*, those to the Colossians and Philippians, were composed in the time of, and partly with reference to, the earliest Gnostic errors, nothing prevents us supposing that precisely this error urged the Apostle so much the more powerfully to declare the truth. The case would certainly be different if anything were asserted in the later Epistles which was denied in the earlier, or the converse. How little this is really the case is evident from the fact, that the points of departure and commencement for the lines of thought which run through his latest writings are already to be discovered in his earliest.

3. That Paul relates but little of the words, deeds, and events of the Lord's earthly life, strikes us at once, from a glance at his writings. Only to a single

unwritten saying of the Master does this Apostle appeal,* and he only mentions a few traits in the history of His life. The attempt has been made on apologetic grounds to gather a life of Jesus out of the writings of Paul; but the harvest has been only scanty. The First Epistle of Peter contains in itself more reminiscences, *e.g.*, from the history of our Lord's sufferings, than all the Epistles of Paul together. The cause is to be sought in the fact that Paul had no personal intercourse with the Lord, and attaches to this privilege, the want of which had been so richly compensated in his experience, but a subordinate value.† Not the teaching and suffering, but the risen and glorified Christ, is here above all brought into the foreground; he has less to do with Jesus in himself than with Jesus as *the Christ*. With the proclamation of this truth he comes forth immediately after his conversion.‡ He defends it, in presence of Jew and Gentile, by an appeal to Holy Scripture;§ and though he repeatedly lays stress upon the circumstance that the Lord sprang from David's seed,|| this is doubtless because His princely descent was an absolutely necessary condition of His Messiahship.

4. There is no ground for supposing that Paul doubted in any respect the true humanity of the Lord. He describes Him as being born of a woman,¶

---

* Acts xx. 35. † 2 Cor. v. 16.

‡ Acts ix 20, where 'Ιησοῦν is to be read instead of Χριστὸν, ar d *Son of God* must be understood as a title of the Messiah.

§ Acts xvii. 3; xviii. 5. || Rom. i. 3; 2 Tim. ii. 8. ¶ Gal. iv. 4.

partaker of the weakness of our nature,* and sets His mind and feelings as an example before the eyes of His followers.† But just as little can we doubt that Paul saw in the Lord one who was more than man, and that not merely in the middle or at the close of his Apostolic labours, but at their very beginning. He had, indeed, beheld the persecuted Nazarene in more than earthly glory,‡ and at once recognised that He whom the Jews had crucified was nothing less than the Lord of Glory himself.§ Shall this only indicate that He is now living in glory? Even the peculiar manner in which Paul speaks of the human nature in Christ, leads to the supposition that such an explanation is too weak. He calls him, indeed, the second man, but the one who is "from heaven," ‖ and declares that God sent his Son "in the likeness of 'sinful flesh."¶ It would, at least, sound strange if this Son had claimed no personal pre-existence, and had not very clearly distinguished himself from sinful flesh. That this latter also is the view of the Apostle is increasingly clear, when we hear him designate Christ as the image of God, in whose countenance the glory of God is seen;** God's own beloved Son,†† as such beyond doubt, declared (proclaimed) with power by the resurrection from the dead;‡‡ proclaimed, but by no means *constituted*, the Son of God thereby. How else were it possible that He was already

* 2 Cor. xiii. 4. † Phil. ii. 5.
‡ Acts xxvi. 13, and following. § 1 Cor. ii. 8.
‖ 1 Cor. xv. 47, according to the shorter reading.
¶ Rom. viii. 3. ** 2 Cor. iv. 4-6.
†† Rom. viii. 32; compare Ephes. i. 6. ‡‡ Rom. i. 4.

working under the old covenant,* yea, as the Apostle plainly teaches, was rich with God even before His voluntary incarnation?† Certainly he distinguishes the Son from the Father, and places Him in regard to the Father in a relation of definite dependence;‡ but, nevertheless, he does not hesitate a moment to speak of Him as the mediate cause through which all, without exception, has been called into existence,§ tacitly to apply to Him that which in the Old Testament is spoken of God,‖ and to exalt Him—for only thus can we at least read or understand the words, Rom. ix. 5—as God, above all blessed for ever.

5. We regard it as a hopeless undertaking, in presence of such expressions of the Apostle's mind, to persist in the assertion that the Christ of the four universally acknowledged epistles is nothing but the heavenly man (Baur). Even the connection into which His name is brought with that of God the Father on the one hand, and the Holy Spirit on the other, leads us to a higher conception; yet the metaphysical domain of the Pauline Christology is still further cleared up, if we direct our attention to later utterances, and observe in them, instead of conflicting ideas, the fairest harmony and development. This is seen to be the case in the *locus classicus* of the Epistle to the Philippians,¶ where he represents the Son of God first in his pre-mundane existence,

---

* 1 Cor. x. 4, 9.
† 2 Cor. viii. 9.
‡ 1 Cor. iii. 23; xi. 3; Ephes. i. 17.
§ 1 Cor. viii. 6.
‖ Rom. x. 13.
¶ Phil. ii. 5-11

then in his earthly humiliation, and finally in his heavenly glory; and describes the incarnation as a voluntary laying aside of this original form of God in which He could abidingly live and reign. We think, however, especially of the exalted words in the Epistle to the Colossians,* in which the Apostle places the Son of God's love in a relation, on the one hand to the Father, on the other to the world, and again to the kingdom of God, which would be absolutely inconceivable, unless in Him, as in a holy temple, the fulness of the Godhead† dwelt bodily. Only if this latter was really the Apostle's idea, can we understand how he speaks—as an unbiassed exegesis seems to require us to understand his words—of "our great God and Saviour,"‡ and consecrates to Him (at the close of his Apostolic course) a doxology§ which he, the strict monotheist, would, without doubt, have been the first to condemn as a sinful deification of the creature, had not Christ, according to his conviction, possessed a nature and dignity which raised Him above all created beings.

6. And yet, however certain and important all this may be, it does not explain the entirely unique position which Christ occupies in the Pauline scheme of doctrine. Not as a supernatural manifestation or Divine person itself, but as *man, the* man by way of excellence—precisely because He is from heaven—is the Lord all things to Paul, not only for His faith and life, but also for His thought. It is more than an accident that he

* Colos. i. 15-20. † Colos. ii. 9.
‡ Titus ii. 13. § 2 Tim. iv. 18.

greets the mediator between God and man with so great emphasis as the man Christ Jesus;[*] the whole work of redemption had been for Paul entirely inconceivable were this man human only in appearance. The philosophic spirit of the Apostle manifests its striving after unity notably in the fact, that in the history of humanity he repeatedly discovers a point of unity, and as from the first Adam he sees sin and death, so from the second he sees redemption and life proceed.[†] He places Christ over against Adam, as the higher over against the lower, as the spiritual over against the merely natural principle of life.[‡] Because He was perfectly Divine, He could be perfectly human, and, in so far as humanity enters into a personal union with Him, at the same time, the Creator of a new principle of life. On this account Paul attaches so great a value to the absolute purity and sinlessness of the Lord.[§] There lies in this also the ground for the supposition, that if Paul does not mention the supernatural conception and holy birth of the Lord, he yet cannot have denied or doubted it. In connection with his doctrine of sin, it is also inconceivable that, according to his view, the second Adam came less immediately than the first, through a miraculous intervention of Divine power. As the faultless head of a new humanity, Christ has for Paul of the highest, yea, an everlasting importance. And

---

[*] 1 Tim. ii. 5. [†] Rom. v. 12-21; 1 Cor. xv. 21-22.
[‡] 1 Cor. xv. 45-47.
[§] 2 Cor. v. 21; Philip. ii. 8; compare Rom. viii. 3; xv. 3.

here we reach the point at which we can understand the peculiarity of his whole Soteriology.

Compare our *Christologie N. V.*, pp. 214-250. Beyschlag, *Zur Paul. Christol.* in the Studien und Kritiken, 1860, p. 431 and following. *Christologie d. N. T.*, p. 201-256. E. W. Koltoff, *Vita Jesu Christi a Paulo Apost. adumbrata* (1842). J. J. Räbiger, *Comment. de Christol. Paulinâ contra Baurium*, Bresl. 1852. On Philip. ii. 6-8, the Commentaries of Meyer, Alford, and Ellicott. On Colos. i. 15-20, see the Doct. Dissert. of S. Hofmeijr, *de Πρωτοτόκῳ*, Traject. 1856; and of J. Cramer, *de Arianismo*, Traj. 1858.

POINTS FOR INQUIRY.

CONNECTION between the Pauline Christology and the doctrine of predestination.—Nature and importance of that which Paul communicates regarding the history of the Lord. —Exposition and defence of the most important texts here referred to.—Critical review of the texts in which, according to the ordinary reading and exposition, the title of Θεός is given to the Lord.—Harmony and **difference** between **the first and the second Adam, according to Paul.**

SECTION XXXIX.

The Work of Redemption.

THE whole earthly and heavenly life of Christ —especially His voluntary self-surrender to the death of the Cross, and His glorious resurrection on the third day—has the definite aim of redeeming humanity from the guilt and dominion of sin, and thereby restoring to man the salvation he had forfeited through the disobedience of the first Adam. At the same time, the way which the Gospel opens to this goal is diametrically opposed to that which the law presented: the justification of the sinner herein proclaimed is a justification only through faith.

1. The soteriology of Paul is not only richer than his Christology, but it bears, besides this, a highly peculiar character. This peculiarity is manifest even in the first Apostolic missionary address of his with

which we are acquainted.* The Pauline doctrine of redemption is, above all things, a doctrine of justification (compare Sec. xxxiii. 3), a doctrine which he presents with evident preference, in the Epistle to the Romans more thetically (*i.e.* by way of statement), in the Epistle to the Galatians more polemically, and which he, once even,† proclaims as the essential doctrine of the Gospel. By the term "righteousness of God" (δικαιοσύνη Θεοῦ) Paul understands in this connection no attribute of God's nature, but a condition before God; a righteousness conferred by God through grace—in the way of imputation—upon the sinner, whom God regards and treats as just; and which is consequently diametrically opposed to any self-righteousness before God, which the sinner seeks to establish by the most exact fulfilment of the demands of the law.‡ With his eye fixed upon the distinction once conferred upon Abraham (Gen. xv. 6), the true Israelite—especially the Pharisee—knew no higher blessing than that of being righteous (צַדִּיק) before God. Paul himself had formerly long sought this in the way of works,§ but had recognised the folly of this attempt, and had acknowledged the highest value of the Gospel precisely in the fact that it opens up an entirely different way to the desired end. He mentions, it is true, and glories in, other blessings conferred by God in Christ,‖ but nevertheless justification occupies the highest place¶ in his estimation.

---

* Acts xiii. 38, 39.
‡ Rom. x. 3; Philip. iii. 9.
‖ 1 Cor. i. 30.

† Rom. i. 16, 17.
§ Philip. iii. 4-8.
¶ Rom. x. 4.

In Christ the sinner, who regards personal participation in the favour of God as the highest of all the blessings of salvation, finds that which he would everywhere else seek in vain.

2. If we ask the Apostle what Christ has done and is yet doing to this end, we find that even the Lord's coming in the flesh is regarded by him as connected with the judgment of sin, but at the same time with the restoration of the sinner.* He likewise directs us to His precept and example as the rule of the new life.† But, above all, he presents, as of supreme importance, the death of Christ and His resurrection from the grave; two events between which he sees the closest connection.‡ Precisely this is the truth which he first proclaims to the Corinthian Church, and of which he has afterwards to remind them.§ On this account he directs them, that he may present in a single sentence the burden of all his preaching, to Jesus Christ the Crucified.‖ Yet he does not attach any less value to the life of the Lord in His humiliation than to His life in glory. Let us see how he insists on the connection of both with the work of salvation.

3. That Christ has truly died is nowhere proved by Paul, because, equally with his resurrection from the dead, it was never doubted. But so much the greater stress does he lay upon the fact that He must suffer;¶ and far from finding therein only a mysterious lot, he

---

* Rom. viii. 3, 4; 1 Tim. i. 15. † Gal. vi. 2; Phil. ii. 5.
‡ Rom. iv. 25. § 1 Cor. xv. 3, 4.
‖ 1 Cor. i. 23; ii. 2; Gal. vi. 14. ¶ Acts xxvi. 23.

presents the Lord's giving of himself up for the suffering of death rather as an act of the highest moral significance; an act, however, in no degree arbitrary, much less separated from the whole life which preceded it. The later theological distinction between the active and passive obedience of Christ, is least of all to be justified by an appeal to our Apostle. The whole life of the Lord is for him *one* act of obedience, which finds its point of culmination in the death on the Cross.* He was not merely delivered,† but gave himself up,‡ according to the will and counsel of the Father; moved thereto by a love which passeth all understanding,§ and which, glorified in the unworthy, bears the character of grace (2 Cor. viii. 9). Precisely because the Lord's death *is* such a moral act, is it a sacrifice which could be only well pleasing to God ‖ On account of this perfect harmony of both, the Apostle could elsewhere say, God spared not His own Son, but delivered Him up for us all (Rom. viii. 32).

4. As to the true nature of this sacrifice, Paul does not leave us long in uncertainty, when he writes that God set forth the Saviour as a propitiatory sacrifice (ἱλαστήριον)¶ through faith in His blood. For the same reason, he calls the Christ in His death the Paschal Lamb of Christians;** for the Paschal Lamb also was originally a sin-offering. Manifestly he implies that by the self-sacrifice of Christ was really effected

---

*Phil. ii. 8.   † Rom. iv. 25.   ‡ Gal. i. 4; ii. 20.
§ Ephes. iii. 9.   ‖ Ephes. v. 2.
¶ Rom. iii. 25.   ** 1 Cor. v. 7.

that which was symbolically represented by the Mosaic ritual.* Such a covering of guilt before the eye of God was necessary on God's side for the manifestation ($ἔνδειξις$) of His righteousness, on account of the passing over of sins formerly committed;† and indispensable for man, in order to procure for him that blessedness which he had forfeited through his sins. There is, consequently, according to Paul, a direct connection between the Lord's self-surrender and the sins of the world.‡ Not merely by means of sinners, but on behalf of sinners,§ did Christ die; and the consequence which this act at once brings with it is, that these sinners, on their entering into communion with Him, no longer need to die for their sins. Death is the punishment of sin, and precisely from this revelation of wrath are they delivered in Christ. Through His blood we have redemption ($ἀπολύτρωσις$), and this is concentrated in the forgiveness of sins, because in forgiveness is already contained (in principle) every other blessing.

5. The extent of this blessedness will be treated of hereafter. Here the remark must suffice, that all righteousness ($δικαιοσύνη$) before God which is the portion of the believer, is a fruit of justification ($δικαίωσις$), and this, in turn, is the fruit of the shed blood of atonement. No wonder that the price at which such a salvation was obtained is called by the Apostle great;‖ a statement which is only apparently

* Colos. ii. 17.   † Rom. iii. 25.   ‡ Rom. iv. 25.
§ 1 Cor. xv. 3.   ‖ 1 Cor. vi. 20.

in conflict with another statement, namely, that we are saved by grace. The former has reference to the immediate cause; the latter to the source and primary cause of the benefit. If we ask the Apostle as to the connection between the propitiatory death of the Lord and the justification of the sinner, he replies that the righteousness in which alone the sinner can glory is an imputed righteousness, that of the righteous and holy Christ. By virtue of the law of an innermost communion of life, all which is ours becomes His, and all which is His becomes ours. He is treated as personal sin,* in order that sinners in Him may be regarded and treated as righteous. He bears on the cross the curse of the law, in order that He may redeem us therefrom.† Paul, then, doubtless conceives of the Lord as dying *on behalf of* ($\dot{υ}πέρ$), and at the same time *instead of* (*e.g.*, $ἀντίλυτρον$), but of whom? In general he mentions "ungodly ones,"‡ without any restriction assures that God wills the salvation of all men, and glories in Christ as the Mediator—a word which is found only with Paul, and in the Epistle to the Hebrews—between God and men.§ But especially is it Christians who know that One has died for them all, in consequence of which they now all live.‖ There is no contradiction between the one statement and the other, if we simply observe a just distinction between the purport and the fruit of the Lord's propitiatory death. Where this fruit is

---

* 2 Cor. v. 21. † Gal. iii. 13. ‡ Rom. v. 6.
§ 1 Tim. ii. 4, 5. ‖ Rom. viii. 32; 2 Cor. v. 15.

enjoyed, there the self-surrender of the Son of God is at the same time regarded as the highest revelation of a love which saves the sinner by the self-same act by which it righteously condemns the sin. The idea of a conflict between God's righteousness and grace is of later origin, by some centuries, than the writings of Paul.

6. The expiation of sin (the ἱλαστήριον implies an ἱλασμός) is the basis of the reconciliation (καταλλαγή) between the sinner and his holy Creator. In this latter sense, also, the atonement proceeds from God, who on this account is called not only "the Justifier"[*] but also "the Reconciler;"[†] and who has in Christ reconciled the whole world (κόσμος) to himself, yea, has brought about a reconciliation in divided humanity,[‡] and has thus restored peace between heaven and earth.[§] For the enmity existed not on the part of God, but only on the part of men,[||] and is now, by the manifestation of the highest love, vanquished and slain on the Cross.[¶] Thus, by the death of the Lord, the broken bond is restored as well between man and his God as between Jew and Gentile, and the power of darkness vanquished and led in open triumph;[**] while, on the other hand, all believers are, through the love of Christ, united into one holy communion.[††].

7. The community, whose guilt is thus covered, is

---

[*] Rom. viii. 33, ὁ δικαιῶν.
[†] 2 Cor. v. 19, ὁ καταλλάσσων.
[‡] Ephes. ii. 14-16.
[§] Colos. i. 20
[||] Rom v. 10; viii. 7.
[¶] Ephes. ii. 14-16.
[**] Colos. ii. 14, 15.
[††] Ephes v. 25-27.

The Work of Redemption.

at the same time in Christ delivered from the dominion of sin; the forgiveness of sin, the great aim of His death, becoming thus the means to a higher aim—the sanctification of all His people. In the Apostle's conception, the one is inseparably connected with the other. On the one hand, it is certain that Christians, on account of the death of Christ, no longer need to die for their sins; on the other hand, that they have, with Him, died to sin.* The communion of faith between the Lord and them, symbolised in baptism—is so close that because He has died to sin they may be regarded as being, with Him, dead to sin.† The cruel tyrant, whose wages they once received (in Him), has, in consequence thereof, lost all right to them, and all claim upon them. They are henceforth to regard themselves as dead for sin, that they may live exclusively to God. The death of Christ is not only the life of His people, but also the crucifixion of their old man. Their spiritual unity with Him, in other words, renders it impossible for them any longer to serve sin; through faith in Him, its dominion is, in principle, destroyed. That this is indeed the ultimate aim of the Lord's death we are reminded by the Apostle in various ways in his epistles from the earliest to the latest. (Compare, for example, 1 Thess. v. 10; Gal. i. 4; ii. 20; 2 Cor. v. 15; 1 Cor. vi. 20; Rom. viii. 4; Ephes. v. 2; Colos. i. 22; Titus ii. 14.) Not only to individuals, but to the whole community, does this

---

* 2 Cor. v. 14, Greek text. † Rom. vi. 3-11.

gracious purpose extend.* And it can and will be so much the more certainly accomplished, as Christ is not merely the Dead but also the Risen Christ.

8. Far from separating for a moment the Lord's death from His new life, Paul rather brings both facts into such close connection, that one might almost doubt which of them takes with him the first place. It is at least certain that for him the resurrection is not of *less* soteriological importance than the death of our Lord on the Cross; yea, that in some respects he gives the pre-eminence to the former.† No wonder, since the resurrection is, on the one hand, the pledge for the certainty and perfection of the completed atonement; on the other hand, the fountain, the type, and the power of the new life of those who are spiritually one with the risen Christ.

9. We cannot feel surprise that Paul, not less than Peter (Sec. xxvii.), places in the foreground‡ the resurrection of the Lord; yea, with warmth defends it.§ For him also was the new life born out of the contemplation of the Risen One, and the whole Gospel stood or fell for him with the recognition of this indisputable fact.‖ Yet we must not overlook — what has indeed been arbitrarily denied — that he everywhere regards this resurrection very definitely as a restoration to the life of the body and a return from the grave. What does it matter

---

* Ephes. v. 25-27.   † Rom. iv. 25; v. 10; viii. 34.
‡ Acts xiii. 30; xvii. 3, 31; xxiii. 6; 2 Tim. ii. 8, and often elsewhere.
§ 1 Cor. xv. 4-8.   ‖ 1 Cor. xv. 14-20.

The Work of Redemption.

—if this is not to be firmly held—that he declares to the Corinthians that the Lord was buried, that He rose again the third day, and appeared unto His disciples? Between the continuance of a purely spiritual existence which He has in common with all the dead, and "our justification,"* no rational connection is conceivable. Besides, only a real, *i.e.*, bodily resurrection, could be a prophecy of the future bodily resurrection of believers.†

10. Through the resurrection, the Lord, after a previous humiliation, has passed over into a condition of glory in which—troubled no more—he can henceforth live unto God.‡ Only twice does the Apostle mention the circumstance of the visible ascension of the Lord;§ in the latter of these (as it would seem), in opposition to his descent into the region of the dead, which we found also referred to by Peter (Sec. xxvii.) So much the more emphatically does he dwell upon the work of the Redeemer in heaven, which—not less than His earthly life—is consecrated to the salvation of His people. Exalted to the right hand of the Father, He intercedes for them; ‖ but also hears and answers them when they on their part call upon Him.¶ He reigns not only through the moral power of the truth, but immediately and personally in the Church; and is, at the same time, head over all for the Church, to make all subject to His power,** and to fill all

---

* Rom. iv. 25.
† Rom. viii 11; 1 Cor. xv. 21-23; Phil. iii. 21, and following.
‡ Rom. vi. 10. § 1 Tim. iii. 16; Ephes. iv. 7-10. ‖ Rom. viii. 34.
¶ 1 Cor i. 2; 2 Cor. xii. 8, 9; compare Acts xxiii 11.
** Ephes. 1 20-23.

things with His life-giving energy.* Only He is excepted from this dominion, from whom it proceded, to whom it will one day return,† and in whose glorification it must of necessity end (Philip. ii. 9-11).

11. The exaltation of Christ is consequently for himself the reward of His perfect obedience, but for all His people the fountain of salvation. Reconciled to God through His death, they are saved by His life, yea, themselves live in consequence of the power which unceasingly flows forth and passes over from the head to the members.‡ Thus it is seen that the saving work of Christ on earth and in heaven is, according to the view of Paul, an inseparable whole,§ and that through the obedience of the second Adam the disobedience of the first is more than made good.‖ His righteousness becomes theirs; but only in so far as through faith they have become personally one with Him. As opposed to an impossible justification by works of law, there is brought in a perfect justification by grace alone *through* faith, not even *for the sake of* faith.¶ The doctrine of the Apostle concerning the nature and fruits of this faith, we shall presently proceed to investigate.

[On the exaltation of Christ, see the eloquent chapter of the author's *Christologie*, pp. 241-272 of the German translation. Hamburg, 1864.] For particular points, C. Tischendorf, *Doctrina Pauli, Ap. de vi mortis Chr. satisfactoriâ*, Lips. 1837. Lipsius,

---

* Ephes. iv. 10.
† 1 Cor xv. 24-28.
‡ Rom. v. 10; Ephes. i. 22, 23.
§ 1 Tim. iii. 16.
‖ Rom. v. 18-21.
¶ Rom. iii. 28.

die Paulin. Rechtfertigungslehre, Leipz. 1853. Rauwenhoff, *Disscrtatio de loco Paulino qui est de* Δικαιώσει, Lugd. Bat. 1852. Bok, *Disquisitio exhib. Pauli. Ap. doct. de τῇ* 'Απολύτρωσει, Amstel. 1856. Bonnard, *de la Resurrection de Christ dans la Theol. de St. Paul*, Strasb. 1862.

POINTS FOR INQUIRY.

Is development and progress to be observed in the Apostle's teaching concerning the work of redemption?—What is the sense of 1 Cor. i. 30?—What is suggested by 1 Cor. i. 13*b* (compare Colos. i. 24) as to the significance of the Lord's death upon the Cross?—Investigation of the most important soteriological utterances.—Wherein lies, according to Paul, the connection between the atoning and the sanctifying efficacy of the death of the Lord?—In what relation does the death and resurrection of Christ stand to the death and resurrection of his people?—In what sense is Christ called "the first fruits of them that are fallen asleep," 1 Cor. xv. 20?—What is the teaching of Ephes. iv. 8-10?—What of Philip. ii. 9-11, as compared with 1 Cor. xv. 24-28?—**The opposition, Rom. x. 4-10.**

SECTION XL.

The Way of Salvation.

THE faith which thus justifies the sinner before God, consists in a confiding surrender of one's self to Christ, and an enduring communion with Him. It is a faith whose seat is the heart, whose author is God, whose manifestation is the new life, and whose priceless fruit is restoration into God's favour and friendship, with all its blessed consequences, even on this side the grave.

1. That faith alone opens the way to salvation is so emphatically expressed* by Paul, that no doubt as to his view is possible. An express definition of this faith (such, for example, as Heb. xi. 1) he has nowhere given, and we must, on this account, infer his conception of faith from scattered intimations. If we do this, we discover at once that with Paul faith is opposed, not to knowledge, but on the one hand to beholding,† on

* Acts xvi. 31; Rom. x. 10. † 2 Cor. v. 7.

The Way of Salvation.

the other to doubting.* Faith is consequently, with Paul, a firm assurance or conviction concerning things which, being either invisible or yet future, fall without the sphere of natural perception, and, consequently, cannot be proved thereby.

2. This faith, inasmuch as it justifies the sinner, has for its object, in the widest sense, God† and His promise—more definitely the Gospel,‡ and the saving truth therein revealed; but constantly, and above all, Him who is the great centre of this Gospel.§ Even where the Apostle speaks of the faith *of* Jesus Christ as the Christian's vocation,|| he has before his mind no other faith than that which is directed to Him as its *object*, and enters into the closest union with Him. Through this faith, however, is attained a living communion with Christ, in which we, so to speak, die with Him and rise to newness of life.¶ This faith surrenders itself unconditionally and confidingly to the Lord, and in turn receives from Him grace and strength.** Without doubt there is in this faith also an intellectual element, which recognises the death and resurrection of the Lord as indisputable facts;†† but these facts, and above all, Himself, it apprehends with the heart.‡‡ The heart is the proper seat of saving faith, which, preceded by an acquaintance with the Gospel, itself leads to a clear and certain knowledge

---

* Rom. iv. 20. † Rom. iv. 3-5, 24.
‡ Phil. i. 27; 2 Thes. ii. 13. § Acts xvi. 31.
|| Gal. ii. 16, 20; Ephes. iii. 12; Rom. iii. 26.
¶ **Rom.** vi. 6; Gal. ii. 20. ** 2 Cor. xii. 9.
†† 1 Thes. iv. 14. ‡‡ Rom. x. 10.

of the things which are freely given of God in Christ.[*]

3. The question how this grace arises and grows in man, Paul answers by pointing out that it is God who brings sinners to Christ.[†] He calls it on this account a faith of God's operation,[‡] and designates it a Divine gift of grace.[§] Without doubt faith comes by hearing,[||] but no planting and no watering can avail unless God give the increase.[¶] The strengthening of the faith is therefore enjoyed as a heavenly gift,[**] and the honour of spiritual growth is rendered exclusively to God.[††] Where God has mediately wrought this faith, there is received, as the fruit of believing, the Holy Ghost,[‡‡] who dwells not only in the whole Church,[§§] but also in each of its members individually,[||||] and unites them most intimately with God in Christ. This Spirit is Himself, at the same time a Spirit of faith:[¶¶] every special measure or every special gift of this faith which manifests itself in the Church is His work;[***] and on that account his enduring communion[†††] is for all Christians the blessing most to be desired.

4. The possession of this Spirit becomes manifest by the fruits thereof,[‡‡‡] and the new life is the development of the faith thus born. Less than perhaps

---

[*] 1 Cor. ii. 13; Colos. i. 9, 10; Phil. i. 9; 2 Tim. i 12.
[†] Colos. i. 12, 13.   [‡] Colos. ii. 12, 13.   [§] Phil. i. 29.
[||] Rom. x. 14-17.   [¶] 1 Cor. iii. 5-7.
[**] Ephes. iii. 14; 2 Thes. i. 11.   [††] 2 Thes. i. 3.
[‡‡] Ephes. i. 13; Gal. iii. 5.   [§§] 1 Cor. iii. 16.   [||||] 1 Cor. vi. 19.
[¶¶] 2 Cor. iv. 13.   [***] 1 Cor. xii. 9; Gal. v. 22.
[†††] 2 Cor. xiii. 13.   [‡‡‡] Gal. v. 22.

The Way of Salvation.

might have been expected, does the Apostle speak in an especial manner of repentance. Without doubt he proclaims it to Jew and Gentile,* and teaches that it is necessary even for Christians after falling anew into sin;† while for unbelievers it is, according to his view, absolutely indispensable, in order to come to the knowledge of the truth.‡ As a rule, however, he is speaking to believers as being now in truth converted,§ and therefore combines in one the demand for repentance and faith.‖ No wonder that man, through faith, is brought into an entirely new condition of life,¶ which gradually developes itself,** and attains its goal only when all that which is old has passed away, and the perfection set before the believer is attained.††

5. It belongs to the peculiarities of the Pauline doctrinal system that he describes the manifestation of the new life trichotomically, as a life in faith, hope, and love; and celebrates this last as the greatest of the three.‡‡ Faith, originally the gift of God as well as the act of man, becomes now a condition of life in which the new man continually moves,§§ yea, a principle which, in its most universal form, gives its true value to every action.‖‖ In its highest development it knows itself, even here on earth, sure of the love of God in Christ for time and for eternity, and thus is naturally one with that hope which is the

---

* Acts xxvi. 20. † 2 Cor. vii. 10. ‡ 2 Tim. ii. 25.
§ 1 Thess. i. 9. ‖ Acts xx. 21. ¶ 2 Cor. v. 17
** 2 Cor. iii. 18. †† Eph. iv. 14, 15.
‡‡ 1 Cor. xiii. 13; compare 1 Thes. i. 3; v. 8.
§§ 2 Cor. iv. 18; v. 7. ‖‖ Romans xiv. 23.

peculiar privilege of the Christian.* As faith has reference to that which is invisible, so does hope especially have regard to those things which are yet future, things which it sees not, but patiently expects.† Its foundation is the promise, its crown the fulfilment, its goal perfect redemption at the approaching coming of the Lord.‡ Since this hope is well-founded and sure,§ the Christian may rejoice in it in the midst of the greatest tribulation.∥ What an exceptionally important place hope occupies in the doctrine of Paul, is evident from many utterances of this Apostle.¶ Yet, above hope and faith rises, in his estimation, love, the crown, the first of all the fruits of the Spirit,** the natural consequence of faith,†† which, without it, is deprived of all value.‡‡ Universal love, also, and love of one's enemies, is emphatically commended;§§ but, above all, is the mutual love of believers the object of his highest praise,∥∥ since it is to be valued more highly than all gifts, yea, is the brief summary of all perfection.¶¶

6. In the new life, which in this manner reveals itself in a threefold form, there is by no means wanting a higher unity. It bears throughout the character of a thank-offering,*** whose final aim is the glorifying of God,††† and whose daily effort is increasing

---

* Gal. v. 5; Ephes. ii. 12.   † Rom. viii. 24, 25.
‡ Rom. viii. 19-23.   § Rom. v. 5; 2 Cor. v. 5.
∥ Rom. xii. 12.   ¶ *E.g.*, Colos. i. 27; Titus i. 1; 2 Tim. iv. 10.
** Gal. v. 22.   †† Gal. v. 6.   ‡‡ 1 Cor. xiii. 2.
§§ Rom. xii. 17-21; xiii. 8-10.   ∥∥ 1 Cor. xiii. 13.
¶¶ Colos. iii. 14.   *** Rom. xii. 1
††† 1 Cor. x. 31; Colos. iii. 17.

progress towards perfection.* It is, on the one hand, a life of liberty; on the other, of voluntary serving†—a life which is not under the law but precisely through which the ideal of the law is most beautifully realised,‡ a life of increasing conflict without doubt,§ but of a conflict with weapons to which at last the victory is assured‖—a life, it is true, still in the flesh, but one which is constantly more penetrated by the Spirit; no life of perfect holiness, but of the ever-continued work of sanctification; a school of exercise, and an arena, which Paul loves to represent under the image of the Grecian contests.¶ The imperfection of this condition, however, detracts in no respect from its worth. In Christ believers are here already in principle perfect,** and are in reality known and loved of God;†† yet this takes place not as though their sanctification, present or in prospect, were the ground, far less the meritorious cause, of their acceptance. The ground of their acceptance lies not within but outside of them, and grace remains the fountain of all. That God, however, notwithstanding their imperfection, and his inviolable holiness, can look upon them and treat them in Christ as righteous, is to be explained only by the fact that justifying faith, which unites them to Christ, is, at the same time, the living principle of renewal and sanctification, which sooner or later comes to full development.

* Philip iii. 12-14. † Rom. viii. 21; Gal. v. 13.
‡ Rom. iii. 31; viii. 2-4. § Gal. v. 17. ‖ Ephes. vi. 10-18.
¶ 1 Cor. ix. 24-27; 2 Tim. iv. 6-8.
** Colos. ii 10. †† 1 Cor. viii. 3.

Paul teaches justification just as little on the ground of, as apart from, personal sanctification (ἁγιασμός).*

7. Even in the present life this living faith becomes the source of a blessedness which is represented by Paul under manifold forms. The justified sinner has peace with God, rejoices in tribulation, and cherishes an unfailing hope for eternity; so that he is rendered perfectly secure in regard to the past, the present, and the future † Justification (δικαίωσις) in the sense of Paul involves not merely, negatively, the notion of the cancelling of guilt, and of pronouncing absolved; but also, positively, the notion of perfect restoration into God's favour and friendship is intimately bound up with this idea.‡ [Justification embraces, consequently, the twofold idea of pardon and acceptance, Ephes. i. 5-7; Acts xxvi. 18.] On this account the idea of justification is closely connected with another, that of adoption into God's family (υἱοθεσία), which is here constantly represented as the peculiar privilege of believers. The conception of a judicial act (in declaring the sinner righteous) underlies the idea of justification; as also is the case in the adoption of him who was originally a servant to the rank and rights of a child, by which an end is for ever put to all slavish service and fear. Yet here, also, the juridical has at the same time its ethical side. As the justified man necessarily lives in righteousness, so are the adopted children at the same time followers of God, who, above all things, in love reveal the

---

* Compare Rom. vi. 22, 23   † Rom. v. 1-5.   ‡ Rom iv. 3-5.

The Way of Salvation.

Father's image in themselves, resemble Him in spirit,* and thereby become inwardly meetened for being his heirs.† This Divine adoption, however, is a blessing which is perfectly realised only in the future, when redemption (ἀπολύτρωσις) shall be enjoyed in its whole fulness.

Compare R. Engels, *Geloofsroem*, 1835. W. Verwey, *Wat God in ons werkt door J. C. volg. Paulus*, W. in L. 1839, iv. Dr. Berlage, *Disq. de form. Paul.* Πίστις Ἰ. Χρ. *significatione*, Lugd. Bat. 1856. Wernink, *Exeg. Stud. over* Πίστις *en* Πιστεύειν *in het N. T.*, Rott. 1858. Coops, *Proeve eener juiste verklaring der woorden: regtvaardigen en regtvaardigheid*, Rott. 1861, pp. 18, and following.

POINTS FOR INQUIRY.

WHAT is the sense of 2 Cor. v. 7?—Explanation of the different formulas Πίστις Ἰησοῦ Χρ., ἐν Ἰησῷ Χρ., εἰς Χρ., &c.— The nature of faith as it is seen in the life of Paul himself, Gal. ii. 19-21.—Is the Holy Spirit, according to Paul, the author, or the fruit of faith?—Life after the spirit, in contradistinction from life after the flesh.—The Christian armour, Ephes. vi. 10-18.—What peculiarity has the doctrine of Paul in regard to υἱοθεσία?—The full compass of the idea of the ἀπολύτρωσις.

* Ephes. v. 1, 2. † Rom. viii. 17.

SECTION XLI.

The Church.

ALL who thus believe form together a spiritual body, whose members are by baptism most closely united to each other and to the Lord; and, through the Supper of the Lord, evermore confirm their fellowship with Him and with each other. Notwithstanding all diversity, is this communion of believers one; notwithstanding all imperfection, holy; spite of all temporary barriers, destined to receive all nations into its bosom; and amidst all conflict, assured at last of the victory in Him whose glorious revelation it expects with ardent longing.

1. Until now we have, under the guidance of the Apostle, contemplated the individual man in fellowship with Christ. In order, however, to estimate at

its true value salvation in Him, we must direct our glance to the union of all those who enjoy the same; in other words, must become more intimately acquainted with the Pauline Ecclesiology. It is especially the Epistles to the Corinthians and that to the Ephesians which here render us important service. But others, also, especially the pastoral Epistles, contain important hints.

2. The church or congregation of the Lord (the two are identical in the language of Paul) is by no means the same as the kingdom of God and of Christ. This latter is a perfectly spiritual society, whose ideal will be fully realised only in the future;* the former is the union of those who are already here on earth, through faith and love, members of that kingdom. When Paul speaks of the church (ἐκκλησία), he means either the Christian assembly which is gathered at a particular place,† or the union of confessors of the Lord in a town or province,‡ or the totality of *all* believers.§ With his presentation of this last we have especially to do.

3. How high the position assigned to the church by Paul, is evident from the names by which he designates it, and by the figures under which he describes it. It is for him the church of God,‖ of Christ,¶ the dwelling-place of the Holy Ghost.** In the first case it is compared by preference to a

---

* 1 Cor. vi. 10; xv. 50; Ephes. v. 5.
† 1 Cor. xiv. 19, 35; compare also the ἐκκλησίαι κατ' οἶκον.
‡ 1 Thess. i. 1.   § Ephes. i. 22.   ‖ Acts xx. 28.
¶ Ephes. v. 25-27.   ** 1 Cor. iii. 16.

cultivated field,* in the second to a body,† in the third to a temple; although the different images here and there run into each other.‡ This last especially is his favourite analogue.§ God is the master builder, Christ the foundation; doctrines of different degrees of value are the different materials of which it is built up, and the household of God are believers, as those who have been received into God's family.‖ If on one occasion the Apostles and prophets of the New Testament are also called the foundation of the building,¶ this is only because they proclaim Christ, who is the living centre. In Him the building of God stands immovably firm, even though within its walls are included objects of the most diverse value.** With no less fitness is set forth the diversity—along with the higher unity—in the church, under the figure of a body. The former is undeniable, but also necessary; the latter is founded in the relation of all to the same Christ. As He can be called, in relation to the whole humanity, the second Adam; so also for the whole church the living, governing, and protecting Head.

4. Into this church the entrance is by means of baptism,†† the initiatory rite of the New Testament, as circumcision was of the Old.‡‡ As Israel,

---

* 1 Cor. iii. 9. † Ephes. i. 23. ‡ Ephes. ii. 20; iv. 16.
§ 1 Cor. iii. 9-17. ‖ Ephes. ii. 19-22. ¶ Ephes. ii. 20.
** 2 Tim. ii. 19, 20.

†† [Debemus in baptismo agnoscere spirituale lavacrum; debemus illic testimonium remissionis peccatorum et renovationis nostræ pignus amplecti; sic tamen relinquere et Christo et Spiritui sancto suum honorem, ut nulla pars salutis ad signum transferatur.—Calvin. in 1 Pet. iii. 21.]

‡‡ Col. ii. 11, 12.

in passing through the Red Sea, was brought into the closest relationship to Moses, so are believers by baptism brought into the closest relationship to Christ, especially as dead and risen. They are called to confess his name, and to form together a spiritual body. Nowhere, indeed, does the Apostle ascribe to baptism in itself a magical power [*i.e.*, without any just proportion between cause and effect], but to such an extent a mystical power, as it is truly a bath of regeneration and renewing,* where—as was the case, as a rule, with those baptized in the Apostolic age— it is believingly desired and received. Baptism is just as little a mere symbol, as it is an immediate source of blessing; it is, however, the mediate cause of spiritual purification, only because it is received in connection with faith.† Infant baptism‡ is in Paul's Epistles just as little forbidden as enjoined; he, however, lays evident stress upon the fact that there is but *one* baptism, as there is but *one* saving faith (Ephes. iv. 4).

5. As upon baptism, so also upon the Lord's Supper, more light is shed by Paul, especially in the First Epistle to the Corinthians, xi. and xii., than by

---

* Tit. iii. 5. [The washing of baptism introduces typically to the new *state* of the believer (compare Matt. xix. 28), while the "renewing of the Holy Ghost" is the efficient cause of the new *life*.—Tr.]

† [Spiritus Dei est qui nos regenerat, facitque novas creaturas ; sed quia invisibilis et occulta est ejus gratia, visibile in baptismo ejus symbolum conspicitur.—Calvin. in Tit. iii. 5]

‡ [Compare, however, the words of Calvin :—Quodsi communi generis humani sorte eximuntur fidelium liberi ut Domino segregentur, cur eos a signo arceamus? si Dominus in Ecclesiam suam eos verbo admittit, cur signum illis negabimus?—Calvin. in 1 Cor. vii. 14.]

any other Apostle. His account of the institution of the Supper* is the oldest which has come down to us, and is the more important since he received the knowledge thereof directly—though mediately—from the Lord (ἀπὸ τοῦ Κυρίου). The Lord's Supper is for him evidently a breaking of bread for the commemoration of the Lord's atoning death, a commemoration ordained by Himself, and to be observed, after earnest self-examination, and in a worthy manner, by His church unto the end of the ages.† But no less is it for him, through the signs of the Lord's body and blood, a feast of innermost communion with the Lord and all His people.‡ It is worthy of notice that baptism and the Supper are at least once mentioned by him in one breath, and placed upon a level;§ though naturally the combining of the two under a sacramental idea is of later origin.

6. The church, which is thus separated from the world by baptism, and by the Supper more closely united to its head, remains *one*,∥ spite of all diversity of gifts, powers, and offices, which manifest themselves in the midst of it.¶ Whilst Paul, in regard to the universal priesthood of believers (1 Pet. ii. 9) throws out only hints,** he is, on the other hand, much more explicit than Peter, where he is called to give directions as to the inner organism of church life.††

---

* 1 Cor. xi. 23-26.   † 1 Cor. xi. 26-29.
‡ 1 Cor. x. 16, 17.   § 1 Cor xii. 13, compare x. 2-4.
∥ Ephes. iv. 1-6.   ¶ 1 Cor. xii. 4-6.
** As, for instance, Rom. xii. 1.
†† Rom. xii. 4-6; Ephes. iv. 11; the Pastoral Epistles.

The Divine origin of the different offices[*] is for him as fully established as the calling of each member of the church to employ the gifts received for the common edification.[†] To this latter end must all be made subservient; even the relative value of the different *Charismata* is very definitely made to depend thereupon.[‡] A sharp line of distinction between the ordinary and extraordinary gifts of the Spirit is nowhere drawn by the Apostle; but he calls upon all to strive in the way of love after the possession of the highest and best gifts.[§] The factious man in the church, on the other hand, falls under the Apostle's severe rebuke,[||] less even on account of his heterodoxy than on account of his egotistic party machinations.

7. While the church is thus one, it is, at the same time, called to holiness, and in reality merits the name of a living church in so far as it corresponds to this ideal. On this account are the highest distinctive titles of ancient Israel bestowed upon it—holy, elect, beloved, &c. Since Paul conceives of the church ideally, there is nowhere made in his teaching a prevailing distinction between the outward and the true church, although he by no means overlooks the distinction between nominal Christianity and living faith.[¶] As a rule, he seeks and finds the power of darkness, not within the church, but outside of it;[**]

---

[*] 1 Cor. xii. 28; Ephes. iv. 11; Acts xx. 28.
[†] 1 Cor. xiv. 26.   [‡] 1 Cor. xiv. 39.
[§] 1 Cor. xiii.   [||] Tit. iii. 10, 11.
[¶] Rom. ix. 5; 1 Cor. iv. 20; 2 Tim. ii. 19, 20.   [**] Colos. i. 13.

and precisely on this account rebukes, with the greatest severity, by word and deed, every manifestation of impurity within it,* while he regards it as beneath the dignity of believers to bring their mutual differences before the forum of an unholy world.† All impurity belongs, as a rule, to that past with which they have no more to do:‡ in principle the church is already perfect, by virtue of its inner oneness with Christ,§ and in reality is destined evermore to become so.‖

8. United and holy, the church is, regarded in the spirit of Paul, also in the highest sense catholic. The middle wall of partition is fallen away; out of the spiritual blending of the different nations, races, and degrees, arises now the true people of Christ.¶ Paul will not, however, in a revolutionary spirit, assail the institutions of social life, much less with one blow overthrow the whole order of the social community.** His own treatment of Onesimus, no less than his directions for servants, wives, and children, proves the very contrary.†† From woman her subordinate place is not taken away,‡‡ but, on the contrary, the duty of subjection is enforced by a humbling reference to the history of the fall;§§ yet, nevertheless, her spiritual emancipation is proclaimed in the Gospel of Paul,‖‖ for the ground-tone of this Gospel is liberty—

---

* 1 Cor. v. 1, and following. † 1 Cor. vi. 1-3.
‡ 1 Cor. vi. 10-11. § Colos. ii. 10. ‖ Ephes. v. 25-27.
¶ Ephes. ii. 14-16; Colos. iii. 11; Tit. ii. 14.
** 1 Cor. vii. 20. †† Ephes. v. and vi.; Colos. iii; 1 Tim. vi.
‡‡ 1 Cor. xi. 16. §§ 1 Tim. ii. 14. ‖‖ Gal. iii. 28.

a liberty* which is bound by no narrow forms, and bows only before the highest law of love.† On this account it is adapted to the case of all, as it is also destined to be brought to all,‡ and was also, even in the beginning, brought to them without restriction of person.§

9. The final triumph of such a kingdom of God cannot reasonably be doubted. The Church itself serves as a pillar and basis of Christian truth, because it confesses and preserves it.‖ In the midst of all conflict, there is, therefore, assured to it a continual growth, a glorious completion of the edifice, but upon the foundation which was laid once for all.¶ Absolute perfection of the kingdom of God before the parousia Paul does not indeed seem to promise; yea, there is no ground for maintaining that he looked for the realization of the ideal in 1 Cor. xiii. 9-12 before the time when the Church has entered upon its eternal state. But yet he sees the fulness (the pre-determined totality of the nations) of the Gentile world soon about to enter into the kingdom of God,** and in consequence thereof all Israel, as a nation, converted and saved.†† Especially from this last event does the Apostle expect, in the spiritual sense of the word,

---

* Gal. iv. 9. † 1 Cor. viii-x.; Rom. xiv.
‡ Rom. x. 14-17. § Colos. i. 23.
‖ 1 Tim. iii. 15. ¶ Ephes. ii. 22; iv. 15, 16.
** [In accordance with this expectation of the Apostle is the petition occurring in the Burial Service of the Church of England: "That it may please Thee, of Thy gracious goodness, shortly to accomplish the number of Thine elect, and to hasten Thy kingdom."—Tr.]
†† Rom. xi. 25, 26.

a new life from the dead.* "Totius generis humani sive mundi conversio comitabitur conversionem Israëlis."—(Bengel.)

10. The prospect of so great events can, from the nature of the case, awaken only lofty expectations. Hope occupies in the Pauline theology a place not much inferior to that which it occupies in the Petrine. The cherishing of the desire for the appearing of Christ, is a prevailing characteristic of the Christian life.† Consciously or unconsciously, all is looking for redemption,‡ and this redemption will not always, yea, will not even much longer, need to be waited for.§

Compare, besides the articles on Baptism and the Supper in Herzog's *R. E.*, Doedes *de leer van het Avondm.*, Utr., 1847, pp. 47 and following. Halley, *On the Sacraments*, London, 1844, 51. Lechler, *l. c.*, pp. 120 and following.

POINTS FOR INQUIRY.

The ἐκκλησίαι κατ' οἶκον in the Pauline Epistles.—Whence the further development of the idea of the Church in the Pauline than in the Petrine theology?—Sense, truth, and beauty of the illustration in 1 Cor. iii. 9-17, compare Ephes. ii. 19-22; 2 Tim. ii. 19.—The unity of the Church, 1 Cor. xii. 26.—The teaching of Ephes. iv. 5, as compared with 1 Cor. xii. 13.—Peculiar character and diverse value of the various charismata.—Union of liberty and order in the Pauline ideal of the Church.—Pauline teaching with regard to Baptism and the Supper, compared with that of the Synoptical Gospels.—The earnest of the future completion of the kingdom of God.

* Rom. xi. 15.
† 2 Tim. iv. 8.
‡ Rom. viii. 19-23; 2 Cor. v. 2-4.
§ Rom. xiii. 12.

SECTION XLII.

The Future.

THE plan of salvation is fully realized with the return of the Lord, an event which Paul, with the whole Apostolic Church, looked for as near at hand, and which—though by no means without previous warning—will at last happen unexpectedly. The resurrection of the dead, the final judgment, and the annihilation of every power which raises itself against Christ, are associated with this great event; in consequence of which the perfected kingdom of Christ finally passes over into the everlasting kingdom of God.

1. As Peter (Sec. xxvii.) and all his fellow Apostles, so does Paul also cherish the living hope of the speedy advent of the Lord. Nowhere does he reckon himself among those who shall be raised at the last day;

repeatedly, on the contrary, does he express himself as cherishing the expectation he may himself even be among the number of those who shall remain alive at the coming of the Lord.* In later epistles, also, the idea is found (expressed, indeed, with less of vivacity) that something similar is possible;† although the more his earthly activity hastens to its close, the more does he become reconciled to the thought of dying before the hour of the Lord's coming shall have arrived.‡

2. However near the parousia may be, the precise period thereof is not to be determined. Unexpectedly,§ but not without warning, it comes: the Man of Sin precedes the coming of the Son of Man. Remarkably enough, the most explicit teaching concerning the Antichrist is found in one of the oldest of all the epistles of our Apostle;‖ another proof how deeply this idea is rooted not only in the teaching of the Lord,¶ but also in the theology of the Old Testament, and the whole cycle of thought of the Apostolic age which was therewith so closely connected. The obscurity of the Apostle's teaching upon this point arises especially from the fact that he is manifestly alluding to circumstances and phenomena in social and civil life, which were much better known to his contemporaries than to later readers. But ever do we find expressed in this mysterious form the equally deep as acceptable

---

* 1 Thes. iv 15; 1 Cor. xv. 51, 52. † 2 Cor. v. 4; Philip. i. 11.
‡ Philip. i. 21-23; 2 Tim. iv. 6-8. § 1 Thes. v. 22.
‖ 2 Thes. ii. 1-12. ¶ Matt. xxiv. 23-24.

thought, that the highest and more individual concentration of the kingdom of darkness will precede the manifestation of the kingdom of light, and that the last mighty effort of the former immediately borders on its deepest humiliation.

3. This humiliation takes place at the last parousia, which the Apostle evidently conceives of as a visible Christophany, which to some extent resembles the glorious Theophany at the giving of the law on Horeb. Christ comes, in a glorified form* from heaven, whither He has ascended.† That He comes henceforth to dwell and reign upon earth, Paul does not say. He expects rather that the believers who remain alive until the parousia will be caught up into the air to meet the coming King of the kingdom of God‡ ($\epsilon\dot{\iota}s$ $\dot{a}\pi\acute{a}\nu\tau\eta\sigma\iota\nu$), in order thus to be ever with Him. On earth or in heaven remains undecided—perhaps we should best express the mind of the Apostle if we should venture on the supposition that, for the eye directed to this future, the boundary-line between the two will be found to vanish. Only from 1 Cor. vi. 2, 3, does it seem to follow that he conceived of believers as taking an active part in the final judgment, the execution of which is now to be accomplished.

4. At this parousia, proclaimed with majesty,§ all

---

* Philip. iii. 20, 21. † 1 Thes. i. 10; iv. 16; 2 Thes. i. 7.
‡ [To meet and return with Him, Acts xxviii. 15. The word itself is clearly a reminiscence of that preserved in Matt. xxv. 1.—Tr.]
§ 1 Thes. iv. 16; compare 1 Cor. xv. 52.

who have fallen asleep in Christ shall be at once raised, and those yet living so changed that, without dying, all that is mortal in them shall be, so to speak, swallowed up of life.* This is the first resurrection,† of which mention is made by Jesus, as also by the Apostle John.‡ It takes place at the end of the age, after a state of separation—beginning immediately at death—has preceded it. Since the Apostle so soon expects the parousia, it is intelligible that he should not more fully describe this condition; he looks beyond it to the end. Only thus much can be said with certainty, that he conceives of this state by no means as a state of lifeless unconsciousness, but as a state of liberation, of repose, and of desirable happiness,§ and cherishes the assurance that death, just as little as life, can separate him from God in Christ.‖ With this departed spirit is the risen body united at the parousia. By the resurrection of the dead, the Apostle understands just as little, merely the immortality of the spirit, as he does a material restoration of the flesh: to the opposite of this latter view he even gives emphatic expression.¶ He conceives of the restoration of the whole man, in consequence of which the liberated spirit receives a heavenly body,** which, essentially identical with the earthly, is yet furnished with very different properties.†† The

---

* 2 Cor. v. 4. † 1 Cor. xv. 23; 1 Thes. iv. 16.
‡ Luke xiv. 14; Rev. xx. 5. § Philip. i. 21-23.
‖ 1 Thes. v. 10; Rom. viii. 38, 39; xiv. 7-9.
¶ 1 Cor. vi. 13; xv. 50. ** 2 Cor. v. 1. †† 1 Cor. xv. 42-44.

possibility of this resurrection, which is founded on God's omnipotence, Paul finds symbolized in the kingdom of nature.* Its certainty is established for him objectively by the resurrection of Christ,† and subjectively by the testimony of the Holy Ghost.‡ Of its glory we obtain in some measure a conception, when we think of the infinite difference between the present earthly and the future heavenly condition. §

5. The end of the present dispensation is, at the same time, the manifestation and glorification of the dominion of Christ on earth.‖ All foes are annihilated, Antichrist also ;¶ last of all death,** which up to this hour had yet preserved considerable power. Here we must, as it would seem, place the general resurrection of the just and the unjust, which Paul also on one occasion†† refers to. But now certainly takes place the great final judgment, which Paul everywhere and always associates with the coming of the Lord.

6. The final judgment takes place on a prophetic day [compare 2 Peter iii. 8] of righteous retribution upon those who have obdurately rejected the Lord.‡‡ The last judgment, absolutely universal,§§ is passed upon deeds good and evil, and is carried out according to the most equitable standard.‖‖ God judges the

* 1 Cor. xv. 36-41.   † 1 Thes. iv. 14 ; 1 Cor. vi. 14.
‡ Rom. viii. 10 ; 2 Cor. v. 5.
§ 1 Cor. xv. 45-49 ; compare Phil. iii. 21.   ‖ 1 Cor. xv. 24, 25.
¶ 2 Thes. ii. 8.   ** 1 Cor. xv. 26.   †† Acts xxiv. 15.
‡‡ 2 Thes. i. 7-10 ; Rom. ii 5.
§§ 2 Cor. v. 10.   ‖‖ Rom. ii. 6-10.

world by Christ,* at whose coming all secret things shall be brought to light.† Nowhere does Paul teach a final determining of the lot immediately upon death: the day of the Lord's coming is for him the day of perfect retribution,‡ and not before this day will also the future glory of believers be manifest in its full brightness.§

7. Highly blessed is the lot which on that day awaits the redeemed of Christ. It is, on the one hand, a perfect deliverance from all that oppresses, especially from the body of death;‖ on the other hand, a knowing,¶ beholding,** enjoying††—a triumphant reigning with Christ‡‡—of which we can here form but a very imperfect conception.§§ No other Apostle describes the blessedness of the future so often as a personal participation in the triumph and dominion of Christ‖‖—a phenomenon which admits of a perfect explanation psychologically, but at the same time an expectation which is based¶¶ on nothing less than the word of the Lord himself. Without doubt, even according to the conception of Paul, this future blessedness and glory has its variously modified degrees;*** but all the children of God will be, in their measure, His heirs, and joint-heirs with Christ.†††

---

* Acts xvii. 31; 2 Tim. iv. 1.   † 2 Cor. iv. 5.
‡ Rom. ii. 16.   § Rom. viii. 23; Colos. iii. 3, 4.
‖ Rom. viii 2, 23.   ¶ 1 Cor. xiii. 12.   ** 2 Cor. v. 7.
†† 1 Thes. iv. 17.   ‡‡ 2 Tim. ii. 12.
§§ Rom. viii. 18; 2 Cor. iv. 17.   ‖‖ 2 Cor. iv. 10; Rom. v. 17.
¶¶ Matt. xix. 28.   *** 1 Cor. xv. 40-44; 2 Cor. ix. 6.
††† Rom. viii. 16, 17.

The Future.

8. On the future misery of the unconverted he speaks less in detail, but expresses himself with equal definiteness. It concentrates itself for him in banishment from the presence (face) of the Lord and in the experience of His terrible displeasure,[*] without a distant prospect of diminution or removal of the chastisement. The doctrine of the ultimate salvation of all finds only apparent countenance in Paul. Guided only by the ring of the words—and not judging after the analogy of faith—one might perhaps find apparent support for this doctrine in certain isolated expressions of the Apostle, divorced, it may be, from their context; but even in this case, every one who decides impartially will admit that dark or vague hints are to be interpreted by the light of more distinct assertions, and not the converse. The second Adam gives life, indeed, to all, but under a moral condition which is not submitted to by all;[†] the last homage rendered by all to Christ[‡] may be a forced homage; and if God is one day to be all in all,[§] the connection of the words forbids us to think of others than those who have already become subjects of the kingdom of God. Mercy, which is shown toward the Gentile and Jewish[||] world in their totality, can be manifested consistently with the perishing of individuals; and the reconciliation of heaven and earth[¶] is accomplished, even though obdurate opponents[**] are not converted and saved. Enough, that,

---

[*] 2 Thes. i. 8-9; Rom. ii. 9-12.
[‡] Phil. ii. 10. [§] 1 Cor. xv. 28.
[¶] Ephes. i. 10; Colos. i. 20.
[†] 1 Cor. xv. 22.
[||] Rom. xi 32.
[**] 2 Thes. ii.

according to the conception of the Apostle, no single hostile power will be able permanently to make a stand against the kingdom of God in its triumph, and that to such an extent every discordant note will be swallowed up in the song of redemption.* "The problem here set before us is, so to conceive of the ἀπώλεια that God's being all in all may yet be in the widest sense possible, and so to explain this latter that the idea of the ἀπώλεια remains unchanged" (Kling).

9. When the kingdom of Christ is completed, the kingly office of the Son has accomplished its special purpose;† and although all things continue to retain their separate existence, they end *for* and *in* God, in the undivided fulness of His being.‡ Upon Paul's conception of the nature of God, full light arises only now we have reached the end of his doctrinal development; and from all we have learnt at his mouth concerning the diverse activity and reciprocal relationship of the Father, the Son, and the Holy Ghost, this conception of God bears no traces of a dry deistical, far less of a superficial Unitarian character. The Trinity of revelation already hinted at by the Apostle Peter,§ comes with him ever afresh into the foreground,|| and however little he is given to abstract

---

* [No more is necessary—in order to realise to its fullest extent all that the Scriptures tell us of the melancholy condition of those that perish—than to be shut up without hope of relief to the consciousness of what one has become through his own transgression, in spite of a provided atonement.]

† 1 Cor. xv. 27. ‡ 1 Cor. xv. 28; compare Rom. xi. 36.
§ 1 Peter i. 2. || 1 Cor. xii. 4-6; 2 Cor. xiii. 13.

speculations, it is manifest that he not only ascribes to the Son of God a Divine nature and dignity (Sec. xxxviii. 4, 5), but also ascribes* to the Holy Spirit a self-consciousness and freedom of action which necessarily leads to the idea of a personal existence. To the Son of God and the Holy Spirit, as distinguished from the Father, he ascribes an activity which is conceivable only if the divinity of their nature is recognised and acknowledged. Yet it is especially the glory of God the Father which is the final goal of all that He accomplishes—even through the Son and Holy Spirit—for the salvation of the sinner.† The "*In majorem Dei gloriam*" is the highest watchword, if of any, certainly of the Pauline theology.

Compare our *Christologie* II., p. 289 and following, with the literature there adduced. The Dutch works of J. P. Briet, *Eschatologie*, II. p. 198, and following. On the Antichrist, 2 Thes. ii., Chantepie de la Saussaye, *Bijbelstudiën*, I., p. 65. The German works of Rinck, *die Lehre der H. S. vom Antichrist*, Elberf., 1867. H. G. Hoelemann, *die Stellung St. Pauli zu der Frage nach der Zeit der Wiederk. Christi*, in his *Neue Bibelstud.*, Leipzig, 1866.

POINTS FOR INQUIRY.

NATURE, basis, and value of Paul's teaching concerning the time of the Parousia.—What is to be understood by the ἀνθρ. τ. ἁμ., 2 Thes. ii. 3, and what by τὸ κατέχον, ii. 8. ?—

* 1 Cor. ii. 10; xii. 11.   † 1 Cor. viii. 6; Rom. xi. 33-36.

Have the ideas of the Apostle concerning resurrection, judgment, &c., been always the same, or is a modification to be observed in them?—Explanation of 2 Cor. v. 1-4, as compared with 1 Cor. xv. 51-54.—What difference is there, according to the teaching of Paul, in the condition of departed believers before and after the Parousia of the Lord? —Does Paul distinguish between a first and second resurrection?—Doctrine of the *Apokatastasis* in the Pauline theology.—Connection of the whole Pauline theology with his conception of the nature of God.

SECTION XLIII.

Kindred Types of Doctrine.

However full and original the Pauline conception of Christianity may be, it stands by no means alone. Its prelude is found in the address of Stephen, its undertone in the writings of Luke, its echo in the Epistle to the Hebrews; and that in such a manner that this last is, on the one hand, a faithful reflex of the spirit of the great Apostle of the Gentiles, and on the other hand, an independent link in the chain of the earliest development of Christian doctrine.

1. In the days of the Old Testament, the founder of Mosaism (Sec. iv.) stood, in a certain sense, alone upon his intellectual and religious height. Paul, however—the Moses of the New Testament—has friends and spiritual kinsmen, who, each in his own manner, proclaim the great principles of Paulinism, although without attaining to the height of the great

Apostle of the Gentiles. One only do we find among them who speaks with such force and dignity that many have thought they discerned in his voice that of Paul himself. Nevertheless, the others may not be overlooked.

2. Like other great men, Paul also has his forerunner. We find him in Stephen, with whom we become acquainted, Acts vi. and vii. The foundation-thought of Paulinism was enunciated by him. Although not fully expressed, and certainly not developed to its consequences, it was yet very forcibly indicated. This is equally evident from the accusation brought against him,* as from single traits in his defence, in which we find a sharp polemic against the same obdurate Judaism, against which Paul afterwards rose so powerfully to plead. In Stephen we see a first, as yet feeble, effort for the emancipation of the youthful Church from the fetters which afterwards cramped her; he had a prescience of that which Paul clearly perceived. In him, also, is apparent that higher intellectual aspiration by which Paul is so greatly distinguished from Peter and his spiritual kinsmen. His hour of death, finally, makes an impression upon the raging Saul, which the latter, even as Paul, never forgot.†

3. The Third Gospel and the Book of Acts, which we ascribe, without any hesitation, to Luke, manifest also a Pauline character. Let any one, for instance, observe the universalistic spirit which they breathe;‡

---

* Acts vi. 14.   † Acts xxii. 20.
‡ See, for example, Luke iii. 38; Acts viii. 35-37; compare i. 8.

the contents and form of many words and deeds of the Lord, which Luke records with manifest preference, and which, in a certain respect, anticipate the Gospel of Paul;* the similarity of their accounts of the institution of the Lord's Supper, of the manifestation of the Lord which was granted to Peter, and other characteristics which furnish indubitable proof that both these writings proceed from the immediate circle in which the Apostle moved.

4. The most manifold traces of Paulinism are, however, to be found in the Epistle to the Hebrews; which has been not inaptly termed "a jewel of the Christian canon," and which, even in itself, but especially in relation to the fundamental ideas of Paul, is worthy of the most careful attention. It is naturally not in place here to enter upon the great number of isagogical questions raised by this epistle—or, rather, treatise. In our judgment, it was written between the years 60 and 70, for those Jewish Christians dwelling in Palestine—not in the Diaspora—with the distinct purpose of pointing out to them how much more excellent is the new covenant than the old, and thereby arming them against the danger of falling back into Judaism. The main thought—the theme— is given, chap. viii. 8-13;† and the way in which this is developed is so surprising, that it will be found worth the labour to become a little better acquainted with the doctrinal peculiarities of this writer. The old

* Luke vii. 50; cap. xv.; xvii. 7-10; xviii. 14; compare Acts xiii. 38-39.

† Compare Jer. xxxi. 31-34.

covenant he places high, but the new dispensation of grace he places yet much higher, and dwells most emphatically upon the vocation of those for whom the former has been abolished and the latter established in its place.

5. How highly the Old Testament is estimated by this author, is at once evident from the point of view in which he regards it from the beginning. It is the fruit of special revelations of God,* which He has formerly granted "at sundry times and in divers manners." Without doubt, He is for him the God of peace,† who reveals His grace in a wondrous manner in the death of His Son;‡ yet this side of the Divine nature does not here come distinctly into the foreground. With the doubtful exception of xii. 7, the name of Father is only once given to God,§ and then in a sense which reminds us of a particular Old Testament utterance. He appears here rather as judge of all, whose judgment upon apostate sinners is terrible,‖ but whose reward of the good required by Him is equally certain.¶ His grace is not passed over in silence;** but the terrors of the Lord, much more than His grace, form the lever and incentive to action. On the other hand, manifest emphasis is laid upon the omnipotence and faithfulness of God, the Creator of all things out of nothing,†† who also doeth wonders,‡‡ and can swear by no one higher§§ than

* Heb. i. 1. † Heb. xiii. 20. ‡ Heb. ii. 9.
§ Heb. xii. 9; compare Num. xvi. 22.
‖ Heb. xii. 23-29; compare Heb. x. 26-31.
¶ Heb. vi. 9, 10; xi. 6, 26. ** Heb. iv. 16; xii. 15.
†† Heb. xi. 3. ‡‡ Heb. ii. 4. §§ Heb. vi. 13.

Kindred Types of Doctrine.

himself; the living God,* as opposed to lifeless idols; in a word the Lord†—just as Christ was before (vii. 14) extolled as *our* Lord—upon whom all things are absolutely dependent.‡ His glory is that of a Divine hypostasis (self-existent being), reflecting itself in the Son,§ and communicating itself by the Holy Ghost, who is here, however, regarded rather as a gift than as a giver.‖ The Trinitarian distinction in the nature of the Godhead is not here so unambiguously brought out as in the theology of Paul or even of Peter. At least, the indication of the [distinct] personality of the Holy Spirit, which has been supposed to be present in iii. 7, ix. 8, x. 15, is more or less doubtful.¶

6. Since such a God has already revealed himself in the Old Testament, it is no wonder that our author prizes very highly the original record of such revelation, especially on account of its prophetic character. He so often introduces Old Testament citations, that his writing in this respect occupies the same place among the Epistles as the Gospel of Matthew among the Gospels. Here and there, no less than Peter, he expresses his own ideas in Old Testament words, without directly citing them as such.** It is, indeed, the Holy Ghost himself who is introduced as speaking in Holy Writ: the expressions *Scripture* and *Word of God* here cover precisely the same ideas.†† And not alone the Hebrew original, the Alexandrine

---

* Heb. ix. 14; xii. 22. † Heb. viii. 2. ‡ Heb. vi. 3.
§ Heb. i. 3. ‖ Heb. ii 4; vi. 4; x. 29.
¶ Compare the use of προϊδεῖν, Gal. iii. 8.
** Heb. xii. 12; xiii. 6. †† Heb iii. 7; x. 15.

translation also, is clothed for the writer of this Epistle with great authority. More closely than any other Apostolic writer does he follow the version of the Seventy; so far, indeed, as to adopt from them even an erroneous rendering—the translation of אָזְנַיִם by σῶμα (x. 5). With slight exception (x. 30) he attaches himself to this version even in the form of his argumentation;* at the same time, he regards rather the spirit than the letter of the words, which he often cites from memory. The whole of the Old Testament is for him one constant reference to the Messiah, whom, by virtue of his peculiar system of hermeneutics, he finds, where more modern exegesis would possibly not even seek Him. From his typico-symbolic stand-point he understands without difficulty of the Messiah even that which primarily was certainly not spoken definitely of Him.†

7. To the narratives, likewise, of the Old Testament he attaches an especial value, because he sees in them not only the account of memorable deeds, but also suggestive types of higher things. Thus, Joshua,‡ as also Melchisedec,§ is for him a type, *i.e.*, a prophetic symbol of the person and work of the Redeemer. On the one hand, he warns against unbelief and disobedience by pointing to the example of the people of Israel ‖ and of Esau;¶ on the other hand, he exhorts to perseverance in the Christian

---

* Heb. ix. 16, 17.
† See, for instance, Heb. ii. 13*b*; compare Isaiah viii. 18.
‡ Heb. iii.   § Heb. vii.
‖ Heb. iv. 1 2.   ¶ Heb. xii. 16, 17.

Kindred Types of Doctrine. 349

race, by pointing to the saints of the old covenant as pre-eminently patterns for believers.* Great stress does he lay upon the spiritual unity of believers of the old covenant and those of the new;† and since precisely this element of faith is for him the highest manifestation of the religious life, he accords also to Rahab, Samson, and others, a place which, measured simply by a moral standard, they would possibly not have deserved. In the high estimate he forms of the dignity of believers under the old covenant, and in the use he makes of sacred history, his practice coincides in a remarkable manner with that of Paul and Peter.‡ Like the latter, also, he mentions with honour the example of Sarah.§

8. In the religious history of Israel, it is especially the sacred rites—notably the sacrifices—on which this writer dwells with manifest preference. The Divine origin of the sacrificial ritual is here everywhere presupposed;‖ and even prayer and alms are regarded from the point of view of sacrifice (v. 7; xiii. 16). Not all kinds of sacrifice, however, are here dealt with; the author directs his attention especially to propitiatory sacrifices and sacrifices for sin—between which he makes no further distinction—as well as to those by which the old covenant was once inaugurated.¶ The great day of Atonement is for him especially important;** as, moreover, whatever concerns

* Heb. xi.   † Heb. xi. 39, 40.
‡ Rom. iv.; 1 Cor. x.; 1 Peter iii.   § Heb. xi. 11.
‖ Heb. xi. 4; compare Heb. v. 4.
¶ Heb. x. 19-21.   ** Heb. x. 1; xiii. 11.

the different acts of the sacred ritual, as the shedding of the blood and the bearing of it for sprinkling into the innermost sanctuary (ix. 22-24). The sanctuary itself is for him a feeble image of the higher heavenly reality (viii. 5), and the high priest who enters therein, performs a symbolical action which stands in immediate connection with the pacification of the conscience burdened on account of guilt.

9. Nevertheless, however great the value of all this —which is evidently described by the writer of the epistle *con amore*, and, as it were, from his own observation—it was, and remained, far from sufficing. It is true the law was proclaimed through the ministration of angels,* but it contains only the shadow, not the substance, of things from its stand-point yet future.† Sacrifice, also, can never sanctify (τελειῶσαι) him who presents it : that is to say, through this the moral goal, for which it is required and offered, is never attained. It is, moreover, offered by priests who, themselves subject to sin and death, continually succeed each other. ‡ It was, besides, only of temporary effect, and must, for this reason, ever be renewed.§ Above all, it procured forgiveness only for sins committed through ignorance, and could produce only Levitical, no higher (moral) purity.‖ It was able, therefore, to preserve the transgressor in communion with the theocratic nation, but could not possibly restore the broken communion between God

---

* Heb. ii. 2 ; compare Gal. iii. 19 ; Acts vii. 53.
† Heb. x. 1.   ‡ Heb. vii. 23, 27.
§ Heb. ix. 25 ; x. 1-4.   ‖ Heb. ix. 13, 14.

Kindred Types of Doctrine. 351

and the sinner.* Thus, it had its highest significance, not as an adequate means of atonement, but as a prophetic symbol: the whole order of Old Testament worship is designed to point to that better thing which is yet future.† No wonder that the old covenant was from the beginning destined to be only of transitory duration.‡ It was, indeed, relatively firm,§ but not immovable.‖ On the contrary, even the prophets had proclaimed a new covenant, an immovable kingdom,¶ and naturally, he who remained at the stand-point of the law, or returned to it, came thereby into conflict with the word and spirit of this old covenant itself. This latter has fulfilled its destiny and attained its ideal in the new; and Christians are consequently the true Israel. The relation in which this true Israel stands to the Church of Gentile Christians is passed over in silence in this epistle. The object of the writer is only to convince Jewish Christians that return to a worship which they had forsaken would be simply an exchange of the greater for the immeasurably less.

10. The dignity of the new above the old dispensation is also manifest from the exalted nature of the person who founded the new covenant. It belongs to the peculiarities of our epistle that this writer, yet more than Paul,** enters upon the way of comparison in order to present before his reader the glory of Christ. He exalts Him (A) far above all saints of the

* Heb. x 4.   † Heb. ix. 8.   ‡ Heb. viii. 13; x. 9.
§ Heb. ii 2.   ‖ Heb. xii. 27
¶ Heb. viii. 8-13; xii. 26, and following.   ** Rom. v. 12-21.

old covenant;* (B) above the high priest, who was weak, sinful, and mortal;† (C) above the mediator of the old covenant, with whom he stands related as the son to the bond-servant of the house;‡ (D) even above the angels, the mediators through whom Moses had received the law.§ As such, He has a more distinguished name than they—that of Son and Lord; performs a higher work than the angels, and must also receive from them the homage of adoration.‖ He is even—upon the support of a very important declaration in the Psalms¶—here termed *God*, and regarded as the mediate cause of creation; the ground of the continued existence of all things, the effulgence of the glory of God.** "God finds himself again, and reflects himself in the Son as His other self" (Tholuck). That from such a Christologic standpoint the personal pre-existence of the Son is understood, even though it be indicated but in a passing way,†† is self-evident.

11. Our author defends the true humanity of the Lord in such a manner that his Christology bears an equally antidocetic character, as, for example, that of Luke's Gospel. Among the testimonies for this glorious truth we must not reckon Heb. ii. 16, since nothing more is there said than that He takes up the case, not of angels, but of Abraham's children. But of so much greater weight is the explicit statement

* Heb. xii. 2.
† Heb. v. 1-3; vii. 23.
‡ Heb. iii. 1-6
§ Heb. i. and ii.
‖ Heb. i. 4, and following.
¶ Heb. i. 8.
** Heb. i. 3.
†† Heb. ix. 26.

Kindred Types of Doctrine. 353

that He became partaker of the flesh and blood of the children of men,* a declaration which was early used by the Church Fathers as a weapon against the Docetæ. Equally remarkable, from this point of view, is the mention of the days of the flesh—of the strong crying and tears of the Lord ;† and of His descent from Judah.‡ Far from being regarded as of no importance, the fact of the Son's being truly man is here brought into immediate connection with the work of redemption itself. He can relieve man's misery only by personally sharing it ;§ and consequently, only by virtue of a unity of nature, can raise his brethren to his own holiness and blessedness, and afford to them the highest example and pattern.‖

12. As true man, nevertheless, the Lord was absolutely not raised above temptation to sin. In no single epistle of the New Testament is His liability to temptation more unequivocally expressed than here.¶ The sufferings of Jesus were, on this account, of great importance, not only for humanity, but also for Himself. Suffering was the great means by which He himself was made perfect, and entirely fitted for His exalted position ; yea, by which He became the ideal of humanity.** Remarkable, again, from this point of view is the special value the writer attaches to that which took place in Gethsemane.†† Naturally, he does not imply that the Sufferer was raised from

---

* Heb ii. 14, παραπλησίως, prorsus. † Heb. v. 7.
‡ Heb. vii. 14. § Heb ii. 16-18.
‖ Heb ii. 11 ; xii. 2. ¶ Heb. iv. 15.
** Heb. ii. 5-9 ; compare Ps. viii. 4, 5. †† Heb. v. 7-9.

unholiness to holiness, but only that through temptation He was raised to the highest possible degree of perfection. Even the recognition of such a faith in God as that through which alone He could stand at the head of a bright succession of heroes in the faith,[*] proves of itself how much he was in earnest as to the true and holy humanity of the Lord. Manifestly, he seeks to bring Him as closely into contact with humanity as this can take place without prejudice to the unconditional acknowledgment of his Godhead.

13. The dignity of the Lord's person stands, according to our Epistle, in immediate connection with His work. Precisely as Son of God was He able to be not merely the highest revelation of God,[†] but also the founder of a new and better covenant. Of this better covenant He became the surety,[‡] *i.e.*, security that it shall certainly be fulfilled. The original word ($\xi\gamma\gamma\upsilon\sigma s$) does not mean that He answers to God for the making good of our obligations, but that He answers to us for the fulfilment of God's promises: not of the payment of a debt is the question here, but explicitly of the founding of a covenant. Only he who is led away by the sound of the words, can here find occasion to speak of the "surety-sufferings" of Christ. It is simply said that in Christ is given to us the pledge of the covenanted promises. In support of this assertion, the eye is directed much less to the prophetic and kingly offices of the Lord than to

---

[*] Heb. xii. 2.   [†] Heb. i. 1.   [‡] Heb. vii. 22.

Kindred Types of Doctrine. 355

the high-priestly functions which He had already discharged on earth and now continues in heaven.

14. The value of the work of the Lord on earth as high-priest of His people, is shown in the form of a sustained opposition between the sacrifice presented by Him and the sin-offerings of the Old Testament. It has, above all things, a more exalted character than these. If there the blood of bulls and of goats was presented, here it is the priest who offers himself by a. moral act of most unconditional obedience. Even the coming of the Lord into the world is the fruit and sign of this obedience,* which attains its glorious culmination in His voluntary death upon the Cross.† To the form in which this death was endured, our author attaches, in itself, no special value. It seems as though, in order as long as possible to spare his Jewish readers the terrible word, he mentions the cross only in passing, and towards the end ‡ of his epistle, and would reconcile them to the thought of Golgotha by the suggestive allusion to the Lord's having there symbolically suffered without the gate.§ There is less stress here laid upon bodily suffering than upon the blood-shedding ($αἱματεκχυσία$) regarded as a personal act; less upon passive suffering than upon the tasting, proving, experiencing of death in all its bitterness.‖ This death is not simply a lot but an act, just as little arbitrary on the part of the Lord as of the Father. On the contrary, this act bears a character perfectly worthy of God; in the ordaining

* Heb. x. 5. † Heb v. 8, 9. ‡ Heb. xii. 2.
§ Heb. xiii. 12. ‖ Heb. ii. 10.

of it according to His will, there were motives which in the highest degree became Him who ordained it.* Therein the grace of God became manifest ;† and in consequence thereof Christ becomes not merely the pledge, but also the mediate cause of salvation.‡

15. This sacrifice has, moreover, a higher aim than all which preceded it. It was not, like these, in part presented for the offerer's own sins,§ but exclusively on behalf of others. The innocent and voluntarily-shed blood becomes a ransom ($\lambda\acute{u}\tau\rho o\nu$), by which an everlasting redemption ($\lambda\acute{u}\tau\rho\omega\sigma\iota\varsigma$) is not only symbolized, but in reality brought in. As a sacrifice, Christ takes away‖ sins, in which statement is implied that He has first taken them upon himself: the taking away (ôter) is a consequence of taking them upon himself (porter), in the sense of making expiation for them, as the sacrificial victim symbolically did for the sins of the offerer.¶ This is especially manifest where the writer says** the death of the Mediator was necessary for the forgiveness of sins which were committed under the first covenant but were not yet expiated; and he thus ascribes to the sacrifice of the Lord a so-called retro-active effect.†† Such an operation of this sacrifice were absolutely inconceivable if anything less than an objective expiation had here taken place. In order to bring this about, the blood-shedding of

* Heb. ii. 10, 17; x. 10. † Heb. ii. 10.
‡ Heb. v. 9. § Heb. vii 27.
‖ $\dot{\alpha}\nu\alpha\phi\acute{e}\rho\epsilon\iota\nu$, Heb. ix. 28. ¶ Compare Isaiah lui 11.
** Heb. ix. 15. †† Heb. ix. 26

Christ was indispensable; but even this would not have been able to effect its object, had it not been, at the same time, the highest moral act of unconditional obedience. For this offering He was qualified by the eternal Spirit which was in Him,* and in this sacrifice He is accepted as representing His people who, now spiritually united to Him, are well pleasing to the Father.† For each of them‡ has He tasted death—*on their behalf*, in the sense that they are now delivered from this punishment of sin. But precisely on this account there remains for the man who obstinately despises Him, no more propitiatory sacrifice.§ In any case, the Levitical sacrifice is for ever abolished, and Christ cannot be offered a second time.

16. But so, also, does this sacrifice produce richer fruit than all which have preceded it. The Lord himself was thereby rendered inwardly perfect, and led up by this path to glory. At the same time He thus became meet to be a Saviour for His people, because, by virtue of innermost sympathy, He entered wholly, so to speak, into their condition.‖ As concerns them, our author expresses their privilege in a peculiar manner when he says they are, by this one offering, for ever *made perfect*.¶ It is not easy perfectly to define the whole meaning of this word (τελείωσις). Thus much is at once clear, that it must be understood not in a purely subjective, but in an

---

* Heb. ix. 14. † Heb. ii. 11.
‡ ὑπὲρ παντὸς, Heb. ii. 9. § Heb. x. 26.
‖ Heb. ii. 16-18. ¶ Heb. x. 14.

objective sense, and must be clearly distinguished from the sanctification of believers. Christians are sanctified (ἁγιαζόμενοι) as being separated from the world and consecrated to God through the holy Christ, who sanctifies them (ὁ ἁγιάζων).* But, as such, they are already perfect, *i.e.*, they have become in principle all that they should be. The τελείωσις includes consequently the Pauline justification (δικαίωσις) and likewise redemption (ἀπολύτρωσις); it is the restoration of the normal condition of man before God, with all that follows therefrom. They are thus assured of the purging (καθαρισμός)† of their sins—a word by which their perfect deliverance not merely from the *dominion*, but, above all, from the *guilt* of sin is indicated. Thus brought into a state of peace and freed from an evil conscience, they can now serve God without fear of death; the more so, since the devil, who had the power of death, has been morally destroyed ‡ by the death of Christ. Yea, even suffering need no more trouble them; it is no longer a punishment but a chastening, a sign of God's fatherly good-pleasure.§ To the throne of grace they may draw near with confidence,‖ as children led unto glory,¶ *i.e.*, now made partakers of the perfection which they already in principle possess, and placed in a position corresponding thereto.

17. No wonder that a sacrifice through which so much blessing is obtained has a so much more enduring power than all others; and then, also—in

* Heb. ii. 11.   † Heb. i 3.   ‡ Heb. ii. 14.
§ Heb. xii. 5-11.   ‖ Heb. iv. 16.   ¶ Heb. ii. 10.

opposition to these—needs never more* to be repeated. In the new covenant everything is eternal,† and the kingdom of God an immovable kingdom.‡ It has been wrongly inferred from the references in Heb. vi. 4-6, ix. 15, x. 26, that this writer taught only forgiveness of those sins which had been committed before conversion. As the person,§ so also the work of Christ‖ has in his eye an ever-abiding worth; and precisely the warning against a sin which is never to be forgiven, presupposes that for lesser transgressions, which are the fruit of remaining weakness, no similar judgment is to be apprehended. The less so, because the work of propitiation, once accomplished on earth, is unceasingly continued in heaven.

18. The heavenly activity of the Lord began with His glorification in heaven, to which, on account of its symbolic importance, the highest value is attached in this epistle. Manifestly, the ascension is here regarded as a fact accomplished once for all.¶ Heaven itself is a definite locality,** with which the innermost sanctuary of Israel's temple could in some sense be compared; or rather the heavenly things themselves are invisible realities, of which the earthly form a resembling shadow. Into this heaven Christ is entered to present His own sacrificial blood before the presence of God;†† and Christians see the entrance thither opened through Him, since by His death the intervening veil

---

* Heb vii. 24-27. † Heb. ix. 12. ‡ Heb. xii. 28.
§ Heb. xiii. 8. ‖ Heb. ix. 12. ¶ ἐφάπαξ, Heb. ix. 12.
** ἐν ὑψηλοῖς, Heb. i. 3; viii. 1. †† Heb. ix. 24-27.

has been, as it were, removed from before their steps.*
The work which the Lord there accomplishes on their
behalf is indeed a priestly, but, at the same time, a
truly kingly one.† He represents them by intercession and sacrifice; but is, at the same time—like a
second Melchesidec‡—the priest-king, who is clothed
not merely with the highest honour, but also with
the highest power for the vanquishing of his foes,§
and for the perfecting of the salvation of his friends.‖

19. This vanquishing and this perfecting becomes
manifest at the impending Advent of the Lord. He
is now seen a second time, without henceforth
standing in any relation to sin, which He has here
put away (ix. 28). The certainty that this parousia
cannot be long delayed, gives an exalted importance
to the exhortation to patient endurance.¶ Then will
take place the judgment (according to ix. 27, *after*
death no doubt, but not on that account *immediately
after*) which, in accordance with the Old Testament
standpoint of this writing, is constantly ascribed
to God himself,** without, at the same time, any
mention of Christ. The resurrection of the dead is
here only incidentally referred to,††and is not more
fully treated of. It belonged, indeed, to the first principles,‡‡ sufficiently well known, and regarded, in all
probability, in the same light by this writer as by his
fellow-witnesses. Eternal judgment, however, is here

---

* Heb. x. 19. † Heb. vii. 25; ix. 24; x. 13.
‡ Heb. vii. § Heb. x. 13. ‖ Heb. ix. 28.
¶ Heb. iii. 6, 14; x. 36, 37. ** Heb. xii. 23; xiii. 4.
†† Heb. xi. 18, 19. ‡‡ Heb. vi. 2.

distinctly described as a terrible retribution upon faithless professors of Christ;* whilst the future blessedness of the faithful is represented as participation in the eternal Sabbath-rest of God.† Nevertheless, the eye of faith is not directed exclusively to a yet distant future. Already are the children of the new covenant brought into the closest relation with a perfected fellowship in heaven (xii. 18-24), to which belong the saints who have fallen asleep under the old covenant, but who only now, in communion with believers of the new, perfectly attain to their heavenly destination.‡ Yet a last shock is expected by the writer, in the destruction of the earthly economy, which, like the first dispensation, must pass away. *Then*, however, he sees the coming and remaining of those things which are immovable.§

20. From the possession of such great privileges arises naturally the obligation of corresponding duties. Like the Epistle to the Romans, that to the Hebrews has, after its theoretical, also its practical and paraenetic (hortatory) ‖ division. The conception of the Christian life as a life of faith, of hope, and of love, clearly underlies the teaching of this Epistle.¶ A powerful incentive to active faith is received from xi. 1-40; to patient hope, from xii. 1-13; to holy love, from xii. 14—xiii. 21.

21. The author's idea of faith is as pure as it is

---

* Heb. vi. 8; x. 26, and following. † Heb. iv. 9-11.
‡ Heb. xi. 39, 40. § Heb. xii. 26-28.
‖ Heb. x. 19; xiii. 21. ¶ Heb. vi. 10-12; x. 22-24.

susceptible of application to all believers of the old and of the new covenant. The great object of this faith is God,* whom he regards as faithful,† and beholds with the eye of faith.‡ In this, his faith, the believer has assurance, even in regard to those things invisible and as yet future;§ and, at the same time, he has confidence to draw near to Him from whom he is no longer estranged∥ by trembling fear. Without this faith it is absolutely impossible to enter into communion with God, and to become well pleasing to Him ; but precisely on this account is it also urgently necessary, not merely to persevere, but also to abound therein.¶ As now faith is assured of the reality of invisible things, so hope looks forward to the personal possession of the same in the future. To such an extent is this of importance, that the Christian confession may be called a confession of hope.** Entirely in the spirit of Paul, is it here, also, presented as an object of glorying,†† and as a source of patient endurance, but also of steadfast perseverance.‡‡ Through suffering is this hope purified, but by no means destroyed ; and this suffering itself is a chastening which comes from God, is imposed in love, ministers to higher aims, and ends in glory.§§ The love, finally, which is here commended, extends

* Heb. vi. 1. † Heb. x. 33. ‡ Heb. xi. 27.
§ Heb. xi. 1. ∥ Heb. iv. 15 ; x. 19-22.
¶ Heb. iii. 6 ; x. 22.
** Heb. x. 23. [According to the reading of the best MSS., including the Alexandrine and the Sinaitic.]
†† Heb. iii. 6 ; compare Heb. x. 35.
‡‡ Heb. xii. 1. §§ Heb. xii. 4-11.

to all,* and especially to the brethren,† and of these, again, most of all to the unfortunate and necessitous.‡ Even when the author is commending love, his words have an entirely Old Testament colouring.§ Beneficence and compassion are regarded as sacrifices: the confession of the name of God as the sacrifice of the lips.‖ From this love arises the exercise of all the duties of godliness, and notably those of brotherly exhortation and intercession,¶ of modesty and contentment,** those of obedience towards estimable leaders, and, finally, that of remembering those who are fallen asleep.††

22. The exhortations with which the author urges to the fulfilment of these duties are, in general, based upon the magnitude of the blessings received;‡‡ more especially upon the glorious fruits of fidelity, and the terrible chastisement of unfaithfulness.§§ Such an unfaithfulness he regards as possible where a very high degree of Christian knowledge and experience has been attained; although it cannot be shown that he looks upon those for whom this possibility has become a reality, as being originally true and living Christians. It is remarkable that in the classic text

---

* Heb. xii. 14; compare Rom. xii. 18.
† Heb. xiii. 1.   ‡ Heb. xiii. 2, 3.
§ Heb. xiii. 2 ; compare Gen. xviii 1.
‖ Heb. xiii. 15, 16 ; compare Rom. xii. 1.
¶ Heb. x. 22-24 ; xiii. 18.
** Heb. xiii. 4-6 ; compare Heb. xii. 16.
†† Heb. xiii. 7, 17.
‡‡ χάριν ἔχωμεν (let us have gratitude), Heb. xii. 28.
§§ Heb. vi. 4-10.

in his epistle, which treats on this matter* (Luther calls it "a hard knot"), neither their faith, their hope, nor their love is mentioned. Nevertheless, even for the most advanced, constant admonition is necessary;† and not in themselves, but in God's faithfulness, have they to seek the final cause of their rest and hope.‡

23. Reference to suitable helps, by means of which such a Christian life is nourished, is also not wanting in the Epistle to the Hebrews. In general, grace is mentioned as that by which the heart is strengthened;§ while the means of grace, also, are not passed over in silence. Only once does the author allude to the rite of baptism,‖ and on another occasion he indirectly alludes to the Supper of the Lord.¶ Especially is it recommended to believers, as a powerful means of help, to look back, on the one hand, upon their own former condition and life's experience;** on the other hand, and above all, upon the example of so many ancient heroes of the faith, who, as a cloud of witnesses, surround them in the Christian course. But if they should look upon them, they had yet greater need to fix the eye upon their great Leader,†† and to watch lest they fall from their former height.‡‡

24. From this brief survey of doctrines contained

---

* Heb. vi. 4-6.
† Heb. x. 32.
‡ Heb. vi. 10, 11 ; x. 36-39.
§ Heb. xiii. 9.
‖ Heb. x. 22.
¶ Heb. xiii. 10.
** Heb. x. 32 and following verses.
†† Heb. xii. 1, 2.
‡‡ Heb. xii. 15.

in the Epistle to the Hebrews, it is apparent how this epistle may be called "a faithful impress of the spirit of the great Apostle of the Gentiles." Without doubt, there is between the writer's mode of conception and that of Paul, a difference by no means insignificant. The Pauline doctrine of justification by faith, of spiritual communion with Christ, and the universal destination of Christianity, is here not so much as glanced at; the resurrection of the Lord receives only once a passing mention,[*] and the whole relation of Christianity to the old dispensation is presented in some measure differently from the manner in which it is represented by the Apostle of liberty. The whole conception of the doctrine of sin, above all, appears, in Paul's teaching, to be much deeper. On the other hand, however, it is at once manifest that the author—more than probably a richly-gifted disciple of the Pauline school—contradicts his master in no single respect, but rather attaches himself to the Apostle's doctrinal development, and in his own manner develops, apologetically, the main idea which Paul, in his Epistle to the Galatians, had developed polemically. If the conception of Christ as the second Adam is not found here, yet the truly human, together with the truly Divine nature in Him, is certainly no less insisted on in this Epistle. If with Paul the suffering Christ is more especially a sacrificial victim, while here He is at once priest and victim, the one conception satisfactorily complements the other. Without doubt,

[*] Heb. xiii. 20.

faith is here more especially regarded in its relation to God, while in Paul it is more especially regarded in its relation to Christ; but, in either case, faith properly has reference to the great Divine promises of salvation, whose living centre is Christ. In no case can it be shown that in our Epistle a radically Judaistic and a radically Pauline conception stand in irreconcilable antagonism (Baur). Many an essential difference is to be explained by the entirely exceptional condition of the reader and the definite aim of the writer; and, upon a sustained comparison with Paul, we believe that just as little is a harsh dissonance as an impersonal echo to be observed here.

On the Paulinism of Luke, see our *Life of Jesus*, I., p. 91. On the doctrinal ideas of the Epistle to the Hebrews in general, as well as in relation to Paul, our *Christol.*, N. T., p. 317-359, v. d. Ham.; *Diss. Theol.* (1847); Dale, *Sermons on the Epistle to the Hebrews;* but, most of all, the excellent monograph of Riehm, *der Lehrbegriff des Hebr.-briefs dargestellt*, &c., in 2 parts, Ludwigsb., 1858, 1859. On the Christology of this Epistle, a Latin *Programme*, by C. B. Moll, Halle, 1854, 1855. On the difficult place, cap. ix. 14, the *Diss. Theol.* of Boon Mesch, Lugd. Bat. 1825. On cap. xi., the *Diss. Theol.* of Huet, Lugd. Bat. 1824. On the whole Epistle, the *Bijbelstudiën* of D. Chantepie de la Saussaye, 3 parts, Leiden, 1860. See also v. Koetsveld, *Het Apostolisch Evangelie*, the Hague, 1865. Also the two appendices of Tholuck to his Commentary on this Epistle [*das A. T. im N.*].

POINTS FOR INQUIRY.

To what extent is the discourse of Stephen an anticipation of the Pauline position?—What Pauline elements have the writings of Luke, above those of Matthew and Mark?—In what relation does the investigation as to the doctrinal standpoint of the Epistle to the Hebrews stand to that as to its author?—His doctrine of God and His revelation. —Of man and of sin.—Of the person and work of the Redeemer.—Of the diversity and the connection of the Old and the New Testament. — Christ, as opposed to Melchisedec, Moses, and Aaron. — The Epistle to the Hebrews compared with the standpoint of the Jewish-Alexandrine theology of this period.

SECTION XLIV.

Result and Transition.

NOTWITHSTANDING all diversity of gift and of mental constitution between Peter and Paul and their fellow-witnesses, the unity of spirit between both is so manifest, that the latter, as well as the former, merits the name of a Pillar among the Apostles (Gal. ii. 9). The doctrinal development of Paul, as a whole, stands equally far above that of Peter as the development of Christianity itself in the Gentile world stands above the original Judæo-Christianism. As the doctrinal system of Paul affords the rich fulfilment of the promise given in the Petrine, so does it in turn afford the preparation and transition to the profound Johannine theology.

1. If we look back from the now completed Pauline circle of ideas upon the earlier contemplated Petrine ones, then nothing strikes us more than the greater

breadth of the former above the latter. The more surprising is it, when we observe that the independence of the Apostle's testimony, which fully entitled him to speak of *his* gospel, leads him in no single essential point into contradiction with the earlier testimony of his fellow-apostles. On the contrary, that right hand of fellowship which three of them extended to Paul and Barnabas* is the symbol of a living—and, precisely for this reason, anything but monotonous—unity. The essential difference is to be so satisfactorily explained—partly from the dissimilarity of the individuals, partly from that of the field of labour and of aim in the different witnesses—that it serves much more for the establishment than for the undermining of the Apostolic testimony. Nothing brings out more forcibly the superficial character—with all show of depth—of the modern-romantic reconstruction of the Apostolic age than an impartial study of the different Apostolic types of teaching in the light of isagogics and psychology.

2. The higher harmony of the Pauline with the Petrine type of doctrine detracts nothing from the rich originality of the former. It is nothing less than the first exceptionally successful attempt of a genial philosophic thinker, enlightened by a higher spirit, to reduce to a higher unity the infinite wealth of truth and life revealed in the Gospel. " Never had Christian truth been expressed with so much of wealth and of depth ; never had it put on a form as systematic and as rigorous. It is a totality of facts

* Gal. ii. 9.

and ideas in which everything is bound together and interlaced, and in which the infinite diversity of details reduces itself without difficulty to the unity of a central and fruitful thought, which is, as it were, the corner-stone of the whole edifice. One recognises in this powerful dialectic a spirit nourished by severe studies, and singularly trained to all the exercises of thought. Thus, the teaching of Paul marks an incontestable progress upon that of James and of Peter" (Bonifas). The Pauline Universalism stands related to the theology of Judæo-Christianism, as the spirit of the Reformation of the sixteenth century to the ecclesiastical piety of the Middle Ages. Yea, truly, " Paul serait le prince des philosophes, s'il n'était pas le plus grand des Apôtres " (A. Monod).

3. Yet the highest conceivable development of the Christian process of thought is to be found just as little in Paul as in Peter. The deepest insight into the mystery of godliness is not to be obtained in the way of acute logical development, but in the way of spiritual contemplation. In Peter, it is the voice of memory and experience that speaks ; in Paul, there is united with this last the power of Christian thought, which, where necessary, can also wield the weapons of a fine dialectic ; but it is only John who, with piercing eagle-gaze, penetrates into the deepest depths. The theology of Paul developes itself in a series of most remarkable antitheses ; but the complete reconciliation of these antitheses, which is in itself advantageous, is afforded only from the Johannine standpoint. Apparently, the difference between

John and Paul is much greater than between Paul and Peter. Especially the Epistle to the Hebrews seems to present *one* almost continual contrast to the Johannine ideas. Yet, the development of John's ideas will teach us that many a Pauline element here first attains to its full development, and that not a little which is testified by Peter and confirmed by Paul, is, if possible, by the Patriarch of the Apostles, developed from a yet higher point of view, and yet more profoundly conceived of.

Compare, in addition to works mentioned at end of Sec. xxxiii., the treatise of Tholuck in his *Vermischte Schriften*, II., p. 272-329, *Einleit. Bemerkungen in das Studium der Paul. Briefe*, &c. As also that of Paret, *Paulus und Jesus* in the *Jahrbb. für Deutsche Theol.*, 1858, I.

POINTS FOR INQUIRY.

THE assumed conflict of principles between Paul and his fellow-apostles tried before their own tribunal, Gal. ii.; compare Acts xv.—Comparative view of the Petrine and the Pauline theology in their main points.—Is there ground for ascribing, with Baur, to the Epistle to the Hebrews a reconciliatory tendency, with the view of harmonising Paulinism with the ideas of the Johannine Apocalypse?

THIRD DIVISION.

THE JOHANNINE THEOLOGY.

SECTION XLV.

General Summary.

THE doctrinal teaching of John, the Apostle of Love, occupies not merely the last but also the highest place in the succession of Apostolic testimonies, and to this extent sets the crown upon that which Paul, the Apostle of Faith, and Peter, the Apostle of Hope, had already placed in a clear light It is recognised from the Apostle's own utterances, preserved partly in the Gospel and Epistles, partly in the Apocalypse, which we shall proceed to examine singly, and precisely in this order. In the one and the other he proceeds from

Christ as a centre, and reveals in his peculiar individuality, on the one hand, an apologetic-mystical, and, on the other hand, an Israelitish-prophetic character.

1. As in the natural, so also in the spiritual domain, that which is noblest comes most slowly to perfection. Already have Peter and Paul deposed their written testimony, and left the scene of their earthly activity, before the testimony of John is heard. It is the fruit of personal reminiscence refined by inner contemplation, before which the past reproduces itself; and the mystery of the future also—in consequence of a new revelation—at once discloses itself. No wonder that the Church of all ages has attached the highest value to the testimony of the bosom friend of the Lord, the venerable and profound Apostle John. While the Petrine bears a Jewish-Christian, the Pauline a Gentile-Christian character, we here see the whole opposition between the Gospel and Judaism on the one hand, and heathenism on the other, recede entirely into the back-ground; and Christianity is regarded, in the fullest sense of the word, as the absolute religion. Thus, the highest point is attained; and, at the same time, the future development of Church and theology is sketched in broad outlines. The Petrine type is regarded by preference in the Roman Catholic, the Pauline in the Protestant development of Church and doctrine; the Johannine theology seems emphatically destined to become **the theology of the future.**

2. The doctrinal ideas of John we learn—yet more than in the case of Paul and Peter—exclusively from his own writings. Among these, the authenticity of the Apocalypse, even in the judgment of the Tubingen school, stands incontestably firm, while that of the Gospel and the First Epistle begins to come forth victoriously from the fiery ordeal of the latest attack. That also of the second and third epistles, although of subordinate importance for our purpose, can be satisfactorily defended. Illustrious names show that it is possible to be a truly scientific theologian and yet to regard as authentic *all* the writings which bear the name of John; while, on the contrary, it is ever more and more apparent that the Presbyter John, to whom in contradistinction from the Apostle, a part of these writings has been ascribed, is a highly problematic, perhaps imaginary, person.

3. The order in which the Johannine writings are to be examined is determined by the verdict of criticism as to the time of their composition. For us it is sufficiently certain that the Apocalypse was written, not under Nero, but under Domitian, and, on this account, after the Gospel and the Epistles. "The Johannine writings form a trilogy; the Gospel basis, the organic conformation, the final and eternal future of the Church: Christ who was, who is, and who is to come. The Gospel, the Epistles, and the Apocalypse" (Lange). In the contemplation of the Gospel as a source of knowledge for the Johannine doctrine, we must by no means take into account the utterances of the Johannine Christ, but exclusively those in

which the Evangelist himself appears as witness or defender.* (Compare Sec. xvii. 3.)

4. Scarcely do we, in the light of these utterances, take the first step in the domain of the Johannine theology, when it becomes apparent that it bears, both in point of contents and of form, a highly peculiar character. John stands entirely alone, without any of his fellow-witnesses having exerted on him any appreciable influence, such as, for instance, Paul did on the writer of the Epistle to the Hebrews, or Peter upon Mark. His theology, as we know it especially from Gospel and Epistle, bears the character less of a doctrinal development than of an animated witness. Not dialectics, but intuition; not the intellect, but the feelings; not the future, with its lofty expectations, but the present, with its priceless blessings, enters in the didactic writings of John ever anew into the foreground. Only on a single occasion† is here indicated the opposition between Law and Gospel which occupies so important a place in Paul; with John the Gospel stands not only in diametrical opposition to the law, but also immeasurably above it. The cause of this phenomenon is not difficult to discover. John probably never occupied so strictly legal a standpoint as, *e.g.*, James; much less experienced such a sudden transition from darkness to light as Paul. As the sun causes the

* John i. 1-18; ii. 21, 22; iii. 16-21 (?); iii. 31-36 (?); vi. 64-71; vii. 39; xi. 51, 52; xii. 14-16; xii. 33, 37-43; xiii. 1-3; xix. 28, 35-37; xx. 30, 31; xxi. 20.

† John i. 17.

blossom to unfold, so had the interview with Christ and the continued contemplation of Him* awakened his spiritual life with silent but mighty power; and of this inner life, his doctrine—so far as we can speak of a doctrine in connection with him—is at once the expression and the deciphering. No Apostle has expressed more profound ideas with less profusion of language. The vocabulary of John is comparatively poor, but the value of his experiences far surpasses that of their verbal exponent. " L'auteur ressemble à un grand seigneur, qui ne paye qu'avec de grosses pièces " (Godet). The inscription on Herder's monument at Weimar—" Light, love, life"—embodies also the fundamental idea of John's theology; but who has ever yet perfectly fathomed this in the spirit of the Apostle? This is the more difficult, since the different ideas are here much less distinctly separated than, for example, in Paul, and unconsciously flow into each other. The Johannine theology is less developed in breadth than in depth and height. Light and life, faith and knowledge, sin and the lie, truth and holiness are, with John, so intimately connected, that here, if anywhere, an entire separation of the doctrine of faith and of morals is absolutely impossible.

5. As the Pauline theology bears an anthropological (Sec. xxxiii. 4), so does the Johannine bear an especially Christological character. Without doubt, the Apostle proceeds in his doctrine from God, but only as

* John i. 40.

He is known in Christ. Upon the person of Christ, yet more than upon His work, is here manifest stress laid; the world, sin, the Church, the future, all is viewed in the light of the historic manifestation of Christ. As in James, the opposition between knowing and doing, and in Paul, that between sin and grace, so, in John, the contrast between darkness and death out of Christ, and light and life through Christ, is the axis around which all turns. The historic manifestation of the incarnate Word in the Gospel and Epistle, the future revelation of the glorified Son of man in the Apocalypse, is testified with a power and an emphasis which cannot be surpassed.

6. In the Gospel and Epistle this testimony bears a distinctly apologetic and, at the same time, an exalted mystical character. Without its being necessary to ascribe to the Fourth Gospel a directly polemical tendency (design) as opposed to particular persons or schools, we may yet infer (from John xx. 31) that the aim of the Evangelist was to strengthen the faith of his readers, especially in regard to a time in which already to many a doubtful phenomenon appeared. Now and then, the apology becomes a direct polemic;* but even where he combats error, it is not by means of a new dialectic, but by a powerful witnessing of that which he himself has passed through, and has, in a spiritual manner, experienced. Often he loses himself, as it were, in the contemplation of a past or a future which, for him, has become

---

* 1 John iv. 2, 3; 2 John 9-11.

present; so that it can be said with truth of his theology, "Elle n'est pas un produit de la spéculation, mais bien de la contemplation; c'est une théologie essentiellement mystique, qui n'a besion que d'un petit nombre d'idées et d'une théorie tout-à-fait simple, pour edifier la vie qu'elle veut faire naître au fond de l'âme" (Reuss).

7. In the Apocalypse, on the other hand, the Apostolic testimony takes a higher prophetic flight, but without any sacrifice of its purely Israelitish character. On the contrary, it is manifest that the seer is intimately familiar with the visions of the Old Testament —especially those of Ezekiel and Daniel—and that even the most highly developed of the Apostles at the end of his course, had by no means torn himself from the theocratic-national ground in which he had once been rooted. He who regards it as absolutely impossible that one and the same John should have written the Gospel *and* the Apocalypse, has not duly considered either the wealth of his individuality, or the considerable period of time which had elapsed between the composition of the one writing and that of the other, or the great difference of their contents, aim, and character. A continued investigation leads rather to the conclusion that only an Evangelist like this could have written the Apocalypse, and only an Apocalyptist like this could have written the Gospel.

8. After what has been said, we cannot greatly wonder that the attempts at the treatment of the Johannine doctrinal system have been made in very different ways, and have not always proved successful.

Especial reference is due to the work of Reuss (*L. c.* II. p. 336), which has developed this whole type of doctrine out of 1 John iv. 9, as compared with John iii. 16 (which latter text, however, contains none of John's own words). We believe we shall remain most true to the historic-Christologic character of the Johannine theology if, in the examination of the Gospel and Epistle, we give especial attention to the Apostle's representation of the world out of Christ, the appearing of Christ, and the life in Christ. In the doctrinal system of the Apocalypse, the article of the Parousia is, from the nature of the case, that doctrine which demands the greatest attention.

Compare, on John and his theology, the Art. of Ebrard in Herzog's *R. E.* VI. On the genuineness of the Gospel and the Apocalypse, the prize treatise of Niermeijer, Hague Society XIII. (1852), and the *Inl. N. T.* of Scholten, Leiden, 1856. On the priority of date of the Gospel over the Apocalypse, our *Christologie des N. V.*, p. 366-379; Article of Godet in the *Révue Chrét.* of 1865, p. 239-249 of the *Bulletin Théol.*

On the doctrinal type of John, the frequently-cited writings of Schmid, Messner, Reuss, Lechler, de Pressensé, and others; above all, the works on this subject of B. Weiss, *der Johann. Lehrbegriff in seinen Grundzügen untersucht*, Berl., 1862. Compare also da Costa, *de Apostel Joh. en zijne Schriften*, Amst., 1854, p. 103 and following.

POINTS FOR INQUIRY.

IMPORTANCE of the Johannine theology beside and above every other.—The key thereto in the history of the Apostle's life and growth.— Closer examination, comparison, and estimate of its sources. — The peculiar character of the Johannine theology, as compared with the Petrine on the one hand and the Pauline on the other.—History of the course and the manner of its special treatment.—Wherefore has the treatment of the Johannine doctrinal system been, as a rule, less successful than that of others?—What is, in its examination, according to both sources, to be above all avoided, and what regarded?—Truth and significance of the "volat avis sine metâ," &c.

FIRST SUBDIVISION.

THE GOSPEL AND THE EPISTLES.

SECTION XLVI.
The World out of Christ.

THE invisible God, according to the testimony of John, reveals himself to the world only in and through the Logos, who from the beginning was partaker of his nature and majesty, the mediate cause of creation, the light and life of men. The world, however, under the delusive and tyrannical sway of its Prince, loves darkness rather than light, and is on this account subject to the dominion of sin and death. Nevertheless, there have ever been those of a better mind who are inwardly susceptible of the highest revelation of God in the Logos, which has been of old, especially in Israel, announced and prepared for.

1. In our contemplation of John's teaching, nothing strikes us so soon as the loftiness of the Apostle's conception of God. God is for him the True One,[*] in opposition to all vain idols; light,[†] the sum of all moral perfection, which again concentrates itself in love,[‡] the fountain-head of everlasting life.[§] And of this God he speaks as the Father,[||] without doubt in the consciousness of his filial relation towards Him, but, at the same time, with evident reference to the mystery of the Divine being, revealed only in the Son.

2. For God is not only invisible,[¶] but also is known only so far as He reveals himself; and the centre of this revelation is the Son, so that even the Theophany of the Old Testament was in reality a Christophany.[**] God's revelation in Christ is consequently for John the source of his Divine knowledge and conception of God. The general revelation of God in nature and conscience, of which Paul speaks, is not with him mentioned in this form; all that can be known of God concentrates itself for his eye in the Logos.

3. The Logos is identical in the Johannine system with the Son,[††] and the reason why he designates this Son exclusively in this manner is to be sought in the peculiar character of the Gnosis of his days. The Johannine idea of the Logos has its basis substantially in the Old Testament; its form, however,

---

[*] 1 John v. 20.   [†] 1 John i. 5.   [‡] 1 John iv. 8, 16.
[§] 1 John v. 20.   [||] 1 John ii. 13; iii 1.   [¶] 1 John i 18.
[**] John xii. 41.   [††] John i. 14; compare i. 18.

is to be explained by the Alexandrine philosophy of his time. The difference, however, between his doctrine of the Logos and that of Philo is too great to admit of the former being regarded simply as a feeble imitation of the latter. " The antithesis is absolute ; for that which is for St. John a truth of the first moment, would have been for the Jew of Alexandria a horrible blasphemy. Between Philo's system and the Gospel, the same difference is found as between the Therapeutæ—taciturn and attenuated hermits—and the first Christians, conquerors of the world by their missions and their martyrdoms" (De Pressensé.) Rightly regarded, John says nothing of the Logos but what is elsewhere in the New Testament testified of the Son of God. Only he says this in another manner; and what he says can be supported either by the letter or the spirit of the Lord's utterances, communicated either by him or by the other Evangelists.

4. The Logos, according to the teaching of John, is partaker of the nature and majesty of God, hypostatically pre-existing with Him in the beginning of all things, and is the mediate cause of the creation of all that lives a created life.* John knows no eternal matter owing to the Logos only its present form ; but proclaims an eternal Word of God whereby all things have been brought into being, and in which God has, so to speak, expressed himself. All light and life in the world of men, whether it be natural

* John i. 3.

or moral, has proceeded from Him as its centre; and the whole history of the world before Christ may be regarded as foreshadowing the conflict of this light against the darkness in humanity.

5. For the Cosmos, from the nature of the case, offers to the Logos an obstinate resistance, not because it is composed of material elements (ὕλη), but because it is swayed by the power of sin. It lies in evil,* as the element in which it naturally moves. At its head stands, as the enemy of God, the devil, a personal evil spirit. Whilst there is no further reference either to angelology or demonology in the teaching of John, Satanology, on the other hand, occupies an essential place in the Apostle's doctrinal system. Satan has sinned from the beginning, *i.e.*, as long as there has been sin.† He wrought the first fratricide,‡ and put the betrayal into the heart of Judas.§ Thus he accomplishes his own work, and has his own children, as opposed to the children of God. Men have evil of him, he has it of himself, because he is by nature evil. How he became so, John does not say, but just as little that he always was so. This last he not only did not, but could not say, without at once breaking with the idea of God and the conception of the world, both of the Old Testament and of Jesus himself.

6. Since sin is of such origin, it displays inevitably the same character as he in whom its power is con-

---

* 1 John v. 19. † 1 John iii. 8, ἀπ' ἀρχῆς, not ἐν ἀρχῇ.
‡ 1 John iii. 12. § John xiii. 2.

centrated. The Johannine hamartology is less developed than the Pauline, but not less true and profound. Sin is for him, in its deepest ground, lawlessness, and therefore moral injustice;* sin and the lie are with John as inseparably connected as truth and holiness; and while life is not conceivable without love, the power of evil manifests itself precisely in hatred against the brother,† and in the love of a world alienated from God.‡ In consequence of this the sinner remains necessarily in darkness, for as in love is life, so hatred resembles death. The conception of death also, like that of the world, is with John a thoroughly ethical one, indicative of a condition of spiritual separation from God which naturally leads to physical death, and attains its terrible point of culmination in an absolutely unpardonable sin.§ So great is the power of sin, that even in the Christian it can be by no means regarded as overcome,‖ so that he also consequently stands in need of constantly renewed forgiveness,¶ although absolute freedom from sinning remains the requirement and the ideal of every Christian life.**

7. This universal sinfulness of the world renders necessary a more especial revelation of the truth and grace of God, after the more general one of

---

* 1 John i. 9; iii. 4.   † 1 John iii. 12.   ‡ 1 John ii. 15-17.
§ 1 John v. 16. [From the antithesis, however, between the ζωή and the θάνατος of ver. 16, the ἁμαρτία πρὸς θάνατον would seem rather to be one leading to *the death of the body*. Compare 1 Cor. xi. 30, and James v. 15.]
‖ 1 John i. 8-16.   ¶ 1 John ii. 2.   ** 1 John iii. 4-10.

the Logos before his incarnation. This revelation proceeds entirely from the love of God, which is manifested in a lustre unknown before, in the sending and giving up of the Son.* This, however, took place by no means without preparation being made for his coming; even before his incarnation the Logos stood in a more especial relation to Israel as his own, although He was rejected by that which was by far the greater part of Israel.† The prophetic Scripture had proclaimed Him,‡ and especially the preaching of the Baptist had prepared the way for his arising.§ Of a preparation for his coming in the Gentile world John does not indeed directly speak; he indicates, however, that all light even there has proceeded from the Logos, ‖ and that there were by no means wanting those who were accessible to the light and life which proceeded from Him.¶

8. For according to the teaching of John, mankind —quite apart from its relation to the historic manifestation of Christ—is divided into two originally different classes. On the one hand are children of the devil and of darkness, for whom faith on this account is morally impossible,** and in whose unbelief the Apostle recognises the fulfilment of the secret counsel of God.†† On the other hand, however, are also the better minded, the children of God even beyond the confines of Judaism,‡‡ light-natures,

* 1 John iv. 9, 10. † John i. 11-12. ‡ John ii. 17; xix. 36, 37.
§ John i. 6, following. ‖ John i. 4, 5, 9.
¶ John xi. 52. ** [Compare also 2 Thes. iii. 2.]
†† John xii. 40. ‡‡ John xi. 52.

who hear the Gospel because they are of God,[*] and feel themselves drawn to Him. Here the law of affinity applies: that which is like is attracted, that which is unlike is repelled. Where, consequently, the light arises, the friend of light will seek, recognise, and prize it; whilst, on the other hand, the child of darkness hates and resists it. That, however, this difference in principle stands in no kind of connection with moral freedom and responsibility—so that unbelief, traced to its ultimate source, were a misfortune rather than a fault—is by John nowhere taught. He, on the contrary, evidently regards this unbelief as something entirely inexcusable, and sees in the highest manifestation of the truth at the same time a manifestation of grace and life, of which all, indeed, stand in need, but which also is designed and provided for all.[†]

Compare in general on John's idea of God the treatise of L. G. Pareau in *Waarh. in L.*, 1844, III. On the doctrine of the Logos, our *Christologie des N. T.*, p. 380 and following, the different commentaries on this place, and the work of J. Bucher, *des Apost. Joh. Lehre vom Logos*, Schaffh., 1856. Compare also Philippi, *der Eingang des Joh. Evang.*, and especially —also as opposed to the interpretation of Beyschlag —the important monograph of Dr. L. Th. Schulze, *vom Menschensohn und vom Logos, ein Beitrag zur bibl. Christol.*, Gotha, 1867. On his conception of the two different kinds of men, as opposed to the Gnosti-

---

[*] 1 John iv. 6.   [†] John i. 14-18; 1 John ii. 2.

cising view of Hilgenfeld and others, B. Weiss, *der Johann. Lehrbegriff.*, p. 128-138.

POINTS FOR INQUIRY.

THE peculiarity of the Johannine conception of God.—Why have we not appealed to the authority of 1 John v. 7?—What can be deduced from John's teaching as to the inter-relation of the Father, the Son, and the Holy Ghost?—Are there also found, elsewhere in the New Testament, traces of the doctrine of the Logos?—The sense of John i. 1-18, compare 1 John i. 1-3.—Connection of the Johannine doctrine of the Logos with the canonical and apocryphal writings of the Old Testament on the one hand, and the Alexandrine philosophy on the other.—The idea of κόσμος in relation to that of the Logos.—Was John a Dualist?—What is implied by John xii. 40?—What is the reading of John xiii. 2?—What is the sense of 1 John v. 16?—The difference detween the Johannine Anthropology and that of the later Gnosticism.

SECTION XLVII.

The Appearing of Christ.

THE Logos became incarnate in Jesus Christ, who is true and holy man, but, at the same time, the Son of God in the supernatural sense of the word, the Messiah of Israel, the Saviour of the world. His whole manifestation and work—both before and after His death—is a continued revelation and communication of truth and life, whereby the world must either be saved, or, in principle, even now already condemned.

1. The appearance of Christ on earth is, according to the conception of John, by no means the merely becoming visible of a heavenly being, hitherto invisible, but a real assumption of the human nature by *Him* who had not hitherto possessed it, and who becomes man while remaining Logos. Even before His incarnation, this Logos was the Son,* whose

---

* John i. 14, 18; compare 1 John iv. 14.

intimate relation to the Father is indicated by the Evangelist in a figure derived from his own experience.* As such, He has been from the beginning,† and is manifested upon His coming into the world.‡ Even in speaking of His coming in the flesh,§ and of His being sent by the Father,‖ the idea of a personal pre-existence underlies the statement. So closely is He united to the Father, that it is sometimes doubtful of which John is speaking.¶ In the single epistle in which the expression *Jesus Christ* does not occur, His *name* is referred to in a highly significant manner;** and, only so far as God is known in Christ, is He, as the True One, opposed to false Gods.†† In vain is it sought to weaken the force of these expressions by insisting on the absence of the wonted article before the name of God,‡‡ which, from the first, is given to the Logos. The judgment of the ancient Church, which conferred upon John, as the proclaimer of the Divine nature of the Logos, the name of Theologus, has been perfectly justified.

2. There is no single reason for understanding the well-known formula, "The Word was made *flesh*,"§§ of anything else than of the assumption of the whole true human nature in all its fulness. Without doubt, John also maintains the reality of the human body of the Lord;‖‖ but with equal emphasis does he ascribe

---

* John xiii. 23. † 1 John i. 1 ; ii. 14 ‡ 1 John iii. 5.
§ 1 John iv. 2, 3. ‖ 1 John iv. 14.
¶ See, for example, 1 John ii. 29 ; iii. 2, 3.
** 3 John 7. †† 1 John v. 20.
‡‡ John. i. 1. §§ John i. 14. ‖‖ John xix. 28, 34, 35.

The Appearing of Christ.

to Him a human soul (ψυχή) and a human spirit (πνεῦμα), with its activities and emotions.* A denying that Jesus Christ is truly come in the flesh (this is something more than to appear in a human body) is, in his eye, antichristian.† Not simply in a fleeting manner has the Logos revealed himself, but has tabernacled (ἐσκήνωσεν) for a while in a truly human nature,‡ and His body was, as it were, the temple of an indwelling Divinity.§ Of a miraculous beginning of life, such as Matthew and Luke relate, no express mention, indeed, is made by John; but it is tacitly assumed (postulated) by him in his whole system of Christology, and once, also, as it seems, is alluded to,‖ although but indirectly. In no case, however, can the incarnation of the Logos be regarded as the annihilation, but rather as the peculiar revelation, of His superhuman glory. That in such a personality the liability to temptation,¶ co-existing with the entire absence of actual sin, is conceivable is, from the standpoint of John, self-evident. He, therefore, emphatically terms the Lord the Holy One, the Righteous,** and recognises in Him no sin, not even the least.†† But with this negative result he is not content; on the contrary, he sees realised in Him the ideal of the highest perfection possible on earth,‡‡ as this is revealed, above all, in a love which is combined with

---

* John xiii. 21, πνεῦμα; 1 John iii. 16, ψυχή.
† 1 John iv. 2, 3; 2 John v. 7.   ‡ John i. 14.
§ John ii. 21; compare Colos. ii. 9.   ‖ John i. 13.
¶ John vi. 15.   ** 1 John ii. 1, 20; iii. 3, 5.
†† 1 John iii. 5.   ‡‡ 1 John ii. 6; iv. 17.

the most exalted consciousness of His relation to the Father.*

3. That the incarnate *Word* is the Messiah of Israel, is brought less prominently into the foreground in John than in Paul or Peter. No wonder; the wall of separation between Israel and the Gentile world is, for his eyes, already fallen; consequently, also, Old Testament expressions, like Zion, City of God, heavenly Jerusalem, seed of Abraham, &c., do not occur in his writings. Nevertheless, he also presents the Lord as the one promised to the fathers, in whom the Scriptures are fulfilled; yea, maintains that the recognition of Jesus as the Christ is indispensable for salvation,† and a sign of the birth of God.‡ With evident preference, however, he dwells upon the universal design in the manifestation of Christ, which had already been indicated by the Baptist,§ and had been so emphatically expressed‖ by the Lord himself. And if we asked, What then is, properly, the great aim of this whole manifestation and work? with his Gospel and Epistles in our hands, we answer: negatively, the taking away of sin and the destroying of the works of the devil;¶ positively, the revealing of the truth and the giving of life.**

4. The Father is interpreted ($\dot{\epsilon}\xi\epsilon\gamma\acute{\eta}\sigma\alpha\tau o$)†† by and in the Son of His love. Without doubt, John is here thinking of the instruction ‡‡ of the Lord, but, above

* John xiii. 1-3.   † John xx. 31.   ‡ 1 John v. 1.
§ John i. 29.   ‖ John vi. 33.   ¶ 1 John iii. 5, 8.
** John i. 16-18; 1 John iv. 9, 10.
†† John i. 18.   ‡‡ 1 John i. 5.

all, of the whole personality of Him in whom the Truth and the Life shone forth in unequalled lustre. A high degree of significance, on this account, have, in his estimation, the miraculous deeds of the Lord, as the beamings forth of His glory.* He sees, however, this glory revealed less in single moments of unwonted lustre (the Transfiguration, the institution of the Supper, the Ascension, &c.), which he rather passes over in silence, than in the resistless whole of the historical manifestation of the Christ.†

5. While the sending of the Son of God into the world had as its end the giving of true life to the world,‡ this end is especially attained by the *death* of the Lord. It is remarkable that, while John elsewhere passes over the Old Testament sacrifices in silence, he nevertheless presents the death of the Lord in the definite character of a sin-offering, by which the guilt of sin is covered.§ In the death of the Lord he sees not only the fulfilment of God's counsel, in consequence of which the true Paschal lamb is slain on Golgotha;|| not merely the manifestation of the highest love of the Lord, which calls for and merits imitation;¶ but the means absolutely necessary for the expiation of the sins of the world.** Not merely purification from the dominion of sin, but also from its guilt and curse, he brings into immediate connection with Christ's blood,†† and comprehends in the

---

* John ii. 11. † John i. 14; 1 John i. 1-3.
‡ 1 John iv. 9. § 1 John ii. 2. || John xix. 36.
¶ 1 John iii. 16. ** 1 John ii. 2. †† 1 John i. 7.

proclamation of the forgiveness of sins the main import of the Gospel message.* He represents the Christ as come,† *i.e.*, as revealed in his exalted character—not merely by the water of baptism, but also by the blood of the Cross, whereby the forgiveness of sins is not merely symbolized but actually realized. At the same time, according to his profound observation, ‡ the receptive Gentiles are gathered together into one communion with the redeemed of Israel. No wonder that he regards a death whereby so great salvation is brought in, as the life of the world.

6. Even after the death of the Lord is this his salutary activity continued. Through the Holy Spirit He ceases not to communicate himself to His believers,§ but, at the same time, He himself remains the Paraclete of His people as often as they have sinned anew.‖ Thus, there exists between Him and them a constant communion of life and of spirit ; and one day He will come again to perfect the blessedness thus begun. Without doubt, the expectations of the future in John are much less highly coloured than in Peter or in Paul. The Old Testament language here in great measure disappears; the blessedness of the future is already, in principle, enjoyed in the present. This is a consequence of the exalted mystical character of the Johannine theology, but gives no right to assert that his expectations are essentially

---

* 1 John ii. 12. † 1 John v. 6. ‡ John xi. 52.
§ 1 John ii. 27 ; iii 24. ‖ John ii. 2.

different from those of his whole surrounding. He also knows a last hour*—a day of the revelation of Christ and of judgment†—in which that which is secret is revealed, and the end of redemption is attained. He also regards the Antichrist as the forerunner of the last decision, although—as distinguished from Paul—he discovers the signs of the last apostasy not so much in lawlessness as in the denial of the truth. We find no single reason for seeing in the one and the other nothing but "forms derived from an earlier mechanical view of the world, which show that John had not yet entirely risen above his former Judaism" (Scholten).

7. The result of this work of the incarnate Logos in the midst of the world cannot be other than decisive for the world itself. The appearing of Christ brings about separation ($\kappa\rho\iota\sigma\iota\varsigma$) between the one who has the Son and the one who has Him not;‡ or rather, the difference, already present, unseen is, in consequence of His coming and His work, brought to light. Thus, the Christ becomes necessarily judge, even where He desires to be Saviour; and whosoever rejects Him abides in that death in which he already by nature was, and from which he can escape only in communion with Christ.§ According to John, it is absolutely impossible not to possess the Son and yet to have the Father;∥ to be unchristian, and yet to serve God. And just as little does he open up any

---

* 1 John ii. 18.   † 1 John ii. 28; iv. 17.
‡ 1 John v. 11, 12.   § 1 John iii. 14.
∥ 1 John ii. 23; 2 John v. 9.

prospect in the future to the obdurate rejecter of Christ; on the contrary, he anticipates a very different issue to the world's history than that which absolute Monism pictures to itself. It can hardly be supposed that he looked for a conversion of Antichrist: rather than this must he regard even his annihilation as conceivable.* On this domain, also, the Apocalypse will afford us suggestions which we should seek in vain in the Gospel and Epistles; but those already examined prove sufficiently that he finds no less difference in principle between belief and unbelief than between light and darkness. With what holy indignation he is filled against those who reject the doctrine of Christ is, at least once, emphatically expressed;† although, even in speaking of the unbelief of his contemporaries, next to the tone of deep indignation, that of inner melancholy and intense grief makes itself heard.‡ Where, however, he is called to speak of the blessedness connected with life in Christ, he knows not how to speak of anything less than "grace in return for grace."§

Compare, on the true humanity of the Johannine Christ, Beyschlag, *l. c.*, p. 141 and following. On the Divine nature in Him, according to the testimony of our Apostle, Gess., *die Lehre von der Person Chr.*, Basle, 1856, p. 99-115. On the Johannine Soteriology, Lechler, *l. c.*, p. 219 and following. On the Johannine Christ, our *Apologetical Prelections*, IV.; Liddon's Bampton Lecture, on the *Divinity of Christ*.

* Compare 1 John ii. 15-17.
† 2 John 7, 9-11
‡ John i. 11, 12; xii. 37-43.
§ John i. 16.

POINTS FOR INQUIRY.

WHAT is the sense of 1 John v. 20?—Wherefore is John silent as to the Lord's miraculous birth?—Is there ground for the assertion that the Johannine Christology contains docetic elements?—What Divine characteristics appear especially in the Johannine image of Christ?—What peculiarities are displayed in the Johannine Soteriology as compared with the Pauline?—What connection does the Apostle observe between the work of the exalted Christ and that of the Holy Ghost (John vii. 39)?—The Johannine description of Antichrist.—The exclusiveneness of John's love.—The brief summary of the Gospel of John, i. 16.

SECTION XLVIII.

Life in Christ.

WHERE the highest revelation of God in the incarnate Word is believingly contemplated, and in this manner is truly acknowledged, this faith becomes the source of a life in communion with Christ—and, through Him, in filial relationship towards God—which manifests itself in a walk in the light and in love, and clearly distinguishes from the world, and closely unites to each other all who possess it. Through this, its spiritual principle of life, is the preservation and victory of the Church of the Lord assured; its glory and blessedness, however, is fully revealed only in the day of the coming of Christ.

1. Although in the Johannine doctrinal system the demand for *faith* is not so constantly brought into the foreground as in that of Paul, yet here also faith is spoken of as the chief commandment of the Gospel,

Life in Christ. 399

and the great means for overcoming the world.* It consists in the upright acknowledgment of Him in His whole unique dignity,† and is the sign of a genuine birth of God,‡ whose testimony it unhesitatingly accepts.§ As from the nature of the case it is preceded by knowledge,|| so, on its part, it leads to ever better knowledge in spiritual things, which again places in a position for ever fi mer faith.¶ Believing and knowing stand, therefore, in John so little opposed to each other, that the upright believer is, precisely on this account, the true Gnosticus. " The true faith is in John a recognising, experiencing faith, the true knowledge a believing knowledge " (Lücke). In consequence thereof the Christian has, then, also an inner assurance of the truth and life in Christ, which does not admit of any, the least, doubt, and even seeks no further support beyond itself.**

2. The believing contemplation and recognition of Christ is the source of a life which is the embodiment of the highest possible blessedness. It arises in consequence of an entire inward change as an abiding inner principle,†† so that it is enjoyed even on this side the grave. But, at the same time, this gift is a promise which awaits its complete fulfilment, ‡‡ and an ideal for the future of the believer. §§ This life is found exclusively in personal communion with Christ, so that to have Christ and to have life

---

* 1 John iii. 23 ; v. 4-5.   † πιστεύειν ὅτι, κ.τ.λ., John xx. 3
‡ 1 John v. 1.   § 1 John v. 9. || 1 John iv. 16.
¶ 1 John v. 13   ** 1 John v. 10-12.   †† 1 John iii. 14, 15.
‡‡ 1 John ii. 25.   §§ John xx. 31.

signifies fundamentally the same thing.* At the same time, it brings the Christian into a personal relationship towards God, of which the blessedness surpasses every other kind of happiness.† For John, also, sonship with God is the highest privilege of the believer, though between his conception of it and that of Paul (Sec. xl. 7), the distinction must not be overlooked that John regards this privilege almost exclusively from its ethical side, and especially directs the eye to the inner kinship of spirit between the children and the Father. With both John and Paul, perfect confidence before God is the fruit of this filial relationship; and the assurance of the answering of prayer, of intercessory prayer also, is, from this standpoint, fully warranted.‡

3. The new life of the children of God reveals itself by a walk in the light and in love, without which there can be no question of personal communion between man and the spotlessly Holy One.§ While it is, however, morally inconceivable that one should know God and not keep His commandments, these commandments for His people are not grievous.‖ It is remarkable how John, who elsewhere is raised so high above the legal standpoint, lays such evident stress upon the doctrine and the commandment of Christ; assuredly, according to his view, also, the new life requires a constant rule and bond. To love

---

* 1 John v. 12. † 1 John iii. 1.
‡ 1 John iii. 22; iv. 17, 18; v. 14, 15; compare Rom. viii. 15, 16; Gal. iv. 6.
§ 1 John i. 5-7. ‖ 1 John ii. 3-11; compare 1 John v. 3.

Life in Christ. 401

towards God and Christ he never directly exhorts; he presupposes that it is, in principle, present in believers, but urges them so much the more powerfully, precisely on this account, to manifest it in love towards the brother, since the one must stand or fall with the other.* The love of the brethren—once by the Lord termed a new commandment†—he, at the close of the first Christian century, can already speak of as an old one;‡ but with ever new power does he insist on its being cherished by believers, after their Lord's own example.§

4. This active love is one with personal sanctification—a sanctification which is nothing less than the final aim of the whole work of redemption.‖ It displays itself in a manful struggle against evil, with the renouncing of the vain love of the world,¶ and in a willing fulfilment of all that is well-pleasing to God.** With such a state of mind, boldness before God stands in such immediate connection that it is impossible to possess the latter where the former is wanting, and that there can be no question of *prayer even* being heard while the conscience inwardly condemns.†† One must have read John with peculiar eyes, before he can assert that a conception wherein so much of moral earnestness and tenderness of conscience is expressed, could, even in any degree, conflict with the doctrine of free and unconditional grace.‡‡

---

* 1 John iv. 20, 21.   † John xiii. 34.
‡ 1 John ii. 7.   § 1 John iii. 16-18.   ‖ 1 John ii. 1.
¶ 1 John ii. 14-16.   ** 1 John iii. 22.
†† 1 John iii. 20, 21.   ‡‡ Compare 1 John i. 7; ii. 1, 2.

D D

5. Those who thus walk in light and love stand by no means alone, but enter, on the contrary, precisely thereby, into the closest relationship towards each other. Genuinely Johannine is the presentation of the Christian life as a life of innermost communion, above all, with Christ, but then, also, in Him with God and with fellow-believers.* His whole First Epistle is a clearly discernible echo of the Master's parting prayer.† Christians are as such, brethren; and if he addresses them as children, this has its ground in his age and in his relation to them. Only on a single occasion‡ does he speak of the Church (ἐκκλησία)—everywhere else of the mutual fellowship (κοινωνία) of believers one with another, of which the peculiar mark is found to be the pure confession of the Father and the Son. Those who fall away from this communion show precisely thereby that they never yet truly belonged to it.§ Those who belong to it present a compact unity to the world, which hates and misjudges them,‖ but will not easily seduce them, because their members possess in the Spirit of Truth, which is given to them, an infallible test by which to distinguish truth from error.¶ It is thus also absolutely impossible that the true believer should fall for ever under the power of sin.** The truth remains with the Church for evermore; because the Spirit of Truth is given to her††—that Spirit who

---

* 1 John i. 3.   † John xvii. 20, 21.   ‡ 3 John 6, 9, 10.
§ 1 John ii. 19.   ‖ John iii. 1, 10.   ¶ 1 John ii. 20, 27.
** 1 John iii. 9.   †† 2 John 2.

is so much more powerful than the spirit of this world.*

6. The more perfect the Christian communion, the more full also is the joy.† While constant warning against sin and error is necessary,‡ the abiding in that which they have heard of Christ has the sure promise of a happiness which cannot be lost.§ In principle already a sharer in that which is best, the Christian has yet to expect something higher. That in the Johannine doctrinal system there is nowhere a place for Christian hope (Kostlin), is an assertion which is in itself incredible, and is, moreover, contradicted in more than one place in his Epistle. He, like his fellow-disciples, sees the darkness,‖ yea, the whole world,¶ pass away, because he lives in the expectation of the day of the coming of Christ. The many Antichrists whom he beholds are for him precursors of the *one*, and, at the same time, heralds of the last hour.** While, then, all passes away, the Christian abides eternally††—has full confidence,‡‡ beholds God and becomes in this manner like Him ($\H{o}\mu o\iota o\varsigma$),§§ yet always in such wise that the personal distinction between the Creator and the creature is preserved. Begun by the believing contemplation of the Logos,‖‖ the life in Christ ends with the future contemplation of the Father, and in this way with the completion of that communion with

---

* 1 John iv. 4.   † 1 John i. 4.   ‡ 2 John 8.
§ 1 John ii. 24, 25.   ‖ 1 John ii. 8.   ¶ 1 John ii. 17.
** 1 John ii. 18.   †† 1 John ii. 17.   ‡‡ 1 John ii. 28; iv. 17.
§§ 1 John iii. 2.   ‖‖ John i. 14.

God which has been begun even here below. As to that which the Christian has to look for between death and the Parousia of the Lord, John is silent.

7. A high value attaches itself to the Johannine system as we have thus far learnt to know it, as being—even when compared with the greater wealth of the Pauline ideas—the most profound of the whole New Testament, the crown of the Apostolic testimony, and the perceptible echo of the Lord's own words. Most of all is this the case in our time, as opposed to the arbitrary separation between religion and Christianity, ideas and facts, doctrine of faith and doctrine of morals. Christologically, no doctrinal system surpasses that of the Gospel and Epistles of John; and what is wanting therein eschatologically is satisfactorily complemented by the Apocalypse.

Compare the treatise of Oehler, *der Glaube und die Geburt aus Gott in ihrer Einheit nach dem Johann. Lehrbegr.* in the Tüb. Theol. Quarterly, 1838, IV. p. 599-622. Lutterbeck, *l. c.*, II. p. 290. The Commentaries of Düsterdieck, and also of Braune, in Lange's series. Graham, *The Spirit of Love:* a practical and exegetical commentary on the First Epistle of John, London, 1857. Candlish, *Exposition of the First Epistle of John.*

POINTS FOR INQUIRY.

WHAT is the connection, according to John, between faith and the birth of God (ἐκ τοῦ θεοῦ) ?—In what manner does he connect faith and knowledge ?—What is, according to John,

Life in Christ.

the last and surest ground of faith?—In what relation does he place our love to the love of God towards us (1 John iv. 19)?—What similarity and what difference is there between his doctrine of the fellowship of believers and that of Paul? —On what ground does he look for the preservation and victory of the kingdom of God?—**What is the sense and force of 1 John iii. 1-3?**

SECOND SUBDIVISION.

THE APOCALYPSE.

SECTION XLIX.
Diversity and Harmony.

THE difference between the doctrinal system of the Apocalypse and that of the Gospel and the Epistles is, without doubt, important, but yet of such a kind as is on the one hand easily accounted for, and on the other hand greatly outweighed by many striking agreements. For a just appreciation of the doctrines of the Apocalypse, it is not necessary to bring into the foreground a definite view as to the signification and design of the prophetic visions therein recorded. Even with the greatest difference as to the interpretation and value of the book of Christ's future, it can be shown—spite of much opposition—that with all that it contains of a peculiar or enigmatical character, it reflects (as to its main contents) in a louder echo the testimony of the Apostles and Prophets, and in so far forms a worthy close to the canon of the New Testament.

1. It is not easy to form a just estimate of the Apocalypse. Like other books of the New Testament, this also has passed through a period first of overestimation, then of neglect, which has been succeeded only in recent times by a truer appreciation. We thankfully recognise how, from different sides, light has been shed on this mysterious domain, but at the same time remember that we are not called in this place to seek the key to the enigma of the Apocalypse, but only to develope the doctrinal system of this book.

2. The first impression which the Apocalypse calls forth, as compared with the Gospel and the Epistles of John, is certainly that of the greatest difference. John the Evangelist stands in many respects nearer to Peter and Paul than to the Apocalypticus. The series of oppositions between the John of the Apocalypse and the John of the Gospel, may be continued almost without end. Between the contents of the two writings, the difference is not less than between their language and style. Equally do they differ in their relation to the Scriptures of the Old Testament. We cannot, therefore, be surprised that the composition of these two writings by the same person is doubted even by those who merit no reproach less than that of an arbitrary criticism.

3. Yet critics have not too strongly expressed them-

selves when, in recent times, they have repeatedly asserted that scarcely for the authenticity of any single writing of the New Testament can more manifold proofs be adduced than for that of the Apocalypse. Even the most negative school has defended its Johannine origin. Spite of sharp contrasts in regard to contents, style, and mode of thought between the two writings, there are not wanting remarkable instances of agreement; confirming as well the identity of authorship as the time of composition of the Apocalypse, as not before but after that of the Gospel and Epistles (Sec. xlv. 3.) If we consider that in the one the calm historian ($\dot{\epsilon}\nu$ $\nu o\hat{\iota}$), in the other the ecstatic prophet ($\dot{\epsilon}\nu$ $\pi\nu\epsilon\acute{\nu}\mu\alpha\tau\iota$) arises; that there the spontaneity, here the receptivity of the Apostle is especially active; that the revelation granted him from above attached itself to that of the Old Testament, and that the main lines of thought, begun in Gospel or Epistle, are carried through in the Apocalypse (not the reverse), then it is manifest that here also the opposition is to be found upon the surface, the harmony in the depths.

4. In the Apocalypse, also, the person of the Lord, the Christ as He comes in His kingdom, is the centre of the whole. Not less than in Gospel and Epistle is homage rendered to His true humanity. He is of Judah and David;[*] the child of the Old Testament church;[†] was truly dead, and is yet seen in heaven with the tokens of His having been slain.[‡]

---

[*] Rev. v. 5; xxii. 16.   [†] Rev. xii. 1-5.   [‡] Rev. i. 18; v. 6.

Diversity and Harmony.

But He is at the same time partaker of the nature and majesty of God, and ascribes to himself Divine names and attributes.* It is true He has received everything of the Father,† and into the glorification of this Father is resolved also the homage presented to Him.‡ But yet directly to Himself is the incense of adoration kindled;§ sovereignly does He dispose of the angels as Lord and Ruler,‖ and as Word of God¶ He bears a name of which the deep significance is already known to us from the fourth Gospel. In the presence of such facts some amount of courage is necessary to hold (with Baur) that the Christology of the Apocalypse does not rise essentially above the Ebionite standpoint. The impartial student will agree with a critic of the most advanced school (Reuss): "On doit reconnaître sans hesiter que Christ dans l'Apoc. est élevé au niveau de Dieu."

5. It is nevertheless not so much in relation to the Father as to His Church that the Lord is here presented, and presented especially in His royal character and dignity. It is true, He appears here also as the witness of the truth,** whose commandments challenge obedience,†† and His atoning work is referred to in a like spirit as in the Gospel.‡‡ Not as the Lion, but above all as the Lamb ($\dot{a}\rho\nu\acute{\iota}o\nu$), is the homage of heaven rendered to Him; and even where He is angry He does not deny this

---

* Rev. i. 11, 18; ii. 2, 13, 23. † Rev. i. 1; ii. 28; iii. 12.
‡ Rev. v. 13, 14.   § Rev. v. 8.   ‖ Rev. xxii. 16.
¶ Rev. xix. 13.   ** Rev. i. 5.   †† Rev. xxii. 14.
‡‡ Rev. i. 5; v..8, 9; vii. 14.

His character.* As the priest-king † He reveals himself, who unceasingly loves His church,‡ and watches over its highest concerns.§ But in this, his kingly character, is He clothed, not merely with the highest honour, but also with the most boundless omnipotence,‖ and exercises this not only in relation to the church, but also in relation to the world, which He overcomes and creates anew according to the counsel of the Father, of which the book is placed in His hands.¶

6. In the idea of God as presented in the Apocalypse, this peculiarity is to be observed, that while in the Gospel and Epistles the moral attributes of the Divine nature are brought into greater prominence, here it is the metaphysical properties which are brought into the foreground; a natural consequence as well of the contents of the book as of its manifest attachment to the prophecy of the Old Testament. God's omnipotence, his infinite and unchangeable nature, is here especially referred to. He is the God of the holy prophets, of the Apostles of the Lamb, and of the twelve tribes of Israel;** the God who makes all things new,†† and establishes his dwelling among men.‡‡ Of seven spirits before his throne, mention is also made,§§ as symbolical of the manifold character of the gifts of the Holy Ghost; whilst even in the beginning of the Apocalypse a

---

* Rev. vi. 16. † Rev. i. 9-20. ‡ Rev i. 5.
§ Rev. iii. 19, 20. ‖ Rev. ii. and iii. ¶ Rev. v. 1-7
** Rev. vii. 5; xxii. 16. †† Rev. xx. 5; compare Is. lxv 17.
‡‡ Rev. xxi 3; compare Ez. xxxvi. §§ Rev. iv. 5.

Diversity and Harmony.

trace of Trinitarian distinction is revealed,* without, however—any more than in the Gospel and Epistles —this distinction being drawn with dogmatic severity.

7. As regards the creature, the Apocalypse is as rich in point of angelology† as Gospel and Epistle are poor in this respect; at the same time, the rendering of religious homage to these higher beings is here not less strongly deprecated than by the Apostle Paul himself.‡ The anthropology, on the other hand, is entirely the same. The world, for the Apocalypse, as for the Gospel and Epistle, lies in wickedness, and ripens for the judgment of God; and this as a consequence of Satanic influence.§ The grace proclaimed here,‖ as in the Gospel,¶ is the only one that saves; and the faith which manifests itself by keeping the commandments is the first duty of the sinner.** Works do not precede, but follow believing;†† and perseverance even in the midst of the severest trials is the peculiar fruit of faith.‡‡ The blessedness in this manner experienced is here, as in the fourth Gospel, presented under the image of satisfaction and refreshment,§§ attainable for all without exception; and those who partake of it are spoken of as redeemed unto God out of *all* nations.‖‖ We find in the Apocalypse not even the slightest polemic against the Pauline universalism,

---

* Rev. i. 4-6. † See, for example, Rev. xvi. 5.
‡ Rev. xxii. 8, 9; compare Col. ii. 18. § Rev. xii. 9, 10.
‖ Rev. i. 4; xxii. 21. ¶ John i. 14, 16, 17.
** Rev. xiv. 12; xxii. 17; λαυβανετω δωρεαν.
†† Rev. xiv. 13. ‡‡ Rev. xiii. 10.
§§ Rev. vii. 17; xxi. 6. ‖‖ Rev. vii. 9.

and just as little the giving of direct or indirect encouragement to Jewish particularism.* The position of distinction which is here, in isolated instances, conceded to Israel, is partly only a relative pre eminence, partly is entirely in the spirit of the Lord,† and of the great Apostle of the Gentiles.‡

8. The eschatology is that part of the doctrinal system of the Apocalypse which is by far the most fully developed. It is true there is here by no means wanting the idea of a preparatory and spiritual coming of the Lord;§ but yet the visible coming upon the clouds of heaven is far more loudly proclaimed.‖ Whilst the departed even now consciously live,¶ and while the blessedness of the God-fearing dead is already begun, the final decision for the seen and unseen world is made only at the glorious coming of the Lord. It is not easy accurately to delineate the prospect here opened before us: "The figurative character of the Revelation renders it frequently impossible to arrange with dogmatic precision the underlying thoughts" (Baur). But thus much at least is certain, John regards this coming as nigh at hand,** as in point of time undeterminable,†† as glorious and decisive.‡‡ Its preludes are with him essentially the same as those mentioned by the Lord in his eschatological address of Matt. xxiv., and are

---

* Compare Rev. xiv. 6; xxii. 2.
† John iv. 22.
‡ Rom. ix. 1-5; Gal. vi. 16.
§ Rev. ii. 5; iii. 20.
‖ Rev. i. 7; xiv. 14; and following.
¶ Rev. vi. 9, 10.
** Rev. iii. 11; xxii. 10.
†† Rev. iii. 3; xvi. 15.
‡‡ Rev. xix. 11-16.

Diversity and Harmony. 413

presented under the figures of three successions of seals, of trumpets, and of vials of wrath—symbols of the judicial visitations of God ever increasing, frequently interrupted only by short intervals, but which are constantly responded to by an obdurate impenitence on the part of man. They prepare the way for the coming of Antichrist,* the Beast, with his two confederates, Satan and false prophecy; at the same time he is supported by the hostile world-power, which is presented under the image of an impure woman sitting upon the beast. The conflict of this world-power against the kingdom of God hastens the approaching decision, the fall of Babylon, the millennial kingdom, and the first resurrection.† After this comes the last conflict against the repressed but by no means annihilated world-power, which is followed by the resurrection of all the dead, the general judgment,‡ and the final renewing of heaven and earth,§ after which even the eye of a John sees nothing save an endless blessedness of God's people, and an endless punishment of the enemies of his kingdom.‖ Manifestly, the prophet looks for an enduring period of prosperity and of peace for the long-oppressed kingdom of God, to be broken only once by a final conflict, that after its last perfect triumph this kingdom may shine forth in undimmed brightness in heaven and earth. But even here we meet with glimpses of a future, of which a distant

---

* Rev. xiii. 1 ; compare Dan. vii. 8.   † Rev. xx. 1-6.
‡ Rev. xx. 7-15.   § Chaps. xxi. and xxii.   ‖ Rev. xiv. 11 ; xx. 10

prospect has been before opened to us,* but which has been hitherto less plastically delineated.

9. An impartial survey of the doctrinal system ot the Apocalypse reveals, on the one hand, how many an earlier or later objection to this book rests on a misunderstanding or a prejudice, and on the other hand, how the prospect here opened up by no means stands alone in Holy Scripture, but is, as it were, the crown of that stem whose foliage is spread forth before our eyes in the prophetic and Apostolic writings of the Old and the New Testament. As streams lose themselves in the ocean, so do all the expectations of blessedness opened to us in Scripture unite in the Apocalyptic perspective; and precisely to the latest book of the New Testament the investigation as to the higher unity of the different doctrinal systems attaches itself easily, and, as it were, without any effort.

Compare, on the Apocalypse in general, the Introduction of Lucke; the article of Ebrard, in Herzog's *R. E.* VI.; and the Commentaries, especially Lange, Biblical Commentary IV. Sec. 2 (Introd. to Commentary on John), and the Dissertation of W. H. Krijt, *cum de Apocal. libro, tum de septem quæ illo continertur Epistolis*, Traj. 1861. Compare also Lange, *Apostol. Zeitalter*, ii. p. 448-456; Da Costa, *l. c.*, p. 308 and following. On the Christology and Eschatology of this book, our *Christol. d. N. V.*, p. 416-465, where that which has been here touched

---

* Luke xiv. 14; 1 Thes. iv. 16; 1 Cor. xv. 23.

upon is more fully developed. On the Chiliasm, more especially the Article of Semisch in Herzog's *R. E.*, and the work of Rinck, *die Schriftmässigkeit der Lehre von einem tausendjahrigen Reich* (against Hengstenberg), Elberf. 1866.

POINTS FOR INQUIRY.

EXTENT of the didactic difference between Gospel and Apocalypse.—Is there in reality a higher unity?—The Apocalyptic writer the complement and development, by no means the antipode of the Evangelist.—The testimonies of the exalted Christ concerning himself in the Apocalypse.—Criticism of the Tubingen view as to the doctrinal standpoint of the Apocalypse, especially as regards the Christology and the Particularism.—The doctrine of John as regards the Chiliasm.—The distinction between the first and the second resurrection.—The indication of the last conflict, compare Ezek. xxxviii.—Must we regard the two last chapters of the Apocalypse as a description of the finally perfected blessedness of heaven, or as a further delineation of the condition on earth during the millennium? (compare xxii. 5.)—What is the sense of Rev. xxii. 2? (compare xxi. 24.) Is, in the Apocalypse, not even the slightest prospect opened up of the "restoration of all things?"—Force and beauty of the conclusion of the Apocalypse.

FOURTH PART.

HIGHER UNITY.

SECTION L.

Harmony of the Apostles with each other.

NOTWITHSTANDING all diversity of contents and form, the doctrine of the different Apostles stands by no means without mutual connection. Not simply in fundamental conception, but also in the presentation of the principal subjects, yea, even in a number of unimportant matters, there is to be observed an unsought and an unambiguous agreement between them. Upon no single question of life does the answer of the one contradict that of the other; and in regard to the way of salvation, it is seen at a glance that each of them proclaimed the Gospel in another manner, but none of them another Gospel, than his fellow witnesses.

1. At the close of our investigation, the higher unity of the different Apostolic systems cannot be passed over in silence. And this not simply because the thoughtful mind seeks unity in diversity, but also on account of the practical importance of the matter. If it could be shown that the teachings of the different Apostles presented, as compared with each other, only an agglomeration of very different opinions, without higher unity (*membra disjecta*), then would be wanting to them not only the highest stamp of truth, but then, also, must the use of the New Testament writings, for dogmatic purposes, be considerably modified. If it is shown, on the other hand, that we have here the right to speak of an "organically connected and gradually progressive cycle of doctrinal development" (Schmid), and to assert that the germs of the higher forms of teaching are already contained in the relatively lower forms, then the conclusion as to the truth and value of the Apostolic testimony lies, naturally, close at hand. We can, however, only throw out hints on this important subject. Our design is not to treat of Biblical dogmatics, but simply to afford a guide to the study of the theology of the New Testament writings. (Compare Sec. i. 3 ; Sec. iii. 2.)

2. It is, *à priori*, probable that there would be found a many-sided harmony between the doctrines of the different Apostles. Doctrine has always its root in the spiritual life ; and however diverse the individuality of the one may be from that of the other, all are partakers together of the same life. They

themselves, therefore, do not imagine that any one will oppose the testimony of the one to that of the other. The one, on the contrary, acknowledges the grace which has been granted to the other, even where there is a difference of opinion upon a particular point.* Peter testifies in favour of his fellow-workers and of the Epistles of Paul;† and the same Paul, who speaks so emphatically of his Gospel, declares expressly‡ that the substance of that which was declared by him, was no other than that which was proclaimed by his fellow-Apostles.

3. Above all, in the fundamental conception with which the Apostles start, the harmony is not to be ignored. They all regard man as sinful, and guilty before God; recognise the Christ, promised of old, in Jesus, in whom they all see the only Saviour of lost sinners; and present faith in Him, united with true conversion, as the only means of salvation. According to the teaching of all, they who thus believe form a circle which is manifestly distinguished from the unbelieving world, and, in the midst of all conflict, look for a glorious future as near at hand. All either assume, or expressly state, that after the Gospel of the kingdom no higher revelation of truth and grace is to be looked for; and see in the grace of God the source, in Christ the centre, and in the Holy Ghost the power of their spiritual life.

4. An equally perfect harmony in regard to each particular article of doctrine would, however, be ex-

* Gal. ii. 7, 8. † 1 Peter v. 12; 2 Peter iii. 15, 16. ‡ 1 Cor. xv. 11.

ceedingly unnatural. In doctrinal types and figures, each Apostle has so much peculiar to himself, that here we can only speak of a relative harmony, however great the unity in things essential. In order, however, to comprehend all the value of this real agreement, it must, above all, not be forgotten that not one of the Apostolic writers thought of furnishing a compact system of truths or duties; that their doctrine, even in regard to things most important, was, as a rule, presented only incidentally and as occasion demanded; that, moreover, the silence of the one or more in regard to any part of the truth is by no means the same as a questioning or ignoring of the same; that conception of the truth from a particular point of view is by no means a negation in principle of another point of view; and that, in a word, here no cycle of ideas is so systematically complete as to leave no room for the admission of other ideas, sprung from another, but kindred cycle of thought. If we add to this, that the Apostles, as a rule, wrote independently of each other, every point of agreement which manifests itself must be regarded as doubly remarkable. From a few single instances we will endeavour to show that this harmony is indeed " unsought and unambiguous."

5. The conception of God in the writings of Peter and James, and the Epistle to the Hebrews, manifests much more of an Old Testament colouring than, for instance, in the Gospel and First Epistle of John. Yet, in the first-named, the evangelical conception of God is by no means wanting; while the Apocalypse,

on the other hand, presents descriptions of the majesty of God which may be compared with the grandest of the Old Testament. The Trinitarian distinction made especially by Paul, is also found in Peter, and even in John is not sought in vain.*

6. The doctrine of man and of sin has been most fully treated by Paul, and the connection between the corruption of humanity and the fall of Adam has been exclusively traced by him. Yet there is no even probable ground for the supposition that either of the other Apostles favoured an opposite opinion. With all, sin is disobedience and transgression of the law; according to all, it is extended through Satanic influence, and leads to temporal and everlasting destruction. While Paul fixes the eye more on the sinful principle, James regards rather the sinful act; it is clear, however, that the latter also regards sinful lust as anything but a matter of indifference; whilst by all, without exception, the new birth of the individual is represented as the indispensable condition of entering into the kingdom of God.

7. As far as concerns the Christology, it has been often said, and reiterated, that two ways of regarding the person of the Lord are found in the New Testament. According to the one view, He was a mere man; according to the other, infinitely more than man. An attentive comparison of the doctrinal teaching of the different Apostles will make manifest the injustice of this assertion. In the estimation of

* 1 Peter i. 2; Rev. i. 4-6.

none of the Apostles is the Lord either a mere man, or man only in appearance; according to the teaching of all, He bears a name and claims a homage which, without idolatry, cannot be rendered to any creature. The doctrine of the Logos is to be found exclusively in John; but what does he testify of the Logos which has not been already proclaimed by Paul of the Son of God? And what do both confess which has not, at least, in principle, been indicated from the standpoint of Peter? No Apostle thinks of presenting a by any means complete enumeration of the miracles of our Lord's life; but the miraculous beginning of life, spoken of by Matthew and Luke, is so evidently presupposed in the Pauline and the Johannine doctrinal system, that it is impossible to speak of a denial or ignoring of this wondrous event from this standpoint. Paul and Peter harmonize in the most beautiful manner with the Apocalypticus in the high value attached by him to the Lord's resurrection from the grave; and, if the author of the Epistle to the Hebrews, in accordance with his whole figurative style, lays the chief stress upon the Lord's ascension, he affords, at least upon one occasion, a clear testimony to the value of his resurrection.* And if further the historic fact of this ascension is mentioned only by some of the witnesses, all agree in the fact that the Glorified One stands in continued personal relation to His Church on earth, and soon will come again as Judge.

8. In that also which the Apostles testify in regard

* Heb. xiii. 20, 21.

to the work of redemption, we look not in vain for a higher agreement. When we speak of a threefold office of Christ, we cannot ignore the fact that James lays by far the greatest stress upon His prophetic word. But he represents the Teacher as also the Lord of glory,* and it is inconceivable that he, who certainly was not less than the other Apostles penetrated by the spirit of the Old Testament, should have overlooked the atoning power of the Lord's death. The redeeming and sanctifying power of Jesus' death is spoken of with equal fervour by Peter, Paul, and John; and, even in the song of the Lamb of the Apocalypse, is heard no other undertone than that which is present in the whole Apostolic proclamation. If, in the Epistle to the Hebrews, the moral value of the obedience is insisted on, while, in the Epistles of Paul, it is rather the actual bearing of chastisement on the part of the suffering Christ upon which the emphasis is laid; the one conception is the complement of the other, and nothing which is asserted on this side is therefore on that side ignored. Entirely peculiar to Peter is the mention of the Lord's appearing, after His death, in the spirit-world; yet there are not wanting, as it would appear, traces of this thought also in the Pauline doctrine.† If Paul traces back more clearly than any other, personal participation in the salvation which is in Christ to the sovereign purpose of God, he finds nowhere less contradiction in this respect than in Peter and John.‡

* James ii. 1.   † Ephes. iv. 9.
‡ 1 Pet. i. 2; ii. 9; Rev. xiii. 7, 8.

According to all, salvation is completed only through the kingly dominion of Christ, which is described by none as a purely moral sway, but by all as a personal reign, by most, as at the same time a priestly as well as kingly rule, redounding to the salvation of His redeemed ones, and destined to triumph over all opposition.

9. The demand for faith and conversion is, in the proclamation of all Apostles, one and the same, and if the latter is, in the epistles, comparatively seldom mentioned, it is simply because these epistles are addressed, as a rule, to those who are already true believers. The conception and life of faith is most fully presented by the Apostle Paul; but along with his, the conception in the Epistle to the Hebrews naturally takes its place; and when the innermost life of the communion of faith is to be described, John is found to yield nothing to Paul. The connection between faith and justification is certainly somewhat differently indicated in Paul from what it is in James (compare Sec. xxxi. 5). "With Paul, faith, because it is justifying faith, is the source of good works; with James, faith, because it is the source of good works—and in them shows itself living and active—is justifying faith" (Kern). From this it does not, however, follow that the one is in conflict with the other, much less that it is impossible to find between both conceptions, which regard the matter from different sides, a higher unity. With no Apostle is sanctification the meritorious ground of justification; with all, is it the sign of a filial relationship towards

God, of which each one of them speaks as being of supreme importance.

10. Upon a superficial observation it might appear as though the Apostles differed considerably in their eschatology; yea, as though even a Paul did not always remain consistent with himself in this respect. More accurate examination, however, leads to a result more favourable, and shows that the more realistic conception of Paul differs from the more spiritual one of John—not in principle and ground-conception, but only in measure and degree. According to all the Apostles who express themselves particularly on this point, the blessedness of believers—enjoyed in its beginning immediately after death—is completed only at the second coming of the Lord; this coming will be an unexpected, personal, glorious one, and is followed by an absolutely universal and endless recompense. All look for a resurrection of the body, yet not until the end of the ages; all expect a world-judgment, held by the same Judge and determined by the same standard. Surprising are the prospects opened up in the Apocalypse—surprising, and yet not without a point of connection with what has been earlier spoken (Sec. xlix. 8); terrible indeed are the judgments there predicted, and yet not at all in conflict with that which especially Peter and Paul lead us to expect in "the last troublous times."

11. If in anything all the Apostles agree, it is in the intimate connection of doctrine and life which we find in them all. It is true, this is especially seen in John (Sec. xlv. 4), who significantly speaks of "*doing*

the truth;"* but yet the remark applies in a greater or less degree to all. "Dans le Christianisme des Apôtres le dogme se transforme en morale, et la morale ramène au dogme à son tour. La morale Chrétien n'est en definitive que le dogme Chrétien passé dans la vie; c'est le surnaturel de la conduite correspondant au surnaturel de la foi; c'est l'extraordinaire dans la vie humaine provoqué par les dispensations extraordinaires de l'amour de Dieu; ce sont les miracles de la grâce produisant les miracles de la charité" (Bonifas). And precisely in this is manifested the practical unity of the Apostolic doctrine, even when it has proceeded from very different points. James, for example, stands not wholly in the same relation to the law as Paul; nevertheless, we are surprised in the former by the remark that the Gospel is the perfect law of *liberty ;*† while the other describes the Gospel as the *law* ‡ of the Spirit of life in Christ Jesus; and both—the one in the name of liberty, the other of authority— describe one life; a life as peculiar as the grace which has been received is unmerited and inestimable. In the conception of John, the centre of gravity falls within the present life; in that of Peter, within the future. Yet the the latter knows, even here, a joy of hope, which supports amidst all sufferings;§ and the former glories in the hope of a future, in comparison with which even the present is as nothing.|| The Pauline trilogy—"faith, hope, love"—is not precisely

* 1 John i. 6. † James i. 25. ‡ Rom. viii. 2.
§ 1 Peter i. 8. || 1 John iii. 2.

co-extensive with the Johannine—"light, love, life;" and yet a parallel may easily be drawn between them, and in both the differently modified fruit is produced from a common stem.

12. The copiousness of the material precludes even the endeavour after completeness. The instances given are presented, not with a view to rendering further investigation unnecessary, but of stimulating to it. At every new step in this domain, we perceive ever more fully, that the whole conception of the Apostolic Epistles, as written with a certain bias (*Tendenzgeschriften*)—for the combating or reconciliation of adverse schools—belongs not to the domain of history, but of romance.

The subject of this chapter is passed over in silence by Schmid, Reuss, Scholten, and others. It is treated of, on the other hand, by Messner, *l. c.*, p. 382-421; Lechler, *l. c.*, p. 232-271; Bonifas, *l. c.*, p. 201-282; Köstlin in the treatise before referred to (Sec. I.) A remarkable proof of the harmony of the Apostolic writers in regard to the death of the Lord is that of Dr. J. Tideman, *Theol. Studiën*, Amst., 1863, p. 79-126.

POINTS FOR INQUIRY.

THE true conception of the harmony of the Apostolic doctrine.—Nearer comparison of the doctrine of Paul with that of James, Peter, John.—Comparison of the doctrine of John with that of his predecessors.—What value is to be attached to presentations of doctrine which are made only by one, or some, of the Apostles?—Historico-critical significance of the result obtained.

SECTION LI.

Harmony of the Apostles with the Lord.

THE remarkable unity of the Apostolic proclamation finds its historico-psychological basis in the personal life-communion of all with Him who had called them, formed them, and by *one* Spirit had led them into the whole truth. Their doctrine contains the spiritually normal development of the fruitful germ deposed in his utterances, and stands in relation to His as the stream to the fountain. Without doubt His doctrine is in theirs developed in a many-sided manner; the influence also upon the contents and form of their preaching, of many circumstances within and without their own minds, is by no means to be lightly esteemed. But with all development, the original fundamental character remains, with all difference, the higher unity is to be recognised; and no single case presents itself in which it is necessary, in order to accept their word, to reject that of the Master, or *vice versâ*.

1. The harmony which is found in so many diverse persons, and in so comparatively many writings independent of each other in origin, and separated by so many years, is a phenomenon so remarkable, that we find no counterpart to it in the history of humanity and of religion. The question as to the cause of this phenomenon finds its answer when we regard the person and work of the Lord; and in this answer is presented at the same time a reverential homage to *Him* who forms such disciples, and unites them in such a manner.

2. The doctrine which is to call forth life can be born of life alone. Thus the Apostolic proclamation has its root in the communion of all with Him who called them all to be His witnesses, and baptized them with the Holy Ghost. So mighty is the impression of His appearing that they cannot possibly cease speaking of it;[*] so powerfully does His Spirit operate in their hearts that they have received—with varying clearness and depth—essentially the same impression of His person and work, and independently reproduce it. The Spirit leads them forward upon the path of a development willed by God, but at the same time back to the words of the Lord himself.[†]

3. Not all Apostles stand in the same relation to the person and work of the Lord. The difference

[*] Acts iv. 20.   [†] John xvi. 15.

is at once manifest in this respect between Paul and his fellow-witnesses; but even these latter are stars of different magnitudes, placed at different distances from the central sun. James attaches himself more to the moral, John to the mystical side of the Lord's teaching; and, while John evidently penetrates most deeply into the spirit of the Master's own testimony, we find again in Peter the living reminiscence not so much of His words as of His deeds and sufferings. With Paul it is less the teaching, suffering, or dying Christ, than the glorified one, with whom he feels himself most intimately united, and who, by continued revelation, gives him to see ever new light (compare Sec. xxxv. 5; Sec. xxxviii. 3). But yet the answer of all to the question as to the last ground of their testimony would have been a unanimous reference of the inquirer to the word, first of the Old Testament, but then, above all, of the Lord, and to the teaching of the Holy Spirit, by which they were led gradually to the full knowledge of the whole truth.

4. That the doctrine of the Apostles, especially of Paul and John, is extensively more full than that of the Lord, scarcely requires mention. It by no means follows from this, however, that intensively it equals (or even surpasses) His doctrine in power. On the contrary, it can be shown that the Apostolic testimony concerning salvation contains nothing which has not been in principle—if not actually expressed, at least —indicated by Him. It lay in the nature of the case that the full truth concerning the exalted dignity of His person, the power of His death, and the brightness

of His glorification, could only come to light after the close of His earthly manifestation. So much the more remarkable is it, that no Apostle expresses anything which cannot be justified by an appeal either to the letter or spirit of the Lord's own words. As the oak is contained in the acorn, so does the Apostolic doctrine of the Atonement lie in words like Matt. xx. 28; xxvi. 28; and their whole eschatology in Matt. xxiv. and xxv. What in His word had for wise reasons not yet been expressed,* His Spirit gave them later to understand; and in that this Spirit testifies, His word again is inwardly revealed and explained.

5. Without doubt the Apostolic teaching contains more than the expansion and development of the doctrine proclaimed by Jesus. The stream which widens in its progress from the fountain-head, and hastens forward in its course with increasing depth and breadth, receives into its bosom other tributaries also. The individuality of the Apostles, their greater or lesser degree of culture in the school of Scripture and of science, the influence of current thought, of circumstances, and of personal experiences, all these are factors which must be taken into account in answering the question, how the doctrine of the Apostles has, in point of contents and form, become that which it is. But yet, after full allowance has been made for all this, the preponderating influence of the Lord's own word and Spirit upon their testimony is not overshadowed, but simply more nearly

* John xvi. 12.

defined; and all the beams, divergent in direction, varying in colour and intensity, radiate unceasingly from the same centre.

6. The observing of the harmony between the doctrine of Jesus and the Apostles—just as little dead uniformity as irreconcilable antagonism—is not merely an admirable proof of the justice of the words, "He that heareth you heareth me;"* but is also in our day of great importance in opposition to the one-sidedness of those who would oppose the testimony of the one to that of the other, and would compel us to choose between the religion of the amiable Rabbi, and the wisdom of a few well-meaning but narrow-minded zealots, who stand infinitely beneath him. Where the alternative so manifestly rests upon a preconceived opinion, the decision may be spared without loss. The inner unity of the Apostolic witness with that of the Master is a fact which cannot be denied; and this fact is for Christian faith and Christian science of no small significance. It proves that the Christian church has not without reason conceded to the doctrine of the Apostles an entirely unique position, above that of all others, and not without good cause, ever afresh returns to it. "Only *the whole* (body) is also the sound (body), and *each* of the Apostolic doctrinal systems is given to Christianity as a pattern, and for its improvement" (Lechler), namely, in its connection with the living totality.

Compare, on the inner unity of the Apostolic

* Luke x. 16.

doctrine, Schaff, *l. c.*, I. p. 640 and following; our *Christologie des N. T.*, p. 447-480. On the wisdom of Jesus, in the formation of his Apostles, our *Lev. v. J.* II. p. 213, and the literature there cited.

POINTS FOR INQUIRY.

CONNECTION between doctrine and life, between progressive enlightenment of the Apostles and their increasing holiness.—Sense, force, and fulfilment of the promise, John xvi. 12-15.—The greater or lesser differences between the doctrine of the disciples and that of the Master.—The Apostolic testimony the expression of a sanctified individuality.—The harmony of the disciples with the Lord, in its historic, dogmatic, and practical significance.

SECTION LII.

Harmony of the Lord and the Apostles with the Scriptures of the Old Testament.

As the doctrine of the Apostles has its basis in that of Jesus, so has that both of Jesus and the Apostles in the sacred Scriptures of the Old Testament, which are by all regarded from essentially the same point of view. Between the theology of the Scriptures of the Old Testament and that of the New the distinction is undoubtedly as great as it is important; but, at the same time—apart from the difference of persons and times—the higher unity in regard to the way of salvation is so unmistakable that both present more and more one organic *whole*, the result of more than human wisdom.

1. The contemplation of the theology of the Apostles (Part III.) leads us back not merely to that of the Lord (Part II.), but also to the Old Testament

basis on which the doctrinal structure of both reposes. What we have earlier said as to the way and manner in which the way was prepared for the Gospel of the kingdom by Mosaism, Prophetism, and Judaism (Sec. iv.-vi.), becomes now at the close of our examination not merely manifest but also confirmed, and furnishes us at the same time with the last key to the phenomenon observed in Secs. l. and li.

2. In deriving the unity between the teaching of the Lord and that of the Apostles from the relation of both to the Scriptures of the Old Testament, we do not mean by any means to assert that these Scriptures were by all explained and cited in the same way. The use of Scripture by the Evangelists and Apostles of the New Testament is different, and affords in its peculiarity important material for comparative criticism. And yet the Apostles in their contemplation of Scripture agree so entirely not only with each other but with the Lord, that their testimony concerning the way of salvation is in a certain respect only the continuation, exposition, and confirmation of the word of Moses and the prophets. According to all, the Scripture of the Old Testament is the documentary record of an especial Divine saving revelation; the Messianic expectation thereby awakened the expression of the deepest want of humanity, and the way of salvation now revealed that which was already indicated in its first principles under the Old Covenant. Allusion or appeal to the prophetic word occupies also in the discourse of all a more or less important place, and just as little the Apostle of

Hebraistic as of Hellenistic culture severs the bond which unites his whole conception of the way of salvation with that of earlier ages.

3. In order to fathom in its entire compass the influence of the Old Testament upon the teaching of the Lord and His Apostles, it suffices not to regard single peculiarities (for instance, the connection of the theory of sacrifices with the Evangelical doctrine of the Atonement), but we must rise to the main and dominant ideas which in both parts of the Scripture appear unceasingly in the foreground. For the ideas, *e.g.*, of life and death, sin and grace, light and darkness, calling and election, sonship and inheritance, righteousness and truth, which we find not less in the teaching of Christ of the Synoptics than in that of the Johannine Christ, in Peter and James not less than in Paul and John, the common basis lies in the sacred Scripture of the Old Testament. In the Scriptures of the New Testament they are developed, completed, and applied as never before; but in order to understand the original sense, one must ever trace them back to the pre-Christian period. Even John* has no more outgrown his reverence for ancient prophecy than Peter; and Paul, for whom the ancient had passed away, shows, with manifest predilection for Old Testament examples, that Abraham and David were justified by a method essentially the same as believers of the New Testament.† The whole Epistle to the Hebrews especially is one continued proof that Christianity is the realisation of

* See, for example, John xix. 24, 36, 37.   † Rom. c. iv.

the highest aspirations of Hebraism and Judaism; and it is impossible to leave the Apocalypse without observing how the circle of Scripture at the end manifestly returns to its point of commencement.

4. No proof of the harmony between the Old Testament and the New is of any value unless it proceeds from the unconditional acknowledgment of the diversity which exists between them. The "*concordabit Scriptura*" is inconceivable unless the "*distingue tempora*" has obtained its due observance. On the other hand, however, every view is one-sided which has regard only to the difference, without discovering beneath and beyond this the higher unity. "Not the contents but the form, not the certainty but the distinctness; it is this in which the prophetic and Apostolic testimonies of salvation differ the one from the other. The whole theology of the New Testament is in its deepest foundation an Israelite theology."

5. A harmony, as it here reveals itself before our eyes, between such different men and writings, separated from each other by centuries, appears inexplicable, unless we assume that the fundamental thought, of which the Old Testament may be termed the proclamation, and the New the fulfilment, is the fruit of a special Divine saving revelation, gradually made known by its interpreters in such a way that later revelations did not contradict the earlier ones, but rather explained and completed them. The inner unity of Scripture is the great proof that we have here to do with something very different from

sporadic remains of Jewish and Christian literature. A whole like this is not the product of human reflection and research, but is the gradually developed fruit of a higher guidance. And the whole now completed structure of the theology of the New Testament Scriptures merits in itself, and in connection with that of the Old Testament, the inscription, " He that built all this is God." The fuller amplification and practical application of this thought belongs, however, no longer to the purely historic domain, whose limit is here reached.

Compare P. Mounier, *Disq. de locis nonnullis Evang. in quibus V. T. libri a Jesu laudantur*, Amst. 1856. The literature cited, Sec. xiv. 8. Our *Christol.* I. p. 37 and following; II. p. 480-485.

POINTS FOR INQUIRY.

COMPARISON of the different ways in which the Scriptures of the Old Testament are used and explained by the writers of the New.—History of the exaggeration and undervaluing of the higher unity of the Old and the New Testament on the part of Christian theology.—Apologetic value of the result obtained.—The theology of the New Testament Scriptures in its significance and value above every other.

INDEX OF GREEK WORDS.

ἁγιάζειν, 358.
ᾅδης, 119.
αἱματεκχυσία, 355.
ἀλήθεια, 156.
ἁμαρτία, 94, 151, 245, 272.
ἁμαρτωλός, 94.
" καθίστασ-θαι, 272.
ἀμνός, 222.
ἀναφέρειν, 356.
ἀνομία, 94.
ἀντίλυτρον, 309.
ἀποκάλυψις, 287.
ἀποκατάστασις πάντων, 55.
ἀπωλεία, 279, 340.
ἀπόλλυσθαι, 119, *note*.
ἀπολύτρωσις, 308, 323.
ἀρνίον, 409.
ἄρχων τοῦ κόσμου, 153.

δεκτός, 217.
δικαιοσύνη Θεοῦ, 305, 308.

δικαιοῦν, 310.
δικαίωσις, 308, 322.
δόξα, 279.
δοῦλος, 208, 223.

ἔγγυος, 354.
ἐκκλησία, 114, 221, 325, 402.
ἐκκλησία κατ' οἶκον, 325.
ἐκλογή, 236.
ἑλκύειν, 164.
ἐλπίς, 225.
ἔνδειξις δικαιοσύνης, 308.
ἐν ὑψηλοῖς, 359.
ἐξηγεῖσθαι, 392.
ἐπίγνωσις, 234.
ἐπιθυμία, 245, 275.
ἐπιστροφή, 110.
ἐσχάτη ἡμέρα, 172.
εὐδοκία 291.

ἱλασμός, 310.
ἱλαστήριον, 307.

καθαρισμός, 358.
καλεῖν, 164.
καταλλαγή, 310.
κλῆσις, 291.
κοινωνία, 402.
κόσμος, 272, 310.
κρίσις, 395.

λίτρον, 356.
λύτρωσις, 356.

μάρτυς, 207.
μετάνοια, 110, 318.
μυστήριοι, 287.

νόμος, 276.
νοῦς, 282, note; 408.

τὸ ξύλον, 212.

ὅμοιος τῷ Θεῷ, 403.

παῖς, 208.
παλιγγενεσία, 55.
παράπτωμα, 94.
παραλαμβ. ἀπὸ, 327.
παροιμία, 177.
παρουσία, 120.
πειρασμός, 94.

πιστεύειν, 160, 399.
πίστις, 111, 317 2,
πνεῦμα, 274, 283, 391, 408.
πρόγνωσις, 291.
προσκυνεῖν, 147.
προορίζειν, 291.

σάρξ, 274.
σκάνδαλον, 94.
σκηνοῦν, 391.
σπεύδειν, 236.
σπουδάζειν, 236, note.
σῶμα, 274.
σωτήρ, 287.
σωτηρία, 220.

τιμᾶν, 147.

υἱοθεσία, 322.
υἱός, 226.
ὑπὲρ ἀδίκων, 212.
ὑπὲρ παντὸς, 367.

φανέρωσις, 287.
φθορά, 284.
φύσις, 273.

χοϊκός, 273.

ψυχή, 138, 274, 391.

INDEX OF SUBJECTS.

(The number refers to the page.)

Adam, the organic connection of the human race with, 272.
Adoption into God's family, 322.
Angels, personal nature of, 87.
    " their place in the last judgment, 123.
Antichrist, 334, 394, 412.
Ascension of Christ, 313.
Atonement, the, 307.

Baptism, its institution, 115.
    " a symbol of life through death, 219, 326.
Believe, *see* Faith.
Believer comes not under judgment, 157.
    " his body a temple of the Holy Ghost, 325.
Believers, sons of God, 322, 399.
    " have died to sin in the death of Christ, 311.
    " are purged from an evil conscience, 347.
    " are preserved unto everlasting life, 171, 322, 402.
    " their relation to the law, 222.
    " their perfection the work of Christ, 357.
    " shall judge the world, 335.
    " their final blessedness, 124, 338, 403.
    " have different degrees in glory, 338.
    " universal priesthood of, 222.
Birth, the new, 165.
Call, the, into the kingdom of God, 109, 163.
  " into fellowship with Christ, 291, 318.
Children of darkness and children of the light, 154, 386.
    " of the Evil One, 93.
Chiliasm of the Apocalypse, 412.
Christ, divine and human nature of, 140.
    " the Paschal Lamb of the new covenant, 307.
    " the light of the world, 156.

Christ, the object of faith, 111, 159, 317.
" the goal of the law, 288.
" the one Mediator, 301, 308.
" the surety of the better covenant, 354.
" the glorified head of the new humanity, 301, 314.
" stands no longer in any relation to sins, 230.
" the prophetic office of, 103, 156.
" the high-priestly office of, 359.
" the kingly office of, 313.
Christianity a new life, 320.
" its influence on the social relations, 330.
Church, character of the, 114–16, 220, 311, 325.
" an ideal society, 329, 402.
" the body of Christ, 325.
" indwelt by the Holy Ghost, 325.
" final victory of the, 402.
" offices in the, 328.
" doctrine of the, not developed in the Epistle to the Hebrews, 365.
Coming of Christ, the, takes place unexpectedly, 121, 335, 360 394.
" nearness of the, 126, 227, 332, 333, 412.
" glory of the, foreshadowed on the Mount of Transfiguration, 235.
" as conceived of in the fourth Gospel, 171, 173.
Conscience, 274.
" becomes darkened by sin, 274.
Consummation of all things, 340, 412.
Conversion, a change of heart followed by a corresponding change of life, 110.
" necessary for all, 93, 99, 219.

Death, Pauline conception of, 279.
" Johannine conception of, 385.
Death of Christ, a propitiatory offering, 307
" a ransom price, 104, 307.
" the channel of pardon, 104.
" a sacrifice for the sin of the world, 58, 393.
" the condemnation of the world and its prince, 157
" fruitful in blessings, 158, 289.
Disobedience, its climax, 274.

Eternal life, 102, 170, 399, 402.
" conferred here, 219.
Evil spirits, 88.

Index of Subjects.

Faith, its nature, 316–17, 362, 398.
" the condition of obtaining salvation, 111, 314, **316.**
" the element in which the new man lives, **319.**
" manifested in following Christ, 112.
" how produced in the heart, 318, 319.
Fatherhood, the, of God, 81, 145.
Fellowship with Christ, its fruits, 166, 400
Filial relationship of believers, 399.
Flesh, the material body, 336
" the body of the sacrificial victim, 158
" human nature in its finite condition, 299, 352, 391.
" human nature as exposed to suffering and temptation, 93.
" unsanctified humanity, as opposed to all that is of **God,** 274.
" as distinguished from body, 274, *note*.
Flesh, the (in the moral sense), the true seat **of** sin, 274.
" the ruling power in man before conversion, 152, **274.**
Fleshly-mindedness, 274
Future punishment, its degrees, 125.
" its duration, 95, 283, 339, 395

Gehenna, 119.
God, as the final cause of all things, 145.
" as the author of salvation, 287.
" glory of the end of redemption, 340.
" his thoughts interpreted by Christ, **392.**
" the eternal purpose of, 289.
" all in all, 339.
Gospel, the, a revealed mystery, 287.
" of Paul, 258–60, 344–5.
Grace, what, 306.
" election of, 289.

Heart, the central point of the personality, **90, 274.**
Heaven, the Father's House, 171.
" a definite locality, 359.
Heavenly inheritance, the, its character, 227.
Holy Ghost, the, divine nature of, 84.
" promised to believers, 167.
" the earnest of future blessedness, 336.
" work of, 84.
" " in relation to the world, to disciples, **and to** the Lord, 167.
" " does not render unnecessary the heavenly activity of the Lord, 168.
" the one baptism of, 326.

Hope, its place in the believer's life, 225, 319, 362, 403.

Immortality, *see* Eternal Life.
Inner conflict, the, of Rom. vii., 282, *note*.
Intermediate state, the, 119, 336.

Jesus Christ, the heavenly origin of, 58, 136, 207, 299, 382, 389.
" sinless humanity of, 76, 137, 299.
" Messiahship of, 74–6, 139.
" in relation to the prophetic Scriptures, 99, 352.
" in relation to the law, 100.
" made perfect through sufferings, 353.
" obedient unto death, 158, 359, 394.
" activity of the separate spirit of, 213.
" exaltation of, 106, 214, 313, 359, 394.
Johannine theology, its character, 373.
" conception of the church, 164, 402.
Justification, its nature, 258, 305, 322
" by works of law impossible, 270, 276.

Kingdom of God, the, 68–73, 164
Kingdom of Christ, its manifestation, 121–4, 331, 357, 412
" its last earthly stadium, 340, 412.

Logos, the sharer of the nature and majesty of God, 383.
" dwelt in fulness in Christ, 391.
Love, the fruit and crown of faith and hope, 319, 362, 400.
" of Christ's appearing, an essential characteristic of believers, 332.

Man, his place in creation, 90
" his moral freedom, 90, 155, 274.
" his receptiveness for that which is of God, 90.
Messiah, God's perfect servant, 207.
Messiahship of Jesus, evidence for the, 160.
Messianic expectations under the old covenant, 41.
Messianic judgment, the, 123, 157, 337, 360.
" inwardly takes place now, 157.
" manifested at the end of the ages, 157, 178.
Moral perfection the goal of believers, 113, 320, 401.

Obdurate impenitence, its characteristics, 94, 152, 274.
" without excuse, 155.
Offering of Christ, the, an oblation and a sacrifice, 306.
" needs not to be repeated, 358.

Index of Subjects.

Perversion of heavenly gifts adds to condemnation, 363.
" leaves no means of restoration unexhausted, 358.
Petrine conception of the Church, 220.
Predestination, the doctrine of, in the teaching of Peter, 220.
" in the teaching of Paul, 289.
Providence of God, the, 83.
Purpose, the, of salvation, not a consequence of the entrance of sin, 289.
" its extent, 293.

Reconciliation of the world, what, 338-9.
" how effected, 310.
Redemption, 307.
" the, of the body, the hope of believers, 319.
Renewal of all things, 123.
Repentance, 319.
Resurrection, the, of Christ, a bodily resurrection, 214, 312.
" of the dead, 122, 337.
" the first, 336, 412.
" of the just, 122.
Resurrection and the life, Christ the, 156.
Restitution of all things, 226, 339.
" in what sense an unscriptural expectation, 340.
Risen Christ, the object of apostolic testimony, 210, 312, 365.

Salvation, its nature, 102, 314.
" attainable only through Christ, 217, 392.
Satan, 88.
" the prince of this world, 153.
" rests not in the truth, 153.
Sin in its nature lawlessness, 94, 385.
" not an eternal necessity, 153-4.
" its universality, 92, 218, 266-9.
" its introduction by Satan, 93, 272, 384.
" its degrees, 152.
Sins, how purged, 357.
Son of God, 77, 300, 351.
" term, how used in the fourth Gospel, 142.
" pre-mundane existence of the, 142, 147.
" the highest revelation of the Father, 143, 386, 392.
" one with the Father, 143.
" entitled to Divine honors, 147.
" His will and working in harmony with that of the Father, 144-5.
Son of man, 75.
" subject to temptation, 353.

Index of Subjects.

Son of man, appearing of the, 121.
Soul, the sentient nature in man, 77.
" sometimes used of the whole immaterial nature, **91, 187.**
" the, its everlasting existence, 91.
" does not sleep at death, 119, 336.
of Christ, the, a ransom for many, 104, 391.
Spirit, the higher nature in man, 91, 274.
" the, stands in need of renewal, 274.
" is in bondage before conversion, 282.
Spiritual life a fellowship with Christ, 164–5, 311, 399
Suffering, the design in, 357.
Superiority of the new covenant over the old, 350.
Supper of the Lord, its institution, 115, 326.
" a commemoration of the atoning death of Christ, 328.

Time of the final decision, 337, 412
Trinitarian distinction in the New Testament, 84, 207, 340, 410, 419.
To be spiritually minded, what, 321.

Unbelief originates in a perverse bent of the heart, 161.
Unbeliever, the, dead in trespasses, 152, 279.

Washing of the disciples' feet, how enjoined, 164
" of regeneration, what, 327.
Word of God, the, a factor in the new birth, 92.
Work of Christ, the, in its universal aspect, 69, 109, 156, 219, 392
World, the term, how used, 151.
" the, under the dominion of **Satan, 153, 272.**
" opposed to God, 384.

www.ingramcontent.com/pod-product-compliance
Lightning Source LLC
Chambersburg PA
CBHW071137300426
44113CB00009B/1002